The principal objective of THE MATHESON TRUST is to promote the study of comparative religion from the point of view of the underlying harmony of the great religious and philosophical traditions of the world. This objective is being pursued through such means as audio-visual media, the support and sponsorship of lecture series and conferences, the creation of a website, collaboration with film production companies and publishing companies as well as the Trust's own series of publications.

The Matheson Monographs cover a wide range of themes within the field of comparative religion: scriptural exegesis in different religious traditions; the modalities of spiritual and contemplative life; in-depth mystical studies of particular religious traditions; broad comparative analyses taking in a series of religious forms; studies of traditional arts, crafts and cosmological science; and contemporary scholarly expositions of religious philosophy and metaphysics. The monographs also comprise translations of both classical and contemporary texts, as well as transcriptions of lectures by, and interviews with, spiritual and scholarly authorities from different religious and philosophical traditions.

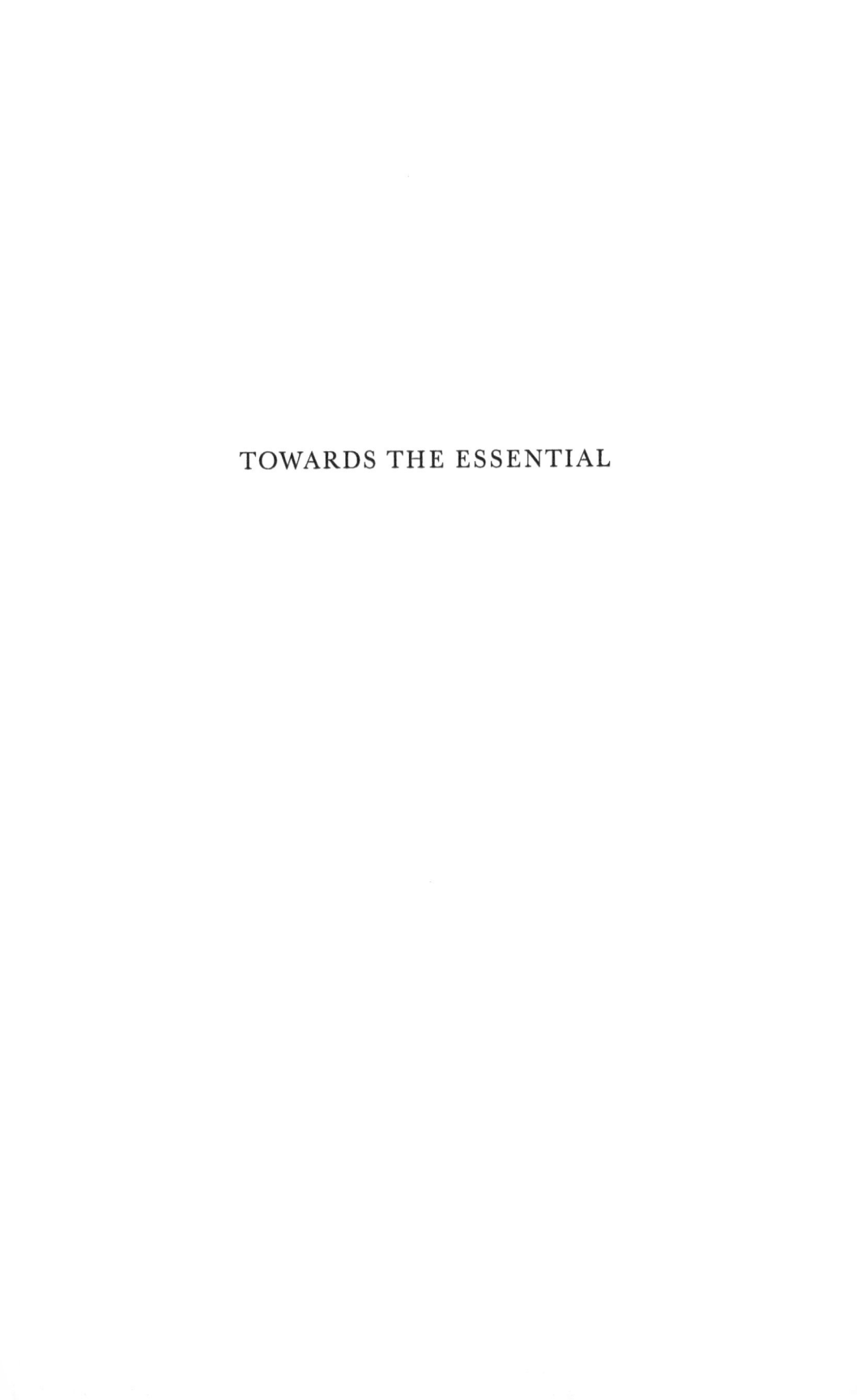

TOWARDS THE ESSENTIAL

Un Détail: vous me demandez si j'ai voulu dire dans un de mes livres "That intelligence cannot discern truth without reference either to esoterism, on the one hand, or the Revelation and its commentators on the other, beginning with Sayyidina Muhammad". Ce que j'ai voulu dire est la chose suivante: en principe, l'intelligence pure — l'intellect — peut connaître tout le connaissable; elle peut, en principe, le connaître par elle-même, sans l'intervention d'un enseignement extérieur. Mais en fait, il y a beaucoup de chances que même l'esprit le mieux doué ne puisse tirer de soi toute la métaphysique; si un _Shankara_ avait grandi dans une totale ignorance, s'il n'avait jamais entendu parler du _Vêda_, d' _Âtmâ_, de _Mâyâ_, peut-on affirmer avec certitude qu'il aurait pu tirer ces notions de lui-même? La Révélation, védique ou autre, est là, non seulement pour nous communiquer des idées-clefs, mais aussi, et surtout, pour réveiller ou actualiser en nous les connaissances latentes que nous portons en nous-mêmes. Vous dites: "But the Muslim philosophers, like their predecessors in Greece, talked about many things not mentioned by the Prophet and the early notables of Islam..." Évidemment car le Prophète — ou le Koran — n'a fait que donner l'impulsion; les philosophes grecs eux aussi avaient besoin de certains stimulants traditionnels. Chaque homme a des parents, et les parents ont toujours des idées; je pense maintenant à l'Antiquité. L'impulsion une fois donnée, — koranique et helléniste chez les Arabes, — les auteurs métaphysiciens et mystiques peuvent avoir des idées tout à fait originales, soit par inspiration, soit simplement par réflexion. —

Extract from a letter of 7 July 1979 (60% scale)

TOWARDS
THE ESSENTIAL

Letters of a Spiritual Master

Edited by

Thierry Béguelin

Translated from the French by

Mark Perry and Gillian Harris

THE MATHESON TRUST
For the Study of Comparative Religion

The Matheson Trust
PO Box 336
56 Gloucester Road
London SW7 4UB, UK

ISBN: 978-1-908092-23-6

First published in French as
Vers l'Essentiel : Lettres d'un Maître spirituel
Éditions Les Sept Flèches
Lausanne, Switzerland, 2013

© 2013 World Wisdom
Bloomington IN 47402, USA
www.worldwisdom.com

© 2013 Éditions Les Sept Flèches
1062 Sottens/Lausanne, Suisse
www.editions.7fleches.com

Typesetting and design by Susana Marín

Contents

Preface . . . . *ix*

Letters to Christian Correspondents 1

Letters to Muslim Correspondents 99

Letters to Hindu Correspondents. 157

Letters to Buddhist Correspondents 181

Letters to Native American Correspondents 199

Letters to Novices 217

Letters to His Brother. 223

Letters to Miscellaneous Correspondents 233

Glossary 251

General Index 259

Index of Letters 267

Frithjof Schuon at his desk in Bloomington

Preface

It was in 1976 that I first saw the name of Frithjof Schuon, as author of an article entitled "Le Paradis comme théophanie" (Paradise as Theophany), in the journal *Études Traditionnelles*. I had previously read all René Guénon's works, to which I had been introduced by Bernard Moitessier, a long-distance solo sailor, and it was only after finishing the last book that I learned that Guénon was no longer of this world. I was disappointed, because I thought I had found in him the Master I was seeking. Thus I decided to turn to one or other of the collaborators of *Études Traditionnelles*, a Guénonian journal. But which one?

Passing through Paris at the end of the following year, I visited the headquarters of Éditions Traditionnelles, publishers of the journal, to renew my subscription, hoping at the same time to find out whom to turn to. Noticing my address, the secretary said: "Ah, you come from Switzerland? Wait a moment!" She returned with a small file, took out a card and said: "So you know Frithjof Schuon? There's where he lives, near Lausanne." Somewhat stunned, I remembered the address: 40, chemin de Rochettaz, in Pully. The owner of Éditions Traditionnelles, Mr Villain, had meanwhile come over and I asked him if he knew Frithjof Schuon. He replied, all in one breath: "I have never seen him, but I know that he is very tall and thin and always wears a black suit with a black tie, but his wife is very nice."

After waiting two months—which gave me time to read some of his books—I received an answer from Frithjof Schuon to my letter; he agreed to receive me at his home. It was a striking encounter, such as I had never experienced nor could ever have imagined: an encounter with a man so different from, and superior to, anyone that I had met until then. He was like a prophet. Even before he began to speak, everything in his physique, his demeanour, his clothing and his ambience bore witness to an eminent grandeur and nobility, without the slightest affectation. We each sat down on a pouf, side by side, with a Moroccan brass tray between us, and as he spoke, in profile, his head tilted back slightly as if he were receiving the inspiration for his long monologue from Heaven, I drank in his words, aware of the exceptional character of the situation and dazzled by so much light. I had pictured meeting a philosopher in a black suit, surrounded by books and perhaps able to direct me towards a spiritual master, but I saw neither books, nor suit, nor philosopher (as we understand that term today), but a Master. Over the next hour and a half he reviewed the fundamentals of his message—the message of *religio perennis*, pure esoterism—without ever asking me why I had approached him or what I wanted, because he knew the reason better than I did. On that day I was bound to him for ever.

The life and work of Frithjof Schuon (1907–1998) having been extensively studied and commented on, I shall limit myself to reproducing a few excerpts from a 1987 draft English review, whose content he accepted, thus guaranteeing its value. "*Frithjof Schuon was a German who acquired Swiss nationality in the French part of Switzerland and wrote most of his books in French. To mention this is not without significance, for Schuon's writings have the merit of combining German imaginativeness and profundity with French precision, clarity, and elegance. Another remarkable feature of Schuon's work is the fascinating combination of a rigorous intellectuality with an exceptional artistic sensibility—one might even say a kind of mystical musicality. From earliest youth, Frithjof Schuon's doctrinal starting point was the Vedānta; and his message encompasses primarily the following domains: essential, hence universal, metaphysics, with its cosmological and anthropological ramifications; spirituality in the broadest sense; intrinsic morality and aesthetics; traditional principles and phenomena; religions and their esoterisms; sacred art. Let us add that in his youth, Schuon wrote beautiful lyrical poems in his native German, and that throughout his life he was a very gifted painter; most of his somewhat hieratic paintings portray the Plains Indians, with whom he has a strong personal connection, having even been officially adopted into the Sioux tribe. We shall thus say that Frithjof Schuon's message is as much artistic and existential as it is philosophical and intellectual, both modes being possible and fundamental expressions of concrete spirituality.*" It is worth noting that during the last three years of his life, a particular inspiration was at the origin of a corpus of more than three thousand German poems in which doctrine and spiritual teachings are interwoven.

Frithjof Schuon authorized me to publish excerpts of general interest from his correspondence. The present collection is a compilation from all the French letters currently available, as well as the few English letters that Schuon addressed to Native American chiefs and Hindus. As for his German correspondence, which is almost as copious, its value may one day motivate one of his friends to prepare a second volume.

The interest aroused by Schuon's books and articles, a veritable metaphysical and spiritual summation, resulted in an abundant correspondence to which he responded tirelessly, conscious of his role and the impact of his thought in a world adrift, which doubts everything but its errors. He also responded to the many disciples scattered throughout the world who had only an occasional opportunity to see him.

Like many collections of letters, Schuon's brings a practical development to his published work, and the reader interested in his message will draw invaluable sustenance from it; he will sometimes be surprised by a given response, and often convinced by an evidentness of which he had only a presentiment, echoing a timeless truth buried deep in the soul. One should also note that, due to its private nature, an archive of this kind reveals some of the author's personal traits for the first time, tangible illustrations, as it were, of human and spiritual excellence. Schuon responded to each correspondent according to his capacity of comprehension, as one will notice in the course of reading. Unlike his books, his letters are conversational in tone; he never worried about style or about choosing the best turn of phrase, transcribing his reflections in a single draft, hence the spontaneity, at times close to speech, that characterizes many of his answers. This collection does not require a continuous reading from beginning to end, for each letter forms a whole, allowing both those readers unfamiliar with the author's thinking and those interested in a particular topic to opt for a selective reading by referring to the table of contents or the index.

Given that they were addressing the author himself, the great majority of his correspondents accepted the fundamental idea of a unity underlying all the great revelations—a transcendental, esoteric or metaphysical unity. The universalist perspective of these correspondents notwithstanding, I thought it best to classify the letters according to the religious forms practised by the respective recipients, at the risk of giving those unaware of my decision a false impression of confessional exclusivism. In each chapter, the letters are ordered chronologically. Contrary to academic practice, and in order to encourage the reader's personal involvement in the content of the message, it seemed appropriate to make only sporadic mention of the addressees' names, the best-known being René Guénon, Titus Burckhardt, Martin Lings, Seyyed Hossein Nasr, Léo Schaya, Jean Borella, Marco Pallis, William Stoddart, Rama Coomaraswamy, Joseph E. Brown, Jean-Louis Michon, Michel Valsan and Lord Northbourne. The book includes a glossary of foreign words used in the letters (p. 251); since they appear in transliterated form (with diacritical signs and without capitals), they differ slightly from the phonetic transcriptions adopted by the author. It is perhaps worth noting here that Arabic transcriptions often appear in Arabic characters in the original text. A few remarks in square brackets will facilitate a better understanding of the text.

As well as being a concrete illustration of Schuon's thought, which is concerned above all with the nature of things, thus with That which Is, *Towards the Essential*, due to its relative ease of access, is also intended as a helpful introduction to a message which, in his books, sometimes approaches the limits of the expressible—the impersonal, timeless, essential and universal message of *Religio Perennis*, the doctrinal and methodical esoterism of which Frithjof Schuon is unquestionably one of the greatest spokesmen.

T.B.

Letters to Christian Correspondents

13 May 1949 · SPIRITUALIZING SUFFERING

The facts that you recount in your second letter are indeed miraculous. They highlight the spiritual and providential meaning of the trials that followed them. Such trials have a twofold cause: the exhausting of our past errors—which may come from a former existence—and the cosmic reaction against our current ignorance; there are also sufferings whose meaning is that of a martyrdom and which a saintly man can take on for others. In your case, there is no need for you to worry about your incapacity to concentrate or to meditate: it would have sufficed to have offered your sufferings to God and invoked His Name without concentration. In a great suffering, as in a great joy, it is the experience of it that serves as meditation; and it is the acceptance—in view of God—of a suffering that serves as concentration. I know this myself, for I have suffered atrociously in my life.

In the lives of saints, for example in that of St Theresa of the Child Jesus, suffering due to a near total lack of physical well-being, and above all also due to the cold and illness, plays an important role. Assuming that St Theresa had followed a way requiring intellectual concentration, her attitude towards suffering would have been the same. Suffering is—by a direct "vision"—a meditation on death.

To understand and accept the cosmic and spiritual meaning of pain amounts temporarily to a kind of concentration. It could be said that, in such a case, and under the sole condition of the attitude I have just defined, the angels concentrate for us—exactly as it is said that angels pray in the stead of him whom illness prevents from praying, on condition that he have the intention to do so.

12 July 1950 · SPIRITUALITY

There is no spiritual method that does not wound our nature. Spirituality is both the easiest and the hardest thing. The easiest:

because it is enough to think of God. The hardest: because fallen nature is forgetfulness of God.

31 May 1955 · CHRISTIAN INITIATION

One cannot draw a systematic distinction between the supernatural and the spiritual, because the first necessarily intervenes in the second, in different ways. The intellect too has a supernatural aspect, but this goes beyond the ordinary theological perspective, which recognizes only will and reason in man.

One must not seek anything from priests that is situated outside their functions; therefore one must direct oneself only to their sacramental function and, depending on the case, to their theological authority; but theology can also be found in books.

In Christianity, it is baptism, confirmation, and Communion that constitute what can be termed initiation; the total character of these sacraments excludes the existence, alongside them, of more or less secret initiatic rites that could be superimposed on them—initiatic rites such as are found in Orphism, Sufism, etc. The particularity of Christianity is precisely the open character of the initiatic means; at least, this is a distinctive feature in the Semitic and Western world. There is a disagreement on this point between Guénon's thesis and mine. Indeed, one cannot conceive that there could be, in Christianity, a source of graces that is more profound or more precious than the blood of Christ, or that there could be souls or intelligences for whom this source would not be good enough. The difference exoterism-esoterism is in this case uniquely a question of perspective and method. There is, of course, a purely exoteric participation in the sacraments, so that one cannot without misuse of language describe the collectivity of Christians as "initiates", but monks and nuns are initiates by the fact that they follow a spiritual path; the same applies to priests who are saints, such as the Curé d'Ars. As for the intellective path, namely gnosis, it is represented above all by Clement of Alexandria, Meister Eckhart, and Angelus Silesius; but it is always specifically Christian gnosis, in other words one situated very close to the perspective of love.

Consequently, the two strange occurrences you allude to in your letter cannot be initiations in the literal and technical sense of the term, for Heaven never acts without a sufficient reason; on the other hand, such occurrences can be "accidental"—and at the same time "providential"—contacts with the world of Essences, be it considered in a subjective manner or in an objective and cosmic manner. What might the practical value be of such "encounters" with "higher states"? They are a calling or a vocational prompting for a contemplative life. After having been subjected to these "fissures" in the hardened individual shell, one ought to make of life a continuous and secret prayer. But this is only possible with the help of the Name of God, that is to say the invocation of Christ, namely the "prayer of Jesus". In order to take on such a path, one must have, above all, the indispensable theoretical knowledge, and a purity of intention that excludes all conscious and unconscious individualism; one must be centred on God, not on the ego. There are multiple illusions on this plane. But with God, all things are possible.

31 May 1955 · THE EUCHARIST, INVOCATION

The impossibility of having an esoteric ritual superimposed on the sacraments results from their character of totality, and notably from the nature of the Eucharist. The revelation, in Christianity, is Christ himself; now the Eucharist is Christ, all of Christ. Since Revelation must comprise, by definition, all spiritual modes, and since Christ unifies in his divinity all these modes, including of course those that can rightly be qualified as "esoteric" or "universal", the same applies to the Eucharist, which is the Word incarnate, and not only a "part"—an exoteric part—of the God-Man. Hence it is the central and total character of the Christian dogmas and sacraments that stands in opposition to the Guénonian thesis.

The connection between the invocation and eucharistic Communion is admirably captured in the following liturgical formulas: "*Panem celestem accipiam et nomen Domini invocabo*", and: "*Calicem salutaris accipiam et nomen Domini invocabo*" ["I shall receive the Bread of Heaven and call upon the Name of the Lord", and "I shall receive the Chalice of Salvation and call upon the Name of the Lord": the words of the priest preparing himself for Communion. *Ed.*]. There can be no initiation superior to the Eucharist, for the simple reason that the blood of Christ contains all of the divinity of the Word made flesh; the Eucharist perpetuates the Word incarnate, in totality, not just in part.

In order to invoke without risk—and in the absence of a spiritual master—it is necessary first of all to know the doctrine contained in the Philokalia or, what amounts to the same, in the "Russian Pilgrim" [*The Way of a Pilgrim*, anonymous work. *Ed.*]— an essentially Patristic doctrine—then to invoke the Holy Spirit and place oneself under the protection of the Virgin; one must realize in oneself the virtues of humility and of charity, that is to say to be aware of one's personal as well as of one's existential limitations, and to consider oneself as a stranger while considering one's neighbour as oneself.

As for language, I am opposed to invoking in French or in just any modern tongue, because these languages bear the imprint of the modern deviation; they are "worn-out" by "literature", etc. One must choose a liturgical language. As for the choice of a formula, this is a matter of vocation.

There is pretension only when there is an absence of intelligibility; in other words, man is entitled to that whose meaning he perceives; intuitive and contemplative intelligence is a grace on par with mystical graces. The intellect is a "naturally supernatural" grace, if one may express oneself thus.

The soul is complex and it has need of diversity; there are thus various means to overcome our nature and to obtain transforming and sanctifying fervour and concentration. What I mean is that there are different modes of orison: the Name of Jesus, the Lord's Prayer, the rosary, Psalms, personal prayer; it is above all the latter that, next to the invocation, must not be neglected. In the Name of Jesus, it is in some fashion God Himself who pronounces His Name; there is a great mystery in this. In the canonical prayers, it is man who prays, man as such and not this or that man; whence the use of the plural "we" in the Lord's Prayer. The prayer of man as such is of necessity revealed, it is the prayer God wishes to hear. In the case of personal prayer, however, performed in a vulgar tongue and not in a liturgical tongue, it is a specific person who prays; it is a specific soul that channels its powers towards God. In this prayer, one must tell God everything, even our boredom, even our incapacity to pray, if such be the case. Invocation, canonical prayer, personal prayer: those are the three necessary modes of the way of prayer.

1 June 1955 · *BHAKTI* AND *JNĀNA* IN CHRISTIANITY

In its general form—not in all its possibilities—Christianity is founded upon man's volitive, thus passional, aspect: man is will, and then reason, without which his will would not be free. In its form, Christianity is a *bhakti*, but *jnāna* also finds its place therein, thanks to the universality of Christic symbolism; this is necessarily so, since the Christian tradition is a totality. Before the Council of Nicaea, there was a certain vacillation in perspectives; the Council of Nicaea marks the crystallization of Christianity into a bhaktic perspective, while officially excluding *jnāna*, that is, a path based upon intellective factors and thereby upon the axiom that man is the intellect; according to the same viewpoint, Christ is the incarnation of the universal Intellect, so that inversely, everything that pertains to the intellect pertains to Christ, independently of the contingencies of time and place.

In fact, Christianity has a voluntarist, individualist and sentimental character; these words do not indicate a pejorative sentiment here, but express external traits that Christianity necessarily has, inasmuch as it must suit the Western mentality. In conformity with this mentality, Christian exoterism confers an absolute value upon a historical fact, and inversely, it attributes a relative character to the Absolute; it ignores the degrees of Reality, exactly as is done by the Hindu *bhakti*, for which the world is real. The result is that Christianity attributes great importance, in fact, to intermediate relativities; the cult of the Virgin, prayers for souls in purgatory, masses with such and such a purpose, etc. Being individualist, Christianity concentrates too much on sin and underestimates positive modes of spirituality based on concentration and aesthetic intuition; in general, its mysticism ignores both intellection and concentration, and in practice recognizes only individualist ascesis and sentimentalities; intellectual and technical—or "yogic"—methods seem "easy" to it—as if this were a criterion, and as if things that are easy in theory could not be difficult in practice. Christianity has a certain hostility with regard to intelligence, this being neither indispensable to *bhakti*, nor accessible to every man; its exclusively ascetic and sentimental viewpoint brings with it by way of vulgarization, and in fact invariably, a sort of cult of stupidity and ugliness, and of disagreeableness also. Intelligence then readily seems like "pride", and is always reduced to reason, which is something individual; beauty, for its part, appears in its aspects of seduction, sensuality, sin, or at least pleasure and ease; nature is "of this world", one is always afraid of a "pagan" naturalism. Such a perspective admits of nothing "supernatural" in man, apart from grace, which man cannot call forth; it is fundamentally dualist by the very fact of its theological anthropomorphism. What is of grave concern here is that upon contact with intellectual or jnanic perspectives, a "personalist" mysticism is substituted for suprapersonal metaphysics, and this constitutes an inversion of metaphysical relationships; to save the lower perspective, *bhakti*—which, incidentally, is in no way threatened by *jnāna*, since the latter puts each thing in its place—the higher perspective is belittled, and once again, an absolute character is given to the relative, and inversely.

1956 · CERTITUDE, INVOCATION, FAITH

The best way to escape the difficulty you describe to me is to place yourself at a viewpoint in which it is a matter of indifference if you "feel" certitude or not; that is to say, the question of knowing whether or not there is such a thing as "lived" certitude should appear to you *a priori* as a contingent matter without importance. The "taste" of certitude is a matter of realization; once one becomes engaged in a spiritual "alchemy", certain contrasts become more acute, and one cannot but feel incomplete in some manner or another. The happiness of worldly people, if one may say, is that they do not see all their disharmonies; they dwell in an opaque and easy homogeneity; it is a harmony procured for a pittance. There is nothing unusual about the difficulty you describe to me, it is just a symptom like another; since the man who has not achieved spiritual realization lacks unity and plenitude, then he is bound to sense that lack; there are many forms of inward scission. All told, what you feel has a positive value.

No concept as such is Truth itself; "existential" certitude is the identification with that truth, which is intrinsically certitude. Absolute certitude is God.

However, it is good to be profoundly aware of the metaphysical foundation of invocation; I speak of this in a chapter entitled "Modes of Prayer" which is part of my book *The Stations of Wisdom*; it is due to be published very soon. But apart from the doctrinal lights, it is the invocation that ultimately gives all light and all soothing, provided we persevere. If our thoughts disappoint or bore us, we must replace them with the Divine Name, for it will "think" in our stead, implicitly and infinitely so.

The certitudes that we may have *a priori* need to be nourished by faith; for faith is an attitude of calmness, trust, resignation, "poverty of spirit", existential simplicity. Man is so made that intellectual certitude does not suffice; man is not just a thinking being, he also lives. Life is situated outside our certitudes, thus it must come to meet them through faith. Faith is the feminine element which is added to the masculine element that is certitude. Within a traditional civilization, faith is something easy, it is so to speak in the air one breathes, but in the modern world it is doubt that is in the air, this doubt that exacerbates our need for logical explanations and our critical sense. Faith is a kind of beauty, whereas doubt has something of miserliness and envy, it is a kind of vindictive bitterness. Faith is nourished by metaphysical certitude on the one hand and by life in God on the other; the pivot of life in God is prayer and virtue. Virtue consists in giving up the tension and heaviness that the Fall has superimposed on our primordial nature; prayer is the fixation of the powers of our soul in God; the quintessence of prayer is the invocation, "jaculatory orison"; it could also be called "pure prayer" or "synthesis of prayers".

7 February 1956 · SPIRITUAL LIFE, CONCENTRATION, DEATH
   to a young monk

It was a pleasure to receive news of you. In turn, I express my best wishes of blessings for this new year. I am glad to learn that you have finally found a life setting that suits your aspirations, that is to say a setting arranged in view of the "one thing necessary". "Solutions of convenience"—since you bring up this moral problem and this typically modern way of looking at things—are always legitimate if God is the purpose of these solutions, for "my yoke is easy, and my burden light"; worldly people make a cult out of difficulty which is but one more form—and a fairly hypocritical form at that—of individualism; it is to forget that greatness comes from God and not from man. The greatness of divine qualities reveals itself to one who opens himself to them, if one may express oneself thus. In spiritual life, difficulties often reside in things that are apparently simple; victory belongs to him who, in secret, knows how to persevere in small things. To think of God, to empty oneself for Him, to escape that habitual dream in which the ego gazes at itself and repeats itself, this seems *a priori* simple; what could be easier than to repeat a jaculatory orison? But to do this always, to keep renouncing our dream anew, to acquire the habit of standing in the presence of God, to thus violate the congenital tendencies of our soul—tendencies towards dissipation as well as laziness—this is a great thing whose "dimensions" cannot be measured from the outside. If you read the lives of saints, you will see that they were great above all through attitudes that were simple, but consistent; the more visible glories were, somehow, superimposed upon these. Worldly people like to soothe their conscience by musing about sublime realities, as if by thinking about them they participated in them; it is of course good to think about such realities and one cannot help doing so, however it is important not to let this habit supplant the absence of real virtues. One must dedicate oneself to a discipline that is not above our strength—that may even appear to be beneath it—but one must dedicate oneself wholly to that. And one will then see, over time, that it is above our strength, but that all is possible with the help of God; nothing is possible without this help. There are things that are small in themselves but, when practised with perseverance, lead to great things; this is what is forgotten by some who constantly bring up the reproach of "convenience".

People often speak to me of concentration, and complain that they are lacking in it; this is, above all, a lack of imagination, for he who knows that God is infinitely lovable and that there is nothing to fear outside Him, has little difficulty in maintaining himself in some state of recollectedness. The man sentenced to death has no trouble remembering death, and likewise the man parched with thirst remembers water effortlessly; it is not difficult for the young man to think about his bride-to-be. This is how every man ought to think of God; if he does not do it, it is because he lacks "imagination". And here is the great surprise of death: the moment the soul is wrested from the body and from this earthly world, it is confronted with God, and sees the fulgurating and infinite Essence of all that it loved—or could have loved—on earth. In a word: "to concentrate" on God is to know right now that all that we love, and all that we could love, is to be found infinitely in God, and that all we love here below we love only because of God, though without being aware of this. We attach ourselves to the fleeting reverberations on water, as if water were luminous; but upon death, we see the sun, with immense regret—unless we became aware of the sun in time.

1959 · THE RIGHT ATTITUDE TOWARDS A SPIRITUAL EXPERIENCE

[previous page missing] This is a cosmic accident that poses no problem in the framework of traditional orthodoxy; thus there is no cause for concern. Such an accident is rare; it is like an opening in the soul towards Heaven; it is of no practical interest to define the exact nature or import of this opening. But what one must know is that this cosmic accident can contribute either to salvation or to perdition. Many heresies stem from phenomena of this kind.

He who practises the spiritual method puts into operation what he is able to put into operation; if a given phenomenon is real, it will come to fruition through spiritual practice, on the express condition that the disciple does not seek to use the phenomenon as a basis, nor even probe its nature. If the phenomenon is illusory, it will disappear through practice.

A phenomenon that is real—a major spiritual experience of an accidental or gratuitous character—can lead the disciple to perdition if he behaves differently from any other disciple, that is, if he relies on his experience in the belief that he has realized something.

The disciple—whatever graces he may have received—must rely on metaphysical truth and orthodox spiritual practice alone; then on the necessary traditional prescriptions—the sacraments, where they still exist—and finally on the practice of the virtues, the purification of the soul. It must be repeated a thousand times that he must never rely on a personal experience, however sublime, nor believe that the exact understanding of such an experience has any importance whatsoever on the path.

1960 · EVIL, SOLITUDE, OUR LIFE

You ask me, in substance, why there is evil in the world. This is why: God, being infinite, created the world, that is to say the creation of the world is a necessary manifestation of His infinity and absoluteness. Now the world is not God; not being God, it cannot be perfect; were it perfect, it would be God Himself. And the world unfolds in duration; towards the end, imperfection predominates, whereas at the beginning of humanity, it is perfection that is preeminent. I have spoken of this in my books, better than I can do so here in a few words.

To be alone with God—without bitterness towards anyone, this is a categorical condition—is a wonderful thing; this solitude living from the invocation of the Divine Name. Our life is there before us, and we must live it; we cannot escape it. I know where the difficulty lies: it is easier—or less difficult—to be alone on a desert island, than to be among men who do not understand us. But if we have no choice, then we are obliged to accept the destiny God gave us and to do the best we can with it. Through prayer, we can transmute lead into gold, alchemically speaking; in a certain measure we can even transform those around us.

Your life cannot be without meaning in the eyes of God, for you exist and you have intelligence and free will. That you met H., and that you also know me, must mean something; there is no such thing as chance. We must start with what is certain, and not waste time fretting about how to evaluate what is uncertain; now what is absolutely certain is death, the meeting with God, eternity; then the present moment, the one we are living in this very instant and that we always live in, and in which we are free to choose God, by remembering Him. Things that are uncertain must be ordered in function of those that are certain—which are spiritual—and not inversely.

This with all my best wishes for blessings and peace.

1960 · BITTERNESS, CONFESSION, SPIRITUAL SINCERITY

Even if all of our past was nothing but error and disappointment, we must bless it if now, in this very instant, we have the grace of remembering God. He who stands before God, or withdraws into Him, has never lost anything. "The Kingdom of God is within you." And this Kingdom is now, not yesterday; it is here and not elsewhere; here in the Sacred Name and in this blessed instant.

You tell me, in your letter, that your soul is often sad and discouraged; this is natural; but above all, one must not allow bitterness to enter it, even in a roundabout or indirect manner, for example by objectifying personal experiences. This would also be illogical, since we know that others have had other experiences and that our experience is not more real than theirs.

Certainly, your life is quite agitated, but we must get into the habit of slipping into it the remembrance of God—the "act of love" as Sister Consolata would say—and this can be done in all circumstances.

The world is a battleground, and it is necessary that there be warriors of the Light everywhere, if I may express myself thus. In the meantime, you are where Providence has placed you, and this means that even there—in the chaos in which you live—there must be someone who thinks of God, or in other words, who manifests the "remembrance". We must bear witness, invisibly. In any case we have no choice; each must do what he can.

Regarding confession, it must be envisaged in its strictly sacramental aspect. One can always accuse oneself for one's breaching of the rules, then of one's lukewarmness, if one wants to, but it is not a matter of "sharing personal secrets". The priest is the instrument of a sacramental grace, he is not necessarily a master; it is even very unlikely that he be so, although he should be so and he is so in principle.

Spiritual sincerity is a grace. One can always blame oneself for lacking in it, but in vain; God knows very well that man is human. Therefore one must cling to God and have trust. The worst of errors is to close oneself to Mercy.

May God bless you!

2 May 1960 · IN GERMANY

We crossed the Rhineland, Bavaria, and Wurttemberg; there one finds medieval towns that are still nearly intact, notably Rothenburg ob der Tauber and Dinkelsbühl. The fact that the Germans protect nature everywhere is also very worthy of note; the quasi absence of billboards is a real blessing. This is true also of the English countryside.

7 October 1960 · THE INCARNATION

Thus, according to some of the Greek Fathers and orthodox theologians, the "Incarnation" would have brought about a kind of universal blessing, an effusion of the "Christic" grace even outside the visible Church. In order to give this remarkable doctrine its full scope and complete universality, it is necessary to know that the "Incarnation" can only touch non-Christians on condition of being situated outside History: the "Self" is "incarnated" in separativity or illusion, *Ātmā* is "incarnated" in *Māyā*; it is the entry into *Māyā*—giving rise to *Īshvara*—that constitutes the "Incarnation" *in divinis*, the eternal Incarnation; it is this Incarnation that has saved beings—first as possibilities—from nothingness, if one may say. On a more reduced scale—or at a lesser degree of reality—the Incarnation is *Buddhi*, that is to say the "sacrificial" entry of *Purusha* into Existence; it is the existential *fiat lux*, the illumination of darkness or chaos. In a more particular meaning, which concerns man, *Buddhi* saves in its capacity as Vishnu or Shiva, that is to say through *bhakti* or *jnāna*; *Buddhi* has an existential function and an intellectual function, and it is the latter which can be termed "Christic". Christ manifests historically and through his very person, in a direct manner, these prototypes of the "Incarnation" and the "Redemption"; but every other Revelation manifests them likewise, each according to its manner, depending on the aspects of the Real and all possible perspectives.

Ātmā, by entering *Māyā* as *Īshvara*, has "saved" possibilities from nothingness; *Īshvara* has saved potentialities from Non-Being and virtualities from non-manifestation; *Buddhi* saves—in a converse and ascending manner—beings from negative manifestation, then manifestation as such; it does so objectively through the *Avatāra* and subjectively through the Intellect.

In no wise does any of this exclude the fact that the birth and death of Christ had the effect of bringing about a universal effusion of graces; but the same thing is true for each Revelation; in that case, it is a matter not of decisive and saving graces—those which are already bestowed by the respective Revelation—but of vivifying graces; it is in this sense that the "Descent" (*tanzīl*) of the Koran can be said to mysteriously touch other spiritualities, to wit the Christian one, or that the "Enlightenment" (*bodhi*) of the Buddha illuminated Hindu spirituality. One can even say, paradoxically, that through the mere fact of his advent, Christ vivified the esoterism of the Greco-Roman tradition, even though it was perishing.

Some might object that only Christ manifests the eternal "Incarnation" in a direct mode and that, as a result, the manner of manifesting it is indirect in the other Revelations; we could respond by saying that only the Buddha manifests the eternal *Bodhi* in a direct manner, and therefore that the *Bodhi* appears in an indirect manner in Christ, and so on and so forth. This is due to the fact that we speak of "Incarnation" because of Christ, and of "Enlightenment" because of the Buddha; the possible designations of the prototype of Revelation and of Deliverance are innumerable. There is in manifestation an unfolding of symbols, and each symbol refers to a real aspect of the Divine Model, or the universal models deriving from it; but since it is a matter here of the same principial and primordial reality, namely the entry of the Absolute into relativity—whatever the degree considered may be—the modes or symbols are not mutually exclusive: the entry of the Koranic Revelation into the body of the Prophet can be termed an "incarnation" of the Word, just as the entry of the Holy Spirit—bearer of the Word—into the body of the Virgin is a "descent" of the Divine Book; and likewise, these two words are within the *Bodhi*, and the *Bodhi* is within them.

All of this is obvious for us, but I wanted to formulate it as I have just done. I intend to write on this subject.

23 April 1962 · OVERCOMING BAD HABITS

You ask me what one must do to overcome bad habits. First of all, one needs to be aware of their causes and also of their consequences; one must objectivize them, see them for what they are and know where they lead us. One needs to know in what way they are opposed to the fundamental virtues.

Hindus say that nothing can resist knowledge, that "there is no lustral water equal to it". This is because it is easy to become detached from something that one has objectivized perfectly, that is to say from something that one is able to see from above. It is difficult to become detached from something with which one is identified.

Next, we must pray that God help us. We must describe our state and our difficulties to God.

The Divine Name, independently from our individual problems, helps us and transforms us. One must therefore invoke much, forgetting what we are and investing all of our life and all of our being into the invocation, something moreover which is in keeping with the Supreme Commandment, that of the perfect love of God.

10 January 1968 · MODERN SCIENCE, TRANSUBSTANTIATION

Modern science, insofar as it applies logic and experience to sensory phenomena, would not be blameworthy were it not that it denies all supra-sensory reality—which escapes both logic purely and simply and, with all the more reason, sensory experience—and were it not that it compensates this negation with errors serving as substitutes such as evolutionism, psychologism, etc.

Leaving aside these limitations, nothing prevents one from understanding "scientifically"—that is, in the sense of a rigorous adequation—the fact of Transubstantiation, which is perfectly clear metaphysically. It suffices to know about the degrees of universal Reality—something modern people do not seek to do—and the reciprocal relationships possible between them.

The great harm of modern science—all the other ills derive from this—is to be found in its very principle, namely an outward curiosity that is incompatible with an understanding of total Truth, and a practical application of this curiosity that is incompatible with spirituality and amounts to a pact with the "Prince of this world".

If the discoveries of modern science are objectively real, then it goes without saying that they have a metaphysical meaning, the one they necessarily have as phenomena; but this proves absolutely nothing in favour of this science.

In order not to find "the doctrine of Transubstantiation to be something astonishing", there is no need to have recourse to considerations on logic's modes of procedure, etc.; this diminishes in a certain way the said doctrine while unduly overrating the value of scientific thought. It suffices to know what Transubstantiation is metaphysically, to what order of possibility it corresponds, and why it must manifest in a given form.

Equations between matter and energy operate with elements that are metaphysically equivalent, whereas the doctrine of Transubstantiation envisages realities that are mutually incommensurable; therein lies all the difference.

9 February 1968 · TRUTH IS NOT EVERYTHING

It is indeed a marvellous destiny that has led you to discover universal metaphysics and traditional ideas in the solitude of your mountains. After reading your letter—I can read Italian but not write it—I sent you the Italian translation of some of my articles, published under the title *L'uomo e la certezza* [*Man and Certitude*].

Perhaps it will be possible for you to visit me in Pully, near Lausanne, sometime, God willing.

Truth is not everything—from the human point of view; one must also draw the consequences from it. And the most elementary consequence for man is to cling to God as to a lifeline. And everything converges on quintessential prayer.

29 April 1968 · THE SPIRITUAL PATH

With the practice of quasi-continual prayer, on the basis of universal metaphysical truth and in the framework of Christianity's sacramental methods, you have everything you need, *Deo juvante*. Psychic regeneration is produced in function of these conditions.

In other words:

One must have doctrinal, metaphysical discernment between the Real and the illusory.

One must have continual concentration on the Real; this continuity must at least be symbolized by a certain rhythm; the essential thing is that consciousness of the Real enters our soul, progressively.

These two elements—discernment and concentration—demand a third: virtue. In Christian terms, one speaks of humility and charity. It is essentially a matter of resignation to the divine Will on one hand, and fervour or joy in the spiritual life on the other. That is, we must accept the inevitable with patience, while putting all our joy in what brings us closer to God. Patience and trust; gratitude and hope.

Discernment, concentration, static and dynamic virtue, traditional framework; these are the conditions *sine qua non* of the path. The *Fiat Lux* belongs to God.

16 November 1969 · FORMAL RELIGIONS AND PERENNIAL RELIGION

In principle, it is obviously possible to go from one religious form to another; this presupposes that one be keenly aware of the pillars of the *Religio Perennis*—discernment, concentration, virtue, symbolism—and also that one have a valid motive for carrying out this passage. Formerly, I would never have dreamed of encouraging anyone to go from one orthodox religion to another orthodox religion, quite the contrary; but now, the situation of the Catholic Church is such that I shall not undertake anything to prevent such a change, if leaving Catholicism is the issue. From my point of view, the author of the letter here is free to consider the change he has in mind, if this be the Will of God;

he must therefore pray with this intention, in order that Heaven may guide him.

6 September 1970 · THE CHRISTIAN INVOCATORY PATH
to an Anglican nun

What distinguishes man from animals is 1. a total intelligence, capable of conceiving of the Absolute; 2. a free will, capable of choosing the Absolute; 3. a heavenly soul, happy only with the Infinite. As a result, man is only truly human in virtue of the contents that are proportioned to his intelligence, will, and soul; namely, the spiritual contents that by definition converge on God, or that are God, the Absolute, the Infinite. Hence it is our human nature itself that proves religion; it is only through spirituality that man is truly man.

All religion or all spirituality comes down to these three factors: 1. discernment between the world and God, or between the contingent and the Absolute, or between the illusory and the Real; 2. permanent concentration on this Real; 3. happiness in this Real.

Christianity's originality is to place the accent on the Divine Manifestation: it is therefore Christ who represents and embodies the Real; Christ and in a certain way the Blessed Virgin too. Christ corresponds more particularly to the elements "Absolute" and "Truth", and the Virgin to the elements "Infinite" and "Mercy", or "Beauty". Thus we need to know that in Christ and the Virgin we are oriented towards the divine Reality.

And what does permanent concentration on the Real mean in practice? It is essentially jaculatory prayer, such as it was practised by the Desert Fathers.

And what does finding our happiness in the Real alone mean in practice? It obviously means: to put all our joy into the invocation of God.

Oratio et jejunium, Christ said. That is to say, it is impossible to do what leads to God without abstaining from what removes from God, namely not just sins as such, but also profane distractions, trivial things, reading things that are useless and unworthy, in short just about everything that the modern world has to offer.

And it is impossible, and moreover illogical, to practise permanent prayer—the invocation—without practising the fundamental virtues, for no spiritual activity is possible without beauty of soul. The soul must therefore realize an attitude of poverty or childlikeness; of vigilance; of contentment or patience; of generosity or trust, in short, of fervour; of self-effacement; of inwardness.

That is all; I could end here. But I want to reread your letter, Reverend Sister, in order to answer some possible questions.

There is much talk about concentration nowadays, but it is done in a manner that is extra-traditional, hence in a purely profane and uniquely psychological way. These kinds of pseudo-yogas lead to nothing, be it only because nothing can be done without grace, and grace acts only within methods that are intrinsically orthodox, that is to say within religions.

Hence: the quintessential path is concentration by means of the invocation of God; this path proceeds on the basis of the metaphysical discernment between the illusory and the Real; and it is carried on with the help of the virtues of patience and trust, or with resignation and joy.

The fact that your religious ambiance is sentimental and therefore individualist, does not concern your spiritual life. What concerns you truly is your jaculatory prayer, your invocation of God. Next to this invocation, you have the sacraments; that the Eucharist will be of great help to you, this is obvious, although the invocation of the Divine Names is also a kind of Eucharist. You also have your personal prayer, addressed to Mary or to Christ, in which you speak to those celestial Personages by describing your state of soul, freely and without constraint. When one thinks that one cannot pray, one must say so; but one must pray.

If you deem that you cannot pursue your invocatory path within a religious community which, for various reasons, is an obstacle rather than an aid, you could obviously return to the world, despite your vows, given that those vows would not have been taken in full awareness of the situation. I do not know Anglican monasteries and I do not know if a strictly contemplative path can be practised there without hindrance. One always has the right to claim that a community to which one had made a commitment does not offer what one had expected.

I said that religion should be reduced to what is metaphysically essential, which all in all is identified with the *Sophia Perennis*. And we must choose the conditions of life or ambiance that offer us the maximum of opportunities to follow our path of discernment, invocation, and virtue harmoniously; I could also say: of metaphysical truth, unitive concentration, and heavenly beauty.

5 December 1970 · MARIAN GRACES, THE SPIRITUAL MASTER
to Rama Coomaraswamy

It is true that I received from the part of the Blessed Virgin some extraordinary graces, the nature of which I have described to no one. The authenticity of such graces is proven by the fact that they leave durable traces in the soul, to the point that we are no longer the same man as before; they remove us from the world and draw us toward Heaven. And there is a kind of vision or inward presence that remains. [...]

If the spiritual master is connected directly and consciously to the *Religio Perennis* and is thereby concretely situated beyond forms—which implies that he accepts them in practice and that he knows their worth—and if the postulant, whatever his formal religion may be, is situated within the same perspective, then in such a case there is nothing to prevent the postulant from becoming the disciple of a master belonging formally to another religion. [...]

After rigorous discernment in the name of the Truth, comes permanent concentration in the name of Love.

4 May 1971 · THE ESSENTIAL IN THE SPIRITUAL LIFE

It is clear that Catholicism, and likewise Orthodoxy, offer the means for the highest spiritual realization; the absolute conditions for this are baptism, confirmation, the first Communion, and perpetual orison, that is to say, precisely, the daily invocation of the Prayer of Jesus, or of the Name of Jesus, or of the Names of Jesus and of Mary.

In spiritual life, one must know how to simplify things, which presupposes that one be firmly conscious of the essential elements of the Path. To the Christians who come to me for advice—Catholics and Orthodox—I like to repeat that one must avoid complications, and that the essential, of which one must never lose sight, is this: discernment between the Real and the illusory, between God and the world, *Ātmā* and *Māyā*; then permanent concentration on the Real, or on the Manifestation of the Real, Jesus and Mary; and this presupposes the practice of the virtues, that is to say, the modes of conformity to the Real, for: "Be ye perfect as your Father in Heaven is perfect". Humility is not the fixed and sentimental idea that we are worse than others—such evaluations are often conjectural—but the consciousness of our nothingness before God and then of our limitation on the human plane and with respect to other men; likewise, charity is above all the awareness that the ego of others is not less truly "myself" than our own ego. Humility and charity are above all the virtues of self-effacement and generosity. Aside from the metaphysical significance of virtues, there is their quasi-musical aspect: virtue is not only a question of truth, it is also a question of beauty.

In spiritual life, outward things sometimes amount to much; the ambience in which we live must, as far as possible, be in conformity with the Spirit; one must live in a fragrance of *sattva*.

The Holy Virgin personifies the beauty of Heaven, she is something of the Beauty of God.

24 August 1971 · TAOISM, CHINESE MEDICINE, CHRISTIAN ESOTERISM

Your letter brings up rather complex issues, but I nonetheless want to attempt to answer it in a few words. Thus you are a Catholic and you practise Chinese medicine; you are studying Taoism. It is no doubt logical and useful to have a basic knowledge of Taoism when practising this medicine, but it is not indispensable to have a thorough knowledge of Chinese and to study all the books, all the more as their dialectical style is quite cryptic.

The demarcation line between practical efficacy and firm spiritual rooting fluctuates; one can obviously start from the idea that Chinese medicine is dependent on Taoism and as a consequence it requires an adherence to this tradition, just as one is entitled to admit, on the contrary, that this medicine can be validly practised on a strictly medical plane and thus outside the metaphysical and ritual domain. Moreover, one does not become a Taoist in order to be able to practise Chinese medicine; one is a Taoist because of a calling from Heaven—when one is Chinese—and the medicine aspect will possibly be practised afterwards, should such a vocation arise. Furthermore: Taoism can no doubt be practised, in principle, by men from any race and in any country; but this path requires such a degree of preliminary principial knowledge and sets such conditions of ambience and psychology that it is extremely unlikely Europeans can follow it in Europe; the capacity to follow this path amounts already to a kind of realization. Without even mentioning initiation, I would say that the psychological qualification is a *conditio sine qua non* and it is precisely this that is *de facto* lacking in the West, given the modern deformations; doctrinal knowledge and the techniques are nothing without certain concomitant dimensions that I would qualify as "moral" and "aesthetic".

Another problem is that of "Christian exoterism". Since I do not believe that the sacraments are exclusively exoteric in nature, I accept that a Catholic or an Orthodox Christian who understands the metaphysical meaning of the dogmas and who practises a quintessential method of orison, possesses all that he could need from the point of view of esoterism; the problem here is, on the one hand, that of the spiritual master and, on the other, of the deviation of current Catholicism. I have discussed the question of the spiritual master in my new book *Logic and Transcendence*.

12 January 1972 · A THORNY PROBLEM

The answer to your letter is difficult because there are, in your problem, two or three levels that are combined while diverging; on what plane shall I place myself to take on the responsibility of answering you? Whatever my desire may be to abstain from all criticism, the nature of things obliges me to give my advice on the facts you have submitted; unless I renounce writing to you, but that is not what you expect from me.

Thus, your wife, upon learning of your intention to come and see me, threatens to leave you, taking the children, to go and live in an unknown place. I am not asking to what degree you are attached to your wife; this question strikes me as being without interest here; but I am asking you to what degree you are attached to your children. Your attachment to your children could be a reason not to come and see me; not so your attachment to your wife.

For your wife cannot be unaware that you are the son of A.C.; she cannot be unaware of those intellectual and spiritual axioms on the basis of which you joined the Catholic Church; she cannot be unaware that your father liked me, and that nothing could be more natural than for you to want to come and visit me, just as I visited your mother almost ten years ago. One must be consistent: if she wants to be a Catholic in the way that she is at present—but this is not Catholicism anymore!—then she should have married a man of that kind, a Progressive and a Teilhardian.

I repeat that, logically and spiritually, you have no responsibility with respect to your wife, since she has an attitude that is neither Christian nor even simply human; but it may be that you have some responsibility with respect to your children. At least if it lies in your power to make of them traditional and spiritual men, which seems to me far from certain.

So, you have spoken of this problem to Father D., and you have both concluded that your wife has no real understanding of esoterism, and that her point of view is limited to a sentimental mysticism at most. I do not share this opinion; on the contrary, I think that your wife does not even have a real understanding of exoterism and that as a result there can be no question, in her case, of any Catholic mysticism, whether sentimental or not. For anyone who is "a strong advocate of Teilhard de Chardin's viewpoint" cannot be a Catholic; this is the very negation of even the most exoterist Catholicism. Someone who "considers that traditional concepts amount to a regression as well as an incapacity to adjust to the real world" is not Catholic in any degree. For the traditional spirit is the spirit of Christ; there is no choice here. Either one is Christian or one is not. "My kingdom is not of this world."

"…Why can't I be just a simple ordinary good person…?" But such a thing does not exist in Christianity! As Christ said, quoting the Torah: the Supreme Law, that which applies absolutely to any human creature, is to "love God with all thy heart, all thy soul, all thy mind, and all thy strength." "Narrow is the way", and "few those who find it"; and "whosoever wishes to save his life, shall lose it". There is no other Christianity.

Given that there are your children, I cannot give you any advice. If there were not the issue of your children, I would not hesitate for a second to tell you to come and see me.

You must address yourself to the Holy Virgin. You must tell her your whole story and ask for her help, and do so tirelessly.

9 December 1972 · THE SACRAMENTS, THE BLESSED VIRGIN, CONVERSION

I understand very well that Archbishop Anthony desires the publication of your reply to my criticism, since this reply clarifies the Orthodox viewpoint; a necessary clarification for the reader, given that your article [*Realization: a Christian point of view*] was presented as a "Christian point of view". But what you say in your reply should have been said at once! […]

You recognize that the title of your article was poorly chosen. Perhaps you will also recognize that the thesis was presented imperfectly, that it therefore led to confusion. I am not criticizing your private beliefs at all; my criticism refers only to the "incriminating evidence", that is, the form—or the logically verifiable content—of your article. My reaction to the latter is not that of the Orthodox reader who is supposed to know how to read between the lines—assuming he really manages to do so; it is only the reaction of the reader who expects information on "Christian Realization" without situating himself *a priori* in the context of Orthodoxy. You cannot hold me completely responsible for my reaction; it seems to me that on the contrary, you should recognize your portion of responsibility; but let us be constructive: in all justice, what needs to be said is that my criticism, whatever the value of its argumentation, renders a series of clarifications in the light of Orthodox doctrine desirable or even necessary. I do not believe I deserve a reproach; on the contrary, I think readers of the journal [*Studies in Comparative Religion. Ed.*] deserve your clarifications, at least those that concern intrinsic doctrine. For what renders your clarifications desirable or indispensable is not so much my criticism—prompted by your dialectic—but the elliptic nature of your article: my criticism can only be the occasional cause of explanations which are necessary anyway, and which—given your responsibility—should be presented in a neutral manner, as additional information. [...]

If I say that the sacraments are conditions, I am not saying that this is all they are; I am not denying that they are also methods. From the viewpoint of the method of prayer as taught by the *Philokalia*, the sacraments extrinsically have this aspect of condition *sine qua non*; besides, I am familiar with the Orthodox doctrine of the sacraments and it is not worth splitting hairs. [...]

Concerning the Blessed Virgin, one encounters the two theses in the oldest documents, and moreover, I do not see why the doctrine of the "Immaculate Conception"—upheld by Origen, St Ephrem and others—would be incompatible with the thesis adopted by Orthodoxy. I am telling you this in passing, as I do not have the time to explain it here *in extenso*. In any case, concerning the Blessed Virgin, I do not think one can speak of "spiritual realization" in the technical and methodical sense of the term. She was "full of Grace" from the moment she was greeted by the angel: that is, her sanctity was humanly unsurpassable, which in no way excludes the fact that she had to learn certain things subsequently. [...]

The association of ideas between "the heavens" and futile imaginations is a bad abuse of language; in the continental languages, Germanic as much as Latin, it is the clouds that evoke fantasies, not the sky. Naturally and traditionally, the sky—whatever word may designate it—evokes God's Domain by analogy; the Greek Gospel uses the same word for the visible sky and Heaven; moreover, Christ rose towards the visible sky. In any case, associating a meaning of illusion or phantasmagoria with the beautiful image of the visible sky is not among the glories of the English language.

As a possible title for your article, I had proposed the word "conversion"; this word signifies the passage, not only from one religion to another—or from unbelief to a religion—but also from worldliness to piety, or simply from common negligence to spiritual contemplation. A given saint, though a believer *a priori*, will be said to have been converted to God through the influence of a given event; I do not know if Orthodox believers are familiar with this use of the word "conversion", but the Catholics are familiar with it.

Coming back to "the general conditions of spirituality", let us be concrete: reading what you have written, one has the impression that it suffices to wait for some inner experience or other in order to "realize" something; or one could think that Christian realization is to recite the Jesus Prayer, without sacraments or moral effort. It is to forestall this very common misunderstanding—which you did not take into account—that I speak of the sacraments as "conditions"; I also mention faith, because it can happen that believers want to "try" a given method of prayer, telling themselves that they will have faith if the method succeeds; in addition I mention the virtues, thinking of people who imagine that to obtain a given "realization", it suffices to practise a spiritual "technique". [...]

What I reproach in your article is that you have only thought of yourself, instead of also thinking—even above all—of your readers, including a reader such as myself. You object—as if I did not know this—that the sacraments are spiritual means and not conditions; doubtless, but the sacraments do not interest the commonest category of seekers of "realization"; it is the apparently easy and gratuitous methods that interest them, those that one can get from books.

20 December 1972 · A DISAGREEMENT
to Archbishop Anthony of Sourozh, Metropolitan of the Russian Orthodox Church for Great Britain and Ireland

Your Grace,

During my stays in England, I sometimes have the intention of paying you a short visit, but as I know you are quite busy and since I do not wish to take up your time, I content myself with asking Miss D. to transmit to you my best regards, hoping that she will not forget to do so. That being the case, it is all the more paradoxical that I am suggesting that you read—at least in part—the text included here, which is the copy of my recent letter to Miss D.

The publication of my critique of her article was more or less accidental: I did not have the intention *a priori* of having those reading notes published. But it was impressed on me that I ought to do so. It was also my understanding finally, based on a letter from Marco Pallis, that Miss D. was not opposed to the publication of those remarks; I took note of this, not without admiring her humility and detachment.

I subsequently learned, from Miss D. herself, that she was determined to answer me, or rather that she had already sent her response to the editor of the review. Having read that response, I wrote to Miss D. the pages included here which I am sending you, Your Grace, in order that you be informed exactly regarding my point of view. It seems to me too that Miss D., once having been apprised of my long letter, could be brought to add some nuance to her text sent to the editor, given that some of her opinions do not render adequate account of my intentions.

Thus in principle I am in agreement with the publication of the "clarifications" by Miss D. But the editor will ask me to have the last word; however, I am firmly determined to end this incident "gracefully". I do not wish to "triumph"; rather, what I want is to restore the equilibrium according to the principle of charity, if I may put it so. I nonetheless hope that Miss D. will make my task easier; otherwise, I shall have to add a few more arguments, but shall do so—I repeat—in a wholly neutral manner, by way of information, and by avoiding the impression of a personal contradiction.

The crux of the difficulty is perhaps this overly peremptory opinion of Miss D.: those who believe they know all that they need, will never gain new insights. This is correct from a certain secondary point of view, but one could also say: God does not refuse His graces because we believe we have obtained all that we need; He refuses them only because we do not take advantage of that which we have already received. He reproaches us, not for not desiring more knowledge out of a sense of our poverty, but for not sanctifying ourselves with the knowledge we already possess, which, whether partial or total on its plane, is a loan from God.

It goes without saying, Your Grace, that I do not expect an answer from you, except in prayer.

1973 · INVOCATION AND SOBRIETY

The terms *oratio et jejunium* imply that the invocation of the Name—or of the Names—must always be accompanied by perfect sobriety, which is to say that one must not expect any results during invocation; our entire satisfaction must come from the sole fact that we are practising the invocation or that we are in presence of the Name. One must not hope for any sensible grace; one must behave as if grace would come only at the moment of death. For what saves us is not the awareness of some grace or answer, it is uniquely the fact that we pray. For this we have our whole life; one must therefore be mindful of the equilibrium of the soul so as to avoid the alternations between phases of enthusiasm and aridity. If we are indifferent to aridity, it will dissipate in the end; we must be thoroughly imbued with the idea that what matters is not our states but uniquely our fidelity to prayer. Our soul must not complicate things; when complications arise, one must on the one hand eliminate them through intelligence by trying to understand their causes, and on the other hand combat them through personal prayer by asking for Heaven's help.

If you have temptations of weariness, this proves that you are putting too much psychic effort into the spiritual practice, and this is tiring for the soul; one must invoke in a more impersonal and more detached manner, and not engage oneself overly in the individualism typical of voluntaristic mysticism; one must have the sense of peacefulness. Our sentiments are nothing, perseverance is everything.

On the other hand, ups and downs are natural for the soul; everything that is situated in duration undergoes phases; every continuous motion contains rhythms. Likewise, temptations and reactions are natural for the soul; this should not surprise us, we need simply to entrust ourselves to Heaven and beseech its help.

19 April 1973 · THE RESURRECTION OF THE FLESH, THE POSTHUMOUS DESTINY OF ANIMALS, HELL

As you may well imagine, I was quite surprised to receive a letter from you—I did not know what had become of you—and at the same time I am glad to learn that certain spiritual worries are now behind you; *Deo gratias.*

It is not easy to situate the problem of the resurrection in a few words; first of all, it must be said that what we have here is a cosmic event, the metaphysical cause of which is the state of fall or disgrace of matter. It is a question, all told, of a return to the initial equilibrium: accursed or perverted matter must be replaced with a blessed or regenerate matter, and this change can only take place from within; a new matter will be so to speak projected from the subtle state, and this is the resurrection. It may be impossible to imagine this, but it is no less real for that, and metaphysically necessary; each disequilibrium requires a return to equilibrium.

As for the question of the afterlife—or eschatological destiny—of animals, Semitic and monotheistic theologies deal with it only from the outside and in passing; that is to say, the question does not interest them since they confine themselves essentially to the consideration of the human state, which begins with human birth and is prolonged in the Paradises or the hells of the human species. It is easy to grasp that Paradise is eternal since it opens onto Eternity; but what is the meaning of the "eternity" of hell? This expression signifies, not that it is truly eternal, which would be metaphysically and morally absurd, but only that the damned are definitively excluded from the human Paradise; this definitive character is expressed, precisely, by the wholly symbolic notion of "eternity", which suggests something absolute or rather irreversible. In reality—but theologies are not at all interested in this—the damned will finally leave hell to enter into the lower transmigration, with the possibility of being born in the end into a state analogous to the human state, and which therefore opens onto a Paradise analogous to the human Paradise; but, once again, theologies are only interested in man and account only for that which concerns him. They are no more interested in animals than in the damned, or rather in the latter's post-human destiny; in theological parlance, animals are "destroyed", just as damnation is "eternal"; "and let us be done with this question". Now animals, not being central beings like man, actually continue through transmigration; but there is in this a possible exception, that of noble animals which have lived in the ambiance of a saint or of a sanctuary, and are absorbed, after their death, by the Paradise of this saint, or of the saints of the sanctuary's setting; thus, it is said that Jalāl ad-Dīn Rūmī's cat—filled with *barakah*—went to Paradise after his master. *wa Llāhu a'lam*. [...]

PS. The "resurrection of the flesh" does not concern either Christ or the Virgin, or Enoch, whose bodies were glorified by the Ascension—or the Assumption—itself. There were, of course, other cases of this sort.

4 August 1973 · SEXUALITY, THE FALL OF ADAM

Certainly, the priest's thesis has something appealing, given that it evokes a certain symbolism that is plausible; yet, finally, it is false because it goes against the nature of things and therefore against total and essential symbolism.

First of all, sexual union is in itself a positive reality, I would even say a divine one; Genesis says nothing to suggest the contrary, and Hinduism attributes this union to the Divinities themselves. Secondly, the cause of the Fall is not in a given aspect of nature, it is solely in the fact of separating all the natural aspects from their Divine Source, namely to experience them outside God and to attribute their glory and enjoyment to ourselves.

The priest in question is therefore not completely wrong if he says that God alone has the right to ravish virginity; but he overlooks the fact that in sacramental sexuality, it is precisely God who is operating, whereas man participates in the divine operation. Moreover, this principle of union with God concerns all the aspects of normal eroticism—the Church is metaphysically mistaken in bringing everything back to the concern for procreation, which implies on the one hand a certain hypocrisy and on the other hand a partial falsification—and this union with God also, and even above all, concerns our intelligence and our will in an altogether general way. The sin of Adam was not a specific outward action; this sin was, fundamentally, the fact of being, thinking, willing, acting, and enjoying outside God; in the act of knowledge or of willing, it was to isolate both the subject and the object; it was to separate them illusorily from God, "sole Subject and sole Object", as the Sufis would say.

The sexual behaviour of the human couple in the earthly Paradise, or in the Golden Age, was the same as that of men in other Ages; the proof of this is that a Rāma, a Krishna, a Muhammad were married as ordinary men are, but with the significant difference that sexual pleasure, far from being locked in an individualist passion, at once compressive and centrifugal, was on the contrary a participation in divine Beatitude, on the very basis of the extinction entailed by sexual union, as Ibn 'Arabī noted.

The disturbing aspects that sexuality may contain *de facto* do not come from the thing in itself, they derive from the degeneration of matter or of the flesh, and also from that of man in general; for one degeneracy leads to another. One will note also that most Westerners—unlike Hindus—do not have the innate sense of what I term "the metaphysical transparency of phenomena".

If the priest of whom you speak to me were right, Christ and the Blessed Virgin would not have attended the wedding at Cana; and Christ would not have said: "Wherefore they are no more twain, but one flesh", and he would not have forbidden to put asunder "what therefore God hath joined together". [...]

PS. "The tree of the knowledge of good and evil": this is the separative distinction of the Substance from the accidents considered in themselves.

15 February 1974 · THE FALL OF ADAM, CONCUPISCENCE,
SEXUALITY, MARRIAGE

This is what one can read in the treatise of dogmatic theology by
Father Berthier: "*By elevating man (Adam) into grace, God granted
him excellent gifts, and above all, He freed him from ignorance, concupiscence, old age (from which, according to St Thomas, he could escape
by means of the tree of life); from death, illnesses, and the trials of this
life. The exemption from ignorance is clear: 'He created in them knowledge of the spirit'... The exemption from concupiscence is also clear:
'They were both naked, and were not ashamed'... The immunity from
death is an article of faith: 'God created man to be inexterminable'...
Though he was in the state of innocence, man nonetheless needed food;
he would have propagated himself in the same manner as today... Had
the first man persevered, all of his offspring would have been born in
justice, together with the free gifts we indicated; however, they would
not have been impeccable, nor would they have had all of Adam's
knowledge. Yet they could have acquired it, either by discovering it or
by learning it, but could have done so very easily. And even had the
children of Adam, who remained innocent, sinned, their own children
would have nonetheless been born in justice.*"

This then is the traditional Christian teaching. This calls for
an initial commentary concerning the idea of concupiscence:
concupiscence is neither the desire for enjoyment in itself, nor
enjoyment as such, but both, inasmuch as they are situated outside God and, because of this, they are no longer supports for
spiritual contemplation, nor concrete contemplative participa-
tions in divine Beatitude; on the contrary, enjoyment when sep-
arated from God—due to the Fall—takes one away from God
owing to the fact that it appears as an end in itself; on the one
hand, it is practically speaking an idol, since it takes God's place
and, on the other hand, it puffs up raw individuality; there is
thus something Luciferian about it. Before the Fall, the desire
for carnal union coincided with a spiritual desire, that is to say
with the desire for a particular perception of the Infinite or, formulated differently, with a desire for extinction in the consciousness of the Divine; this primordial point of view, if one may say,
is always accessible in principle on the basis of a certain esoteric

sanctity, as is proven above all by examples such as Krishna, David, Solomon, Muhammad.

Regarding woman, it is not childbirth that comes from the Fall, it is only the pain.

It is absolutely wrong to affirm that original sin is the ravishment of the virgin woman. Original sin is uniquely enjoyment outside God; hence the desire to see and experience cosmic reality—or illusion—in itself and without God. Primordial copulation was a prayer and not a sin.

Regarding marriage in Christianity, there can be no reference here to an ideal couple; the Christ and the Virgin do not constitute a couple. There remains Joseph and the Virgin, then the Holy Spirit and the Virgin; now Joseph cannot be the model, precisely, of a husband, and as for the Holy Spirit, which husband would dare put himself in its place? And which husband would dare touch—in imagination—the Holy Virgin? The model of Christian marriage is either the relationship between Christ and his Church, or the love of the soul for its Creator, or for the divine Infinitude; in this case, the partner—male or female—takes on a mystical symbolism, an example of which is given to us by the troubadours; the case of the *Fedeli d'Amore* is no doubt analogous.

21 November 1975 · THE PERENNIAL PHILOSOPHY, THE TERNARY INTELLIGENCE-WILL-SOUL, CHRISTIAN ESOTERISM

There is indeed only "one thing needful", and it is impossible to avoid it within the framework of the human vocation; given on the one hand that our intelligence is made for the truth and on the other that we have a soul to save.

To understand a religion in depth, one must understand religion as such: now the religious phenomenon is identified, in its essence, with the one universal wisdom, hence with esoterism or with the "primordial tradition", or the *Philosophia Perennis* if one prefers. In other words, esoteric wisdom is based, doctrinally and methodically, on what is common to all religions, or on what underlies each one of them. If I am repeating here something that is obvious, it is to emphasize that one must never lose sight of this fact—for experience proves that the temptation to do so is great—when engaged in the practice of an orthodox spirituality, hence inevitably surrounded by a framework of formalism or mythology.

There are three planes to consider in the human microcosm, namely the intelligence, the will, and the soul. The spiritual function of human intelligence—hence its essential function—is the discernment between the Real and the illusory, the Absolute and the contingent, the Infinite and the finite, the Permanent and the impermanent; this is the one universal Doctrine, and consequently this is the quintessence of all theology and all metaphysics. Then there is the will: the spiritual function of the human—hence free—will, is essentially the concentration—in principle continuous—of the mind on the Real, the Absolute, the Infinite, the Permanent, or else on the avataric manifestation of the Real, which in practice amounts to the same; this is the Method, and it is the quintessence of all possible paths, for "prayer" is everything, and one must pray "without ceasing", according to St Paul. Finally, there is the soul, the character, sensibility, affectivity, the capacity to love: the spiritual function of the soul is essentially the quasi-existential conformation to the Real, namely virtue; this is Morality, not merely extrinsic and social, of course, but intrinsic and contemplative; without beauty of soul—I shall even say: without the sense of beauty—no spirituality is possible, vexing as this may be for the ignorant and the pedants who imagine that with respect to metaphysical realization "technique" is all that matters, that is to say a kind of coldly mechanical yoga. Discernment, concentration, virtue: it is these elements, and nothing else, that one must seek when one has entered a traditional path as a metaphysician; when practising such a path, one must not "be converted" to a given theology or a mythology, although one must love the symbols and their beauty in one's own religious cosmos as in that of others.

Christianity is a bhaktic esoterism become religion; thus it is exoteric by its literalist and dogmatist interpretations, not by its symbolism, nor by its means, which are initiatic in their essence. Baptism and confirmation taken together constitute Christian initiation; according to Guénon, the sacraments later lost their initiatic character, but this is impossible in principle and in fact:

in principle, because God never gives less than He promises—rather, it is the reverse that is true—and in fact, because it is technically impossible to effect such a change, be it only due to the dispersion of the Christians from the first centuries onward. From the point of view of the method, the central means is the jaculatory orison containing the sacramental Name of Jesus, possibly that of Mary or both of them at once; He who wishes to practise this method—dating back to the origins of Christianity—must solemnly promise the Blessed Virgin to do so—in the manner of a vow—in a sanctuary dedicated to her; he must also ask permission from the Virgin and implore her for her assistance; and this will have to be kept secret, at least *a priori* and under usual circumstances. And he will then have to renounce all the dispersing and degrading trivialities of the modern world; we must await death in a little spiritual garden and do so in the midst of our family life and worldly duties, as the case may be. God wants our soul and nothing else; if He demands something more from us, we will know of this with certitude by giving Him our soul.

As there are hardly any valid sacraments left in the Post-Conciliar Church, jaculatory orison—the "Prayer of Jesus" or the "Prayer of the Heart" of the Orthodox—can suffice, for "God knows His own" and the Name of Jesus can serve as a substitute Mass, given that we have no other choice, unless the Tridentine Mass is still accessible, depending on where we happen to live. With respect to the invocation: since it is impossible in practice to pronounce the orison without ceasing, we must do it three times a day at least, and at all other moments if we are reasonably able to do so; we must have an underlying rhythm, but we are free for the rest of the time.

I write all of this, Madame, out of care, so as not to overlook anything; therefore, I must tell you likewise that Islamic esoterism is also accessible in the West, but I have no reason *a priori* to go into further detail regarding it.

That said, let us return to the essential. There are two moments in life, and these moments are everything: it is the present moment, where we are free to choose what we want to be, and the moment of death, where we no longer have any choice and where the decision belongs entirely to God. Now, if the present moment is good, death will be good; if we are now with God—in this present that renews itself ceaselessly while remaining always this sole actual moment—God will be with us at the moment of our death. The remembrance of God—jaculatory orison—is a death in life; it will be a life in death.

Between the present moment, when we remember God, and death, when God will remember us—and this reciprocity exists already in each prayer—there is the rest of life, the duration that extends from the present moment until the last moment; but duration is only a succession of present moments, for we always live "now"; thus, concretely and operatively speaking, it is always the same blessed instant in which we are free to remember God and find our happiness in this remembrance. [...]

PS. Metaphysical truth and perpetual prayer, together with intrinsic virtue—virtue envisaged in terms of beauty—are the fundamental elements of the esoteric path and, in the last analysis, of all spirituality. And the Divine Name contains in principle the totality of all sacramental means.

23 November 1975 · CATHOLICISM AND DISCERNMENT

One cannot without contradiction claim to adhere to the point of view of pure metaphysics and esoterism while affirming the desire to interpret doctrinal and methodical principles in terms of Catholicism, hence in terms of a religious formalism; likewise, one cannot without contradiction claim to be particularly bound to the element "Discernment" while wishing to realize the specifically Catholic type of sanctity which, precisely, is volitive and individualist. For sanctity "within Catholicism" is one thing, and "Catholic" sanctity is another; certainly, all modes of sanctity existed in medieval Catholicism, but when one speaks of "Catholic sanctity", one has in mind that which is specific and characteristic and not that which lies outside this framework and therefore rejoins the imponderable and the ineffable. One must not forget that Catholic spirituality since Bossuet has been considerably impoverished with respect to its scope, owing to a moralism that is hostile to pure contemplation and to everything that appears to threaten theology's schemas and social equilibrium.

What matters therefore is not to interpret the ternary "Discernment-Concentration-Virtue" (or "Intelligence-Will-Soul" or "Intellection-Realization-Conformity") in terms of Catholicism, but on the contrary to interpret Catholicism in terms of this ternary. Be that as it may, Christianity, inasmuch as it insists *a priori* on penitence, asceticism, the rejection of the world, mortifying *bhakti*, bases itself on the volitive element and not on "Discernment"; Islam, on the other hand, with its emphasis on the Principle as such—not on the human manifestation of the Principle—and therefore on the mystery of Unity, opens directly onto pure metaphysics and gnosis; one can opt for Christianity for reasons of affinity or atavism, or of personal experience, but not for reasons based on the element "Discernment"; however, the fact that this element is necessarily found in Christianity too is an altogether separate question.

The relationship between the three planes—cognitive conformity, volitive conformity, affective conformity—is ontological and logical, and is therefore not subject to variations; the question of knowing whether or not there are subjective variations to be found here is without interest, at least *a priori*. The ternary in question must be understood in its objective, principial, and universal reality, and not from the point of view of a given subjectivity or of a particular experience; for instance, when I speak of discernment or of truth, I have a cognitive equation in mind, a pure perception of the nature of things, and not a soothing experience; otherwise the key notions would be rendered inoperative.

You have been told to be "a saint, the greatest saint possible"; for various reasons, I cannot approve of such an unrealistic and ill-sounding formulation, which is moreover very Catholic in its style; a Muslim would never express himself like that. I would have accepted, however, that one tell a newly baptized person: "Be holy, for God is holy."

January 1976 · METAPHYSICS, ATTACHMENT TO GOD

Your metaphysical readings need not worry you; the essence of Truth is simple—and it is this essence that matters—namely: God; eternal life; the obligation to attach ourselves to God. Now we attach ourselves to God through prayer, and by avoiding what takes us away from Him. Metaphysical readings can broaden our horizon and deepen our perspective, but they must not trouble our peace; if something causes us to worry, we must put it aside. What is decisive is our attachment to the Absolute; within the framework of Christianity, it is also necessary to place ourselves under the protection of the Blessed Virgin, for she personifies divine Mercy; moreover she also has an influence in Islam, which, like Christianity, venerates her.

Every man possesses by nature a sufficient capacity to discern between the real and the illusory; everyone notices the impermanence of things, and everyone can conceive of the immutability of the Principle. Metaphysics is a vocation, it is not a condition of salvation; God will not reproach us for not having a particular gift, but He will reproach us for not fulfilling what He requires of every man; He will not ask us to render account about things we have not understood.

You say that you are a [male] nurse in a psychiatric hospital; it might be better for you to work in an ordinary hospital, because the psychic ambience in a psychiatric institution is not easy to bear over time and it may be conducive to a certain disequilibrium. Be that as it may, the most basic thing to do is to get into the habit of praying; this is incumbent upon every man, and it has nothing to do, I repeat, with any metaphysical studies. One must have patience and trust.

22 February 1976 · SALVATION, THE CRUCIFIXION AND THE BLESSED VIRGIN ACCORDING TO ISLAM, ECUMENISM

I come now to the six points of your letter to D.W.

First point: "one has to be a Muslim to be saved." Not only does Islam teach this, but it is even obliged to teach this, otherwise it would not be a religion; this exclusivism is an essential trait of the religious phenomenon, and without it no religion could maintain itself, human psychology being what it is. But just as Catholic theology admits that a non-Christian can be saved by the grace of Christ, so too does Muslim theology admit that a non-Muslim can be saved by the grace of Allah; and in virtue of this very principle, even a true heretic can be saved if his confession contains sufficient elements to provide an objective basis for salvation.

Second point: since the salvific element in Islam is the Divine Essence and our faith, Islamic Christology is a matter of indifference; it cannot but be minimal. In order to fully explain it, one would have to introduce the notions of exoterism and esoterism, something that would take us much too far; I shall limit myself to saying that, exoterically, Islam must leave the question of the God-Christ on the side—its perspective centred on the Essence requires this—but esoterically, the Islamic notion of the "Spirit" or the "Word" rejoins the Christian doctrine of the uncreated Logos. That a sufficient foundation for salvation can be provided by taking into consideration the Divine Essence alone—from the metaphysical and mystical point of view— is proved by numerous Muslim saints and their miracles.

Third point: this is exoterically obvious. Same response as for the first point.

Fourth point: these stories do not have a dogmatic bearing. As Massignon showed, the passage of the Koran—which contains no story—means only that Christ was not "really" crucified, since he overcame death.[1] Muslim commentators seek fanciful and impossible explanations; but in fact the entire issue remains outside Islam's specific perspective.

Fifth point: the Koran is right in a certain way to equate the Holy Spirit with Mary, since Mary, as Spouse of the Holy Spirit, is really its human vehicle. The Blessed Father Kolbe wrote:

---

[1] *Translator's note.* "And because of their saying: We slew the Messiah, Jesus son of Mary, Allah's messenger—They slew him not nor crucified him, but it appeared so unto them; and lo! Those who disagree concerning it are in doubt thereof; they have no knowledge thereof save pursuit and conjecture; they slew him not for certain. But Allah took him up unto Himself. Allah was ever Mighty, Wise." Koran, sura 4 ("Women"), verses 157–158.

"Immaculate Conception is one of the Names of the Holy Spirit, and Mary, Spouse of the Holy Spirit, presents herself by taking the Name of her Spouse to whom she is indissolubly bound; one can affirm that in being wedded to Mary, the Spirit was quasi incarnated in her." The Koran also takes into account the fact that, practically and not theologically—*de facto* and not *de jure*—the Holy Virgin assumes the importance of the Third Divine Person. Moreover, when one religion concerns itself with another, its affirmations are much more symbolic than literal; Muslim legends concerning the Christian world are always types of metaphors; Christian facts, whether real or imaginary, are but pretexts or images meant to illustrate moral, metaphysical, or mystical truths. Intrinsic Islam is only interested in God in His aspect of Unity or Essence, and in the manner in which He is to be served.

Sixth point: what I have just said applies notably to the Parousia and to the eschatological stories; everything there is symbolic, the names of personages play no role.

All that you have written in your book is irrefutable; nothing can compromise you even from the most exclusivist Catholic point of view; you are not defending Muslim dogmas, you are simply relating certain facts that no witness could contest in good faith.

I am completely against ecumenism as it is envisaged today, with inoperative "dialogues" and gratuitous and sentimental gestures that amount to nothing. And yet an understanding between the religions is possible and even necessary, but it is not on the dogmatic plane, it is uniquely on the basis of common ideas and common interests. The common ideas are: a transcendent, perfect, almighty, merciful Absolute; then a hereafter that is either good, or bad, depending on our merits or demerits; all the religions, including Buddhism—Buddhist "atheism" is but a misunderstanding—are in agreement on these points. The common interests are: a defence against materialism, atheism, perversion, subversion, and modernism in all of its guises. I think that Pius XII once said that the wars between Christians and Muslims were but domestic quarrels, compared to the current opposition between the world of the religions and that of militant materialism-atheism; he also said that it was a consolation to know that there are millions of men who prostrate themselves five times a day before God.

30 April 1976 · INTEGRALISM AND MODERNISM, CONFESSIONAL EXCLUSIVISM, THE KORAN

That priests are sending you angry letters because of your defence of Muslims is certainly irritating; yet it is normal for two reasons: first, religions exclude each other, except in their common essence, which is metaphysical and esoteric and which is not affected by ordinary theology; secondly, the taking of sides is a natural weakness of man, except men of the elite; but those, by definition, are rare.

But one should not mix planes. Father Barbara has the immense merit of being a traditionalist, and this has nothing to do with his inability to understand things situated outside the Catholic tradition. It is deeply illogical and unfair to reproach integralists for opinions that, from the point of view of tradition, are immaterial; I prefer the narrow-mindedness of an integralist—he is entitled to this theologically—to the possible broad-mindedness of a modernist. For the modernist who accepts Islam does so on the basis of modern errors, in other words he does so for philosophical and psychological reasons that Islam itself does not accept; whereas the integralist bases himself either on truth as such—which obviously includes the Islamic perspective—or at least on a form of this truth, namely Catholicism, precisely. Better to hold to a truth that is narrow but offers salvation, as I have said, than to be broad-minded while betraying the essential. [...]

To return to the attitude of Catholicism in regard to Islam, one must take note of the fact that one religion necessarily excludes the other; thus, theologies have to remain implacable. I say this as an esoterist, in other words starting from the idea that all intrinsically orthodox religions—not the pseudo-religions, nor merely human philosophies—manifest the absolute Divine Truth which is universal and underlying, as well as transcendent with respect to all forms. It could be said, from this point of view, that the historical Christ manifests the intemporal Logos, but that the Logos can manifest itself also under other historical forms. But one should not try to blend religions!

Massignon, though he was a fervent and even mystical Catholic—and no Catholic knows Islam better than he did—admitted that Islam was an authentic revelation, given on the one hand the promise made by God to Abraham and, on the other, the virtues of Muslims and the phenomenon of sanctity within Islam. [...]

PS. As for the Koran, it is largely incomprehensible without a commentary; everything in it is elliptical and symbolical. For example: the palm tree next to which Christ was born, indicates the middle, the axis of the world. In Christianity, which accentuates the human Manifestation of God, the historical fact has a fundamental importance; in Islam, which places the accent on the Divine Nature, history has no importance, and it is symbolism that takes precedence.

30 April 1976 · DOGMA

The "rigidity of the dogma" can be transcended, but only metaphysically and mystically, that is to say within, not outside; on the theological plane, the dogma has to be rigid, otherwise it disappears; there is in this also a question of collective psychology, which Providence—or the Holy Spirit—always takes into consideration. Esoterism is not syncretism; forms are what they are and have a right to existence. Dogmas, while being exclusive, and thus "narrow" and "rigid", are sacred; and what they exclude on the plane of form, they include on the plane of the metaphysical essence which is one.

1 September 1976 · MODERN CATHOLICISM AND HOLY SPIRIT

One could ask oneself why the Holy Spirit allows the aberrations in the official Church; to which I respond, with all the theologians who have not forgotten their theology: first, because man is free; and secondly, because "for it must needs be that offences come; but woe to that man by whom the offence cometh!" It is enough to read the New Testament to remember that towards the end of the world, the powers of darkness are unleashed; this is so in virtue of a metaphysical law determining that at the end of a cycle of humanity, the most inferior possibilities need to be exhausted; and then comes the divine intervention. All religions teach this in one form or another.

8 November 1976 · CHRISTIANITY AND ISLAM

The Muslim religion is less permeable to modern errors than is Christianity, because Islam has no papacy; even if a religious authority of Egypt were mistaken, this would not implicate the Muslims in Morocco; all that matters in Muslim theology is that which has been taught everywhere and always; each mufti is infallible to the degree that his judgments coincide with those of the majority of the other muftis.

27 February 1978 · ENTERING THE PATH

Your letter contains allusions to spiritual life. Clearly, it is never too late to start a life dedicated to the one thing needful. However, to undertake such a life, it would be necessary to affirm the intention to do so in a prayer addressed to the Blessed Virgin, to ask for her help and her blessing by promising her to remain faithful to the pledge taken; that is to say, the pledge to practise the invocation of a specific sacred formula. Since a life of prayer must have a fundamental rhythm from which we must never desist, one can practise the invocation three times a day, no matter the length of each session; however when one has the time and the strength to do so, one can also recite the Formula or the Name at any moment. Apart from the initial prayer addressed to the Blessed Virgin, one ought to start with a little spiritual retreat of at least two hours in order to pronounce the Formula without interruption; because everything needs to have a beginning; and this retreat can be repeated from time to time. We must never ask if we are "worthy" of such a path, nor if we are sufficiently gifted for it, because we have no choice; we have an immortal soul, and we do what we can.

17 July 1978 · INVOKING LIKE THE BIRDS

You want me to speak to you a little about the manner of invoking God "as the birds do". Well, there is in the invocation a holy gravity and a holy carefreeness. Holy gravity is based on the sense of the sacred and devotional fear; it is to invoke God solemnly, profoundly, contemplatively, worshipfully, and in awareness of his majesty, as if one were to find oneself in the most venerable and most marvellous of sanctuaries. Holy carefreeness on the contrary is based on trust, the sense of Mercy, and spiritual childlikeness: it is to invoke God like a child playing in a garden, or like a bird—precisely—that sings for the sake of singing, or because God makes it sing, or because God is God; in short, without worrying about why things are the way they are. These are the two poles or the two complementary modes of invocation, or simply of prayer.

"I love because I love", as St Bernard would say. And this applies to the serious mode as to the light mode. Love immobilizes him who contemplates Majesty, as it makes him who offers himself up to Mercy sing and dance with joy.

4 September 1978 · MALADJUSTMENT TO ONE'S MILIEU, RESOLVING A PROBLEM

You must not allow yourself to be discouraged by a situation which is easily explained and which consequently poses no intellectual problem; the problem is purely practical: it is moral and spiritual adaptation to an absurd ambience. First of all, you should say to yourself that this human ambience, though so full of assurance and arrogance, is monstrously abnormal, with regard to both its convictions and its tendencies; these people may be unanimous in their errors and vices, but it is you who are normal; so remain imperturbable in the face of this collective hypnosis, and remain completely yourself. In a conceited, icy and stupidly passional world, stay quietly in your little garden; this is a transitory trial. Metaphysically speaking, the emergence of such a dreadful world is an inevitable necessity, according to cosmic laws which require that error be manifested: it *must needs* be that *offences come*, said Christ. You were more or less in a little paradise in Morocco; but one matures through experience, and therefore we must not be surprised by the trials that destiny sends us.

When faced with a problem, one must first of all seek its objective and subjective causes; clearly seeing the outer and inner givens of a difficulty is already much; this allows us to avoid upsetting ourselves excessively, and to draw the necessary consequences. Consequences both practical and spiritual: on one hand, to do one's work and make oneself as anodyne as possible, while remaining unmoved by disdain and hostility; on the other hand, to withdraw into prayer, to become established in it, as it were; to practise individual prayer as well as jaculatory prayer. To live in hope and expect nothing from the world, yet ask God to come to our aid, inwardly and outwardly. It is difficult to be alone, but it is an apprenticeship; it is what Heaven asks of you at the moment.

10 September 1978 · *HABEMUS PAPAM?*

About the question of the papacy, one can find information in the writings of St Robert Bellarmine, St Alphonsus Liguori, Cajetan, and others, the first two being "Doctors of the Church"; they acknowledge, not only that a pope can fall into heresy, but also that, in such a case, he is *depositus* or *deponendus*, which amounts to the same thing. As a result, the question of knowing whether a pope conspicuous for his heresy was elected legitimately or not is altogether secondary; once a pope proclaims a heresy, hence an opinion which is contrary to what has been taught "everywhere and always", or once he takes a measure having the same malignant character, he is *depositus* and his opinions and measures are null and void.

24 January 1979 · BECOMING A MONK TODAY

Someone asked me if it was a good idea to go to a convent; this gives me the opportunity of speaking about what happened with some Carmelites I know. The gate was removed; the habit—that of St Teresa of Avila and of St Therese of Lisieux—was transformed into a costume of Protestant sisters, with shortened dress and a skimpy veil; during the divine offices, the nuns are allowed personal gestures, either to raise their arms or to cross them on their bosom, and other singularities, and to make improvised speeches, spontaneous prayers out loud, as in certain Protestant sects; none of this could have been invented by the nuns! Pentecostalism, which is Protestant in origin and officially encouraged by Paul VI, was introduced among them; but this wave of false mysticism fizzled out, without anyone coming to the obvious conclusion regarding the movement's inspiration; in other monasteries, "Yoga" and "Zen" is being practised, both disciplines being cut off from their traditional roots, of course. It is pointless to add—and it is the same with my brother's Trappist monks—that the old chants have been replaced with trivial modern songs; there is nothing but the new Mass, the new liturgy, the new pastoral teachings, and so on. It is the "opening to the world" and the closing to Heaven.

24 January 1979 · GOD OWES NOTHING TO THOSE WHO ARE LUKEWARM

It is too easily asserted that God "owes" this or that to the "Christian people", and one deduces from this that God "cannot" deprive them of this or that, particularly of a legitimate pope and a valid Mass; a perfectly abusive theological argument is made out of this, while forgetting how fallen these "Christian people" are and how unchristian. Proof of this is their indifference and their insensitivity in religious matters: the fact that they—I am speaking of the majority—accept the most suspicious and the most outrageous innovations that the new religion imposes on them without batting an eyelid. God owes nothing to sheep, nor to somnambulists; "I will spue the lukewarm out of my mouth", the Scriptures say.

For if one stakes a claim to sacred things and to Heaven's benevolence, one must have a mentality and a comportment that conform with those gifts and graces; one must think and act in a way that is correct, and not false; one must think and act in a manner in keeping with the sacred, and not with the trivial; one must lead, amidst the activities in the world and without being the dupe of it, a life of prayer in a holy monotony: in simplicity, poverty, and childlikeness. But always according to the truth.

47

4 May 1979 · ESOTERISM, THE SACRAMENTS AND LEGISLATION IN CHRISTIANITY

In my opinion, there can be no supra-sacramental initiation in Christianity; this strikes me as obvious, since baptism confers the virtuality of the primordial state, and confirmation the virtuality of the *unio mystica* or the *deificatio*; namely, all that we are capable of attaining. It seems to me that in Christianity it is doctrine that constitutes esoterism—not theology, it goes without saying, but the purely metaphysical doctrine, as it appears among orthodox Gnostics and in an incidental way with Meister Eckhart and others—and then it is the spiritual intention of the contemplative. I think that the Christian sacraments offer the keys for all possible realization. Most of the Christian saints are what Hindus term *bhaktas*, but this does not mean that the sacraments cannot also help *jnānis*, even if they are—or were—very few in number, but this has nothing to do with the question of the principle.

Christianity offers an individual all that an integral exoterism offers, and it did so from the very beginning; but it does not offer this to the collectivity. A collectivity needs laws and rules which the disciplined individual can do without if he follows a spiritual path. Muslim criticism is directed at Christian society, not at the Christian individual who is gifted, well disciplined, and well inspired; moreover, this criticism is partly exoteric and because of this it over-simplifies matters. In any case, Christian history proves that there has been far too much wavering and too many improvisations on the plane of exoteric legislation, whereas in Islam everything is fixed in advance; the popes had too much power, the role of the emperor was not clearly defined, some of the papal measures were mistakes—for example, the obligatory celibacy of the priests which perilously cut these off from the lay world and gave laymen the sense of constituting a world of their own, and so on. But all of this, I repeat, does not necessarily concern the Christian individual; the lack of a developed exoteric framework does not affect him, therefore he is missing nothing in this regard.

4 May 1979 · THE EARLY CHURCH

I do not subscribe at all to Guénon's thesis according to which the original Church would have been a closed initiatic society and would later have become a world religion. Christianity, despite and along with its initiatic character, was a religion from the very start; this is its originality. In the early days, when Christians were few in number and were socially subject to Roman laws, the absence of a legal exoterism was not a problem; it is only from the time of Constantine onwards that this absence turned out to be a lack, although only relatively, not absolutely so.

4 May 1979 · THE EGO

There is no such thing as a "being who no longer has an ego"; the "extinction" of the ego is only a manner of speaking, in other words, what is implied is the passional ego, egoism. Christ had an ego; he was, and is, "true man and true God". There is no common measure between the "I" and the "Self", so that the presence of the first does not prevent the realization of the second. If the Holy Virgin can appear and speak, it is not because she might not have "realized the Self", it is because the realization of the Self does not exclude the parallel presence of the "I". There would be much to say about this subject, and I think I have spoken of it in my books, notably in *Logic and Transcendence*, in the chapter "The Servant and Union".

25 February 1980 · THE ESOTERIC PATH

The essence of all religion—of every form of the one religion—is the discernment between the Real and the illusory, then union with the Real, and finally human conformity to the Real, without which neither discernment nor union can bear their fruit. These are the three things that an esoterist seeks in religion; if man seeks something else, he is situated outside esoterism; he is perfectly entitled to this, of course. But one must know what one wants and what one is seeking, or what one is called towards.

The question the esoterist has *a priori* is that of knowing where, in which religion, or in what dimension of a particular religion, he will find what he is looking for; from a theoretical point of view, every religion contains every essential element, but from a practical viewpoint, it may be necessary to extract those elements and in any case to find a master who can indicate how they are to be used. Since we are placing ourselves on the terrain of esoterism, it is not enough that the man who serves as master teach us exercises of piety, that he restrict the path to a form of exclusive *bhakti*, while seeing nothing outside his religion; he must know how to place himself beyond forms and be able to understand the essential nature of the elements of doctrine and the method. Such expertise is unlikely to be found in the Christian world—I mean, among priests—and yet all of the supports are there; which does not mean that a Christian esoteric path cannot in fact be accessible, or that it cannot be found under very particular conditions. Neither does it mean that Eastern paths would be easily accessible for a Western seeker; and more often than not this is not this seeker's fault.

1 March 1980 · ESOTERISM AND RELIGION

As for the second question, concerning the change of a traditional form, the criterion for the legitimacy of such a change is the precision and sincerity of our esoteric intention. The essence of every religion—of any form of the one religion—is first of all the discernment between the Principle and manifestation, or between the Real and the illusory, the Absolute and the contingent, and then operative union with the Real, hence realization; all of this on the basis of our psychological or moral conformity to the Real, because without this conformity—this beauty of the soul or these virtues—neither doctrinal discernment nor the method of union can bear any fruits. These are the three things an esoterist seeks in religion: a metaphysical doctrine, a unitive method, and moral conformity—the first element comprising awareness of traditional universality and of the relativity of the forms. To know whether or not one can change traditional forms, one must have an esoteric intention that is sufficiently strict and sincere; one must then inform oneself about the elements of the new religion; and one must pray to know the Will of God, in the case where there could be some uncertainty of a human order in us.

24 November 1980 · CHRIST AND THE BLESSED VIRGIN

I have been asked more than once about the respective functions of the masculine Logos and the feminine Logos. Now Christ is the "Path", and the Virgin is the "Place of Abiding"; he is the Sacrifice, and she is the Temple. I could say also, as concretely as possible, that Christ personifies the spiritual Perfections, whereas the Blessed Virgin personifies the Retreat; she is the holy ambience without which there is no flowering. This is something I know from experience; the Marian grace excludes all worldly curiosity and all alienating dissipation; she is like a pure and blissful aura which accompanies us everywhere and which we must not leave. And this has some relation with the symbolism of her veil or her mantle, which protects and is the shelter of saints.

9 January 1981 · MARITAL DISCORD

I was disquieted by what you write to me, as I make it a principle never to admit to my community a person whose spouse is directly or indirectly opposed to this admission.

If entering the religious form—in view of affiliation to esoterism—was somewhat hasty for your wife, this was no doubt due to my impending departure for the United States; otherwise there was no hurry, to say the least. First of all, I do not seek to attract anyone, and secondly, I prefer slowness to rapidity, for obvious reasons. Be this as it may, I thought that everything was in order in the case in question, and I hope I have not been misinformed; this would be as regrettable for me as for yourself. I do not have time to take care of everything—I had less time than ever during the three months before I left—and I am obliged to trust the postulants on one hand, and my representatives on the other.

But because the speed of the process is explained by quite external reasons, if I have understood correctly, you should really not feel hurt in this particular regard.

But in all this there is a much more general aspect which escapes my control, and this is the phenomenon—perhaps more frequent than ever—of the ideological divergences that fragment the modern world; these divergences exist and we can do nothing about it. How many dramas there are around us because one spouse converts to an opposed political ideology, or to some unusual preoccupation! In many cases this results in separation; in others, the union can continue, and this is due to the tolerant, patient, serene character of one of the spouses or both. Loftiness of character can fill many gaps and will restabilize many imbalances.

In a certain way you are an extremist, which is your right—I am one also—but to the very extent that we are extremists, we must temper our demands vis-à-vis others; I mean vis-à-vis the people we live with, if their position has nothing intrinsically bad about it. I do not know what your wife's opinions were at the time of your marriage; in any case, given your own convictions—but what good is it to give retrospective advice which is anyway quite obvious—it would have been wise to verify your fiancée's convictions or tendencies, since your exigencies of authority—or other similar intellectual or moral exigencies—are only justified by a quasi-visceral, and so to speak predestined, affinity between you and the woman you chose. In the absence of this *a priori*, you ought to be more indifferent and more serene; less disappointed, as it were.

Be this as it may, there is an element of contradiction in your attitude, in that you seem, by a sort of *amour propre*, to be reproaching your wife for a psychological position that she cannot not have, given your convictions on one hand and hers on the other. Since you sense that Darwinism is not the last word in all possible wisdom, you ought to show yourself even more patient and tolerant, more humble, too, and even bear the situation with a certain humour, that is, without taking yourself so tragically. For it is contradictory to be a scientist, a biologist, a Darwinist, all the while claiming a role that this option—rather narrow, it must be agreed—renders completely uncertain, or even excludes, precisely.

There are several scientists in my community; they do their work meticulously, and their metaphysical convictions do not disturb them in the least; one must have the sense of relativity, and consequently that of proportions. The professors of philosophy who follow me find themselves in the same situation. I mean simply that it is neither Platonism nor Shankarism that prevents anyone from being honest and efficacious on the level of scientific empiricism. Regarding you, I do not see why your preoccupation with biological phenomena obliges you to a kind of quasi-religious option; it suffices to take the facts for what they are and put the speculative side—which science practically and wrongly claims—in parentheses. Many great men of science, Max Planck for example, have this detached, nuanced and altogether realistic attitude.

If the metaphysical doctrines were "mental constructs"—and they have existed always and everywhere—human intelligence would be nothing and its existence could not even be explained; but I cannot insist here on considerations that I have developed to satiety in my books. If the greatest minds have been duped for millenia by "mental constructs", whereas the scientists of Moscow see clearly, I repeat, human intelligence is nothing, and man himself is nothing.

And that one may feel "marvellously at peace", as you say, is obviously no criterion; psychological experience proves it without difficulty. That truth gives peace—after one has overcome the turmoil that it also provokes—does not imply that the mere phenomenon of peace always comes from the truth, nor that one possesses it.

The most difficult thing in life is to rise above oneself; one actually has no choice, in the last analysis; man is condemned to this miracle, precisely because he is man. Intellectually speaking, but also humanly speaking, there is something profoundly contradictory in your attitude, and it is precisely because you refuse to rise above yourself when on one hand your situation, and on the other, your state as a man, invite you to do so. And you have a sort of irrational *amour propre* that makes you too susceptible and too vulnerable; that your wife may be right—supposing that she is—does not prevent you from having grandeur; and moral grandeur is always a kind of participation in truth.

July 1981 · THE RESURRECTION OF THE FLESH, CHRISTIAN
SACRED ART

In the earthly Paradise, Adam and Eve had bodies and souls;
after the Fall, their bodies became mortal; the blessed in Heav-
en no longer have bodies, except for Christ, the Blessed Virgin,
Enoch, Elias and a few others. After the Last Judgment, all the
souls in the hereafter will once more have their bodies, which
will arise from their souls; this is what is symbolically called the
"resurrection of the flesh". The separation of soul and body is
transitory and provisional, and it will end with the current cycle
of humanity. It is a question of cosmology.

The naturalist crucifix, as it has existed since the Renaissance,
is completely illegitimate; even the oldest crucifix, which did
not appear until the 5th century—before that only the cross was
known—is but relatively legitimate; the Orthodox Church does
not accept it, but at least the figure of Christ was very stylized,
he wore a crown; it was the glorious rather than the suffering
Christ. The viewpoint of the Orthodox Church is more perfect:
Christian sacred art should consist only of the traditional image
of the Virgin and Child, then the traditional image—that is, stylized and canonical—of the Holy Face, and finally the Cross; the
images portraying sacred history are secondary, they are periph-
eral—not central—icons. Christ Pantocrator prolongs the icon of
the Holy Face.

3 September 1981 · THE CHOICE OF A SPIRITUAL PATH

You tell me first of all that, being a Catholic, you thought of
dedicating yourself to a religious vocation [...]. You tell me also
that you are interested in Buddhism, which is all very well, and
that you meditate according to the method of Zen, which is impossible; because in order to practise a spiritual method, one
must adhere first of all to the religion to which it pertains—thus
in the case of Zen one must validly be a Buddhist—and then one
must be validly accepted by an orthodox spiritual master. This
amounts to saying that, in practical terms, one needs to go to
Japan and enter a Zen monastery; although one must still make

sure that the abbot is fully orthodox, because the modern influence has penetrated everywhere.

As for Islam—since you ask me—there are no monastic orders,
but there are spiritual congregations whose members, men and
women, live in the world. The spiritual life for the women is the
same as for the men.

At any event, it makes no sense to practise a spiritual method outside the indispensable conditions and traditional rules;
there is even every chance that this would be detrimental. First
of all, one must be sure that such a path is "willed by God" for
us; next, one must realize a psychological, moral, and mental
climate that renders the path possible; this is not just something
that can be done on one's own.

You ask me if you ought to resume studies at the university;
this makes sense only in view of one's professional future, in
which case the choice is a matter of opportunity.

15 October 1981 · SERENITY

We live here [Bloomington, Indiana. *Ed.*] in a wonderful landscape, where everything is vast and pure; there are only fields
and forests; serenity is in the air everywhere. Serenity is to be
above the clouds, above the world; above oneself. Recollectedness and serenity: we must discover these in prayer, and through
prayer.

22 March 1982 · PRAYER, ASCETICISM
to Jean Borella

We must never doubt Mercy; that would be the sin of bitterness.
A life that ends in prayer and in trust is never lost; the most
wretched of human beings finds himself in the antechamber of
Paradise—or under the Blessed Virgin's mantle—the moment he
prays with sincerity and hope. And a man who wonders whether
he is sincere is always sincere. Moreover, even if one happens to
be in a situation where one has no access to a valid sacrament,
prayer suffices; it becomes a sacrament in God's eyes; there is in
this a principle of divine economy, so to speak, and the thing is
in any case obvious, as is proven by the baptism of desire or the

baptism of blood. This particular point notwithstanding, old age homes—or analogous institutions—should be places of prayer, hence of peace and happiness. The greatest possible happiness is faith, hence trust, hope; and consequently prayer, invocation.

I am reading your text *Quintessence of our Path*. You say at the beginning that the manifestation of the Absolute, for Christians, is Christ; it should be specified, metaphysically, that this manifestation is first of all the whole Universe, and within it—more directly—the celestial world; and then, on the human plane, Christ; the Word itself not being human, quite obviously.

What you explain afterwards on the subject of the union to Christ is good; I shall add that the pronunciation of the Divine Name amounts, for the metaphysician, to a metaphysical awareness, and thus it is to "practise metaphysics"; in esoterism, one needs to have a sense of the Absolute, as well as a sense of the Sacred.

And what you say next about the virtues is also perfect. This in fact recalls the problem of asceticism; now we must not forget that the Jews reproached Christ and the Apostles for not being ascetics; Christ answered: "As long as the bridegroom is with them..." Asceticism as such is practised, on the one hand, to extirpate passional inclinations inasmuch as they oppose the love of God, or to do penance, and, on the other hand, to set an example for worldly people, or for all of those reasons at once; but a man who might take Communion every day without committing any sins—I am not speaking here of imaginary sins nor of endless perfectionism—such a man would have no need to practise a privative asceticism; an altogether different matter is the natural sobriety that any good man must heed and with all the greater reason a contemplative. But the presence of the "bridegroom" is not guaranteed by Communion only, it is also realized through prayer in which our heart participates, and *a fortiori* through quintessential prayer, the invocation, in which the Divine Name adds an effectively sacramental element to human merit.

22 April 1982 · THE ORTHODOX CHURCH

I do not know if you have ever visited an orthodox country. The first time I went to Greece, I had this overwhelming impression: here at last is authentic Christianity; here at last are priests, churches, liturgies! Because everything here reminds one of Christ, the Apostles, the Early Church. Orthodoxy, which has always excluded change, innovation, and so-called progress, offers the perfect equilibrium and perfect beauty. [...]

Our spiritual community is not there to offer the happiness, or the sentimental satisfaction, of belonging to a religion; one must therefore neither encourage nor hold on to people who are basically seeking only this, or who do not have a sufficient sense of esoterism, the essential, the universal.

2 May 1982 · DOGMATIC DIVERGENCES, PURGATORY

All dogmas that are intrinsically "orthodox", that is, set down with a view to salvation, cannot but be objectively true, otherwise there would be no contradictions between the religions and the confessions; on the other hand, all dogmas are subjectively efficacious, by their nature if not always *de facto*, in the sense that they determine attitudes of faith or love, or fear according to the case; and it is precisely these attitudes which are meant to contribute to salvation. This is the meaning of the Buddhist term *upāya*, "technical procedure" or "spiritual stratagem"(*Kunstgriff* in German), and it is by virtue of this intention of efficacy and this virtually saving "truth" that all dogmas have their justification and are, in the final analysis, mutually compatible. Thus the Protestant negation of purgatory is a function, not of an appropriate and exhaustive cosmology, of course, but of a mystical economy founded on the saving power of faith, thus of trust in divine Mercy, the latter crystallized in Christ's unique Sacrifice; and it is in the same manner that in devotional and invocatory Buddhism, Amida's grace is supposed to save every sinner, in function of the same symbolism of faith. In such perspectives, the dogmatic concept is not an end in itself, in its informative quality, it is only a means to a result; and in this case one can say without reticence that "the end justifies the means";

the same remark applies to all those religious concepts that are objectively problematical, indeed unacceptable, obviously on condition that we are speaking of archetypal manifestations and intrinsically orthodox religions or confessions. The brutal contrast between the dogmas of Christianity and those of Islam is particularly instructive in this regard; it is obviously impossible that the two factions could be objectively right in their flagrant contradictions, but it is possible—and in fact necessarily so— that both are right, each in its own way and from the viewpoint of the respective "salvific psychology".

In eschatological logic, the Catholic dogma of purgatory is a function of the idea of justification by good works, whereas the Protestant negation of purgatory is a function of the idea of justification by faith. On the Catholic side, it will be objected that the Protestant negation of purgatory leads to lukewarmness and thus compromises salvation; on the Protestant side, the Catholics will be reproached that their idea of purgatory compromises saving trust (the *prapatti* of the Hindus) and leads to the abuses of penitentialism as well as the abuse of indulgences; the two factions are simultaneously right and wrong, according to the cases in question; they are mainly wrong, of course.

I repeat that one must distinguish between "informative" dogmas with direct import, and "functional" dogmas with indirect import: the first communicate metaphysical, cosmological or eschatological information; the second determine moral and spiritual virtues; though erroneous in their literality, they rejoin truth by their fruits.

Here, spring has finally arrived, after a long, rigorous winter. The whole countryside is in flower. How can one doubt for one instant that infinite Goodness is in the very Essence of God? It is because of divine Goodness, and through it, that nature awakens and renews itself.

30 June 1982 · CATHOLICISM AND PROTESTANTISM

It is wrong to wish to define Protestantism—"orthodox", not "liberal"—according to Catholic logic alone; I say "define", since if it were only a question of demonstrating the incompatibility between Protestantism and Catholicism, and affirming Catholicism's right to remain true to itself in the face of the Protestant provocation, I would find nothing to say; for I have never thought that the intrinsic legitimacy of the Lutheran phenomenon engenders the obligation for Catholics to renounce a single one of their rights, extrinsic as well as intrinsic.

Besides, even from the specifically theological viewpoint—which does not suffice to resolve the problem—Catholic logic is not absolute, since there is also the logic of the Greek Church; to say the least, I see no reason to prefer Catholicism to Orthodoxy, since the latter's positions are very strong and allow us to see more clearly that if there is something absolute and intangible in the Catholic viewpoint, there is nevertheless something relative and debatable also. If from the Roman Catholic viewpoint there are elements of heresy in Greek Orthodoxy, the inverse is also true: Catholicism comes across as a heterodoxy to Orthodox believers; esoterically speaking, the two viewpoints have their respective justification. But what I wish to point out here is firstly that certain reproaches made by Luther coincide with those of the Orthodox Church, and secondly, that the latter's attitude towards Lutheranism is surprisingly indulgent, which is not without significance.

30 June 1982 · APOSTOLIC SUCCESSION AND HEAVENLY MANDATE

I come now to the crux of the matter. Religious or confessional phenomena are governed by two major principles, namely "apostolic succession" and "Heavenly mandate"; "sacramental technique" is related to the first, and "attribution of grace", that is, the intervention of an extra-canonical grace, to the second. The "Heavenly mandate" is a Confucian notion: as you no doubt know, it means that authority or investiture descends directly from Heaven, without the intermediary of a sacramental means, and in function of certain conditions of which Heaven is the sole judge; this was the case of the Chinese emperors, and also, as Dante notes in his treatise on monarchy, of the Roman, and later the Germanic, emperors. This investiture, of which, quite paradoxically, the papacy itself is an example—and this is a reason for the Greeks to reject it, since they accept only sacramental, thus "traditional", consecrations—this investiture draws all its authority from the spiritual archetype, which must manifest itself in the human world under certain providential conditions, with the ontological necessity of "possibilities of manifestations", as Guénon would say; but here it is a question, not of just any manifestations, but of positive manifestations "willed by Heaven".

The Lutheran phenomenon, exactly like other analogous manifestations, notably in Hinduism and Buddhism, is entirely a function of the principle "Heavenly mandate", thus "intervention of a salvific archetype"; as such, this phenomenon is completely independent of what governs "apostolic succession" and "sacramental technique", and this independence—the human and confessional mentality being what it is—explains precisely the vehemence of the Lutheran denials, and above all its "extrinsic heterodoxy"; not "intrinsic" since the perspective is determined by an archetype *in divinis*. One could ask me: how can a Catholic, even if he is an esoterist, accept the "intrinsic"—not extrinsic—orthodoxy of Protestantism? With much greater apparent justification, one could also ask: how can a Catholic accept the intrinsic orthodoxy of Islam? For Islam rejects Christianity, as Protestantism rejects Catholicism, but even more fundamentally; and if esoterism allows us to understand why and how Islam can do this, it also allows us to understand why and how Protestantism can act likewise, *mutatis mutandis*. The apparently naive, crude character of the arguments plays no role in this domain; it is symbolism, neither more nor less.

30 June 1982 · EUCHARIST AND COMMUNION

As for the Lutheran Communion, it arises from the same ritual economy as Muslim prayer; it is a minimal fragment of the Catholic Mass from the viewpoint of its content, but it is something entirely different from the viewpoint of the container or form, so much so that Catholic objections fall into nothingness, apart from the self-defence of Catholicism. The Catholic Eucharist offers graces proportionate to the mystical possibilities of a St Bernard; the Lutheran Communion offers a viaticum proportionate to the possibilities, not of just anyone, but of the pious and relatively impeccable man, exactly as is the case in Muslim prayer, which is the only "sacrament" of exoteric Islam, thus proving that it is sufficient. All Catholics must take Communion, but not all are St Bernard; and the very transcendence of the Eucharist brings with it terrible dangers, as St Paul attests. In short, Luther was the instrument of what Guénon attributed to the Holy Spirit itself; he made the "initiatic rite" "descend" to the exoteric level. By way of compensation, the Lutheran world has its hermetists and theosophers—its esoterists—but this is another question that I shall not discuss here. Luther closes a given door, he opens some other door.

Still concerning the Eucharist: the obvious theological *distinguo* between an absolute sacrifice and a relative sacrifice— one sanguinary and the other not—does not suffice to excuse the Catholics for the rhetorical and sentimental over-accentuations—above all in their polemics against the Protestants—which prompted my remark on the supernatural phenomena of Golgotha in connection with the Mass [in *Christianity/Islam*, chapter "The question of Evangelism". *Ed.*]. I come from a Catholic family—a bishop, a monk, two brethren in Christian schools, a Carmelite, a Visitandine—and I know what I am talking about; I know that theological clarifications are one thing and habitual and instinctive imagery is another. I shall add that in the Catholic world, theological ignorance is *de facto* prodigious, even in priests—either through forgetfulness or through the incapacity to think—which moreover proves the current disorder, and the ease of convincing people of no matter what.

2 July 1982 · EXOTERISM

In pure metaphysics, exclusive accentuations—namely "points of view" and "aspects"—are not admissible; to look at things through a coloured glass is not metaphysics. But in exoterism, accentuations or colourations are not only allowed, they constitute the very principle of the exoteric outlook; and they inevitably assert themselves with vehemence and unsparingly. According to Islam, the only sin that will certainly not be forgiven is the fact of associating partners with the One God; in this perspective of Unity, the Trinity appears almost as the worst of aberrations; and this perspective has its rights since exoter-

61

ism does. According to Protestantism, it is the Mass which is an abomination, since it seems to supplant—given that it presents itself as a sacrifice—the unique Sacrifice of the Calvary; here too, the accentuation of an exclusive point of view has its rights, those of exoterism precisely. For Christianity, the worst of abominations is the rejection of Christ: the fact of not accepting that Christ alone saves; that there could be other ways than his. For Judaism, the ultimate blasphemy is to believe that the Torah, which is meant for all of eternity, could actually be abolished and replaced by something else.

2 July 1982 · PROTESTANTISM

Whether we understand it or not, whether we like it or not, we have to accept the fact that exoterism exists by the Will of God—for He knows what men are—and that therefore exoterism has certain rights. Now Protestantism is a fruit of the exoteric perspective; it is not a fundamental fruit, but a secondary one, although one that is nonetheless inevitable, and legitimate on its plane. One of the extrinsic proofs of this is the lightning expansion of Protestantism in the Northern countries, among believers, namely those who, precisely, were Catholics; it is impossible to accept that all of these men, several million in other words, would have been fundamentally bad and that the others, those who remained Catholic, would have been fundamentally good; the extremely serious disorders in the Catholic world of that time are all too well known. Of course, this argument applies only in connection with a truly religious ideology; it loses all its worth when it is applied to an obviously false ideology, such as Catholic modernism—not to mention the political ideologies—because in those cases the motive of their success is altogether different; it does not stem from the power of a spiritual archetype, but from the seduction of error and from men's weakness.

But what is the meaning of the fact that Protestantism rejects Tradition and intends to base itself on the Scriptures alone? This means that, very paradoxically, we are dealing here with a religious possibility, not fundamental but marginal: the argument here is that Scripture alone is absolutely stable, whereas Tradition is variable and sometimes not absolutely reliable; the proof of this is that Catholics, Orthodox Christians, and Protestants agree about the Scriptures, but not about Tradition; in Islam too, the brutal divergences between Sunnis and Shiites involve Tradition and not the Scripture. The New Testament is one, but the liturgies are diverse, and some are even of doubtful authority. Catholics are right, of course, to maintain their point of view, but the Protestants' point of view corresponds nonetheless to a possibility within a certain theological, mystical, and moral context, though not outside this context. What Christ termed "commandments of men" pertained clearly to "Tradition"; the Talmud is incontestably "traditional".

2 July 1982 · LUTHER

Compared to some Catholic liturgists, Luther appears with the greatness of a cosmic force because of the breadth of his human scope and the archetype that he conveys; but to grasp this, one needs to read him and to know his story; he is truly what can be termed a great man. What is more, Luther is entirely a man of the Middle Ages, someone fundamentally religious, not worldly, and unshakeably monarchist; he was tolerant, in his way, and not really iconoclastic—he abhorred excesses—and was always personally devoted to the Holy Virgin. A curious fact: the Fathers of the Council of Trent renounced condemning Luther explicitly, contrary to what the conciliar practices normally required; they preferred not to "close the door definitively to further dialogue", which is significant. I have moreover read—in German—Catholic texts that are full of praise for the personality and the genius of Luther and that refute the conventional calumnies—though this is not difficult to do; now these texts are older than the "Council" [Vatican II. *Ed.*], otherwise I would not attribute much importance to them.

2 July 1982 · CHRISTIAN ART, CIVILIZATIONISM

You say in your letter that Lutheranism engendered a quasi-total destruction of sacred forms; undeniably, it produced a kind of void—although there are temples in the Germanic countries that have their sacral beauty given that they prolong Gothic forms with sobriety—but is this void so much more regrettable than the horrible oversaturation and profusion of the Baroque churches and other deviations of Catholic art? To fully measure the entire horror of baroque art, whose inventor moreover was the very problematical Michelangelo, one needs to have seen not only the cathedrals, but also the sanctuaries of the Greek Church; I have visited many a church in Greece, and I would say that it is impossible to understand and evaluate Christian art in its totality without knowing the sacred jewels of Byzantine art, an example of which is offered by Saint Mark's Basilica in Venice; this also enables us, perhaps, to better understand the full extent and depth of the baroque disaster, or of the Renaissance in general. The centre of the Catholic world is the Vatican; now one fine day, some popes had the fateful idea of destroying the marvellous basilica of Constantine—a jewel of art which was profoundly sacral and profoundly Christic—in order to replace it with a gigantic temple, that was megalomaniac, profane, imperial, pagan and glacial, and just as marmoreal and pretentious inside as it was outside, not to mention the shattering paganism of its statues. And this horror, or those horrors, are something that religious nationalism forces us to admire; it forces us to become insensitive to their falseness; to kill in us a whole dimension of discernment. That people admire at the same time "our cathedrals"—which were scorned in the epoch of the Renaissance and even later—does not change anything, because people admire them without understanding them, partly out of an inane patriotism, otherwise how could one bear at the same time to admire the basilica of Saint Peter or all the other "sanctuaries" of the same style or of the style that came afterwards? Truly, there is something in the average Catholic mentality that "is out of order"; the Eastern Church noticed this long ago. The most general manifestation of this "something" is what I call "civilizationism": it is, all told, the adulteration of the religious conscience with all the ruinous heritage of the Renaissance; in other words, it has become impossible henceforth to dissociate the Christian from the "civilized man", or let us say from 19th century man, and this is all the more dissonant in that this "civilization", which the missionaries were eager to inflict on non-European peoples, is poles apart from the sacred, materially as well as psychologically. Civilizationism produces, even more so among Catholics than among Protestants—because Catholics have the plenary sacraments and the liturgy—a split in the personality and an inferiority complex, without which the most recent "Council" would never have been possible.

2 July 1982 · PROTESTANT PIETY

You accuse Protestants of being pretentious. I lived for forty years in the canton de Vaud [Switzerland. *Ed.*] and I now have lived for two years in the state of Indiana, two Protestant lands, and I can say that I know the mentality of Protestantism, all the more so as I grew up in Basel among Protestants. Mediocrity exists everywhere and, obviously, it can take on a different tone depending on the confessions, but as for Lutheran or even Calvinist piety, I can assure you that it is not at all pretentious in itself, because the danger of pretentiousness entailed by the emphasis on trust or faith is compensated and neutralized, among truly pious Protestants, by a sincere humility nurtured by the Augustinian awareness of our irremediable helplessness; the sole remedy being the grace of Christ to which we have access by means of faith. This Christocentric faith is extended by a morality that appears not as a merit but as a "categorical imperative" which is Biblical in essence; quite simply, virtue enters into the logic of faith. This is an archetypal "reasoning" found also among Amidists, or in the Vishnuite *prapatti*; and also within Catholicism among quietists, although much more precariously. I have met some truly spiritual men among Protestants, and especially among pastors; they are not exactly analogous to pious Catholics, in their *barakah*, but attest unquestionably and quasi-existentially to a living dimension of the Gospel. That such a piety still survives four centuries after Luther means something after all.

The Protestant "pretension" of which you speak—and one finds this unavoidably in a Protestantism that is no longer wholly Lutheran nor completely Calvinist—this "pretension" occurs largely as the result of a contact between a trusting religiousness and the modern world that, in its tendencies, either excludes piety or distorts it; the Catholic mentality, in its turn and in its way, is the victim of the same thing. Apart from blindly patriotic and often stupidly republican civilizationism, there are, in the Catholic universe, more specific flaws, such as the complex of triviality one finds among priests, and monks and nuns—as extensive experience has taught me—which is due to the contrast between the sacred, which the priest must handle professionally, and the trivial, the ugly, and the "modern" which are present everywhere; whence the occurrence among these people of a kind of protestation of "virility" or rather of vulgarity, of profane "realism", of scorn for "bigotry", in short of a deformation that manifests itself in part by a lack of dignity, jokes in poor taste, and by a certain reflexive cynicism, and so on. My wife, who comes from a Protestant background, was very surprised by this when she entered Catholic milieus for the first time; she had never seen anything like this among pastors. I am not saying that one does not find any defects among pastors, I am saying that one finds them everywhere, thus also among Catholics; these are, in every instance, defects that are characteristic of a given milieu, and not purely personal or incidental defects.

[...] I would have no interest, nor any wish, to point it out, nor to say good things about Protestants, were it not that you place all the blame on them.

2 July 1982 · THE ORTHODOX AND PROTESTANT CHURCHES

For Orthodox Christians, the West—which is *a priori* Catholic—is a world of exaggerations, of over-accentuations, thus of oppositions, and consequently of disequilibrium and change, innovation; Protestantism is, for them, basically a Catholic phenomenon; had the Catholics of Luther's time been more realistic and less narrow-minded, less lacking in imagination, less pettily legalistic and also, from another point of view, less decadent, the positive and archetypal possibility manifested by Protestantism in itself could have flowered within Catholicism, without having to sever itself from it. At all events, the Roman Church should have remained far closer to the Greek Church, with or without the schism; it is not the Eastern Church that moved, it is the Western Church; it is the latter which tyrannically imposed the *filioque*; it is the latter which, along with the unspeakable act of ransacking Constantinople, weakened Eastern Christianity in a definitive way and thus delivered it to the Turks.

I would have gladly preferred being spared from having to deal with the problem of Protestantism and from having to write my chapter on Lutheran Evangelism [in *Christianity/Islam. Ed.*], but the Protestant phenomenon exists, and it is huge; consequently, I was obliged, sooner or later, to address it. I would also just as gladly have preferred being spared from dealing with Muslim theology—Lord knows how grating it can be—but I had no choice since Sufism is situated in parallel to this body of doctrine; it was a sacrifice for me, because I am hardly enamoured of exoterisms and would have preferred to deal only with pure metaphysics and the perennial religion; with the *Sanātana Dharma*.

14 August 1982 · TRANSUBSTANTIATION, THE FRENCH REVOLU-TION, NAPOLEON

It is not exact to say that the Lutheran Communion is only "a commemoration", that it denies the ontological relationship between Calvary and the rite; it is Zwingli and liberal Protestants, not Luther, who minimize the Eucharistic mystery in this manner; for the German reformer believed in the real Presence in each of the species. In denying transubstantiation—not inherence—he is referring moreover to St Paul, who speaks of the "bread which we break", and says: "... so let him eat of that bread". Even Calvin affirms that "Christ, with the plenitude of his gifts, is not less present, in the Communion, than if we saw him with our eyes and touched him with our hands." It is not transubstantiation that creates or manifests the ontological relationship in question, it is the real Presence; but that the real Presence can be conceived of as a "transubstantiation"—an elliptical idea if ever there was one—is an altogether different question.

In rereading your letter, I chance on a passage that suggests the following reflection: I was always of the opinion that those who inspired the French Revolution most directly were Voltaire, Diderot, Rousseau, and the Abbé Sieyès; did the French Encyclopaedists really need a Kant? With Rousseau, they have a thinker who is of Calvinist origin; be that as it may, the Revolution took place in Catholic France and not in Protestant Prussia. I shall add, since it occurs to me, that the Italian Napoleon had three great merits: to have been ultimately a monarchist, to have concluded the Concordat, to have died in the Catholic faith. Even though nationalisms derived their inspiration from him, he is not directly responsible for that, he who dreamt of a unified Europe.

26 January 1983 · MEDITATION AND INVOCATION, DISTRACTION AND CONCENTRATION

Thus you can see that there is no need to make a practical distinction between meditation and invocation—the act being nothing without the intention—, nor to seek concentration as if it were an end in itself when it derives merely from the sincere intention, and therefore from the invocatory effort. Besides, God is not interested—if one may say—in our concentration; all He asks of us is to have the correct intention. It is human to be a little distracted; but the intention must always be good, that is to say, it must be in conformity with the nature of things, and that is why there are [our] meditation themes. It is not permissible, for instance, to practise the invocation to personally obtain some kind of sublime realization, or to become a saint, or to overcome defects and to acquire virtues, or even powers; or to try out the invocation to see what kind of effect it produces, or for reasons of spiritual elitism, *et caetera*. But one can—and must—practise the invocation: first to save one's soul, secondly because one loves God and the atmosphere of his proximity, and thirdly because there is finally nothing else to do since God is God and man is man.

There are two ways to banish distractions—to which man has *a priori* a certain natural right—and these are first of all thematic arguments and the fervour of the invocation. By fervour I mean to say that the invocation can be accomplished with a certain psychosomatic violence, using a more rapid rhythm for example and moving the body; this is a kind of "holy war" against distractions. Distractions often arise from fatigue and overwork, and in any case are in no way abnormal; they should not be the cause of any alarm or moral reproach concerning ourselves. In the spiritual life, one must always start anew, with resignation and patience. The invocation is not a chore, it is a joy.

As for the Divine Name, or the divine Names—or the avataric Names that in certain instances replace the divine Names—there is no need to analyze them; whatever their form may be, they always refer to God, to the Absolute, the Infinite, the Sovereign Good. That there is a so to speak "virile" or paternal aspect in God, and one that is so to speak "feminine", maternal and also virginal, this is metaphysically obvious; but this should not allow us to lose sight of the fact that God is one, and that the Supreme Reality is one.

In the spiritual life, one must simplify the means, not make them more complicated; one must always return to the fundamental elements, which alone matter: discernment between the Absolute and the contingent or the relative; methodical practice of the invocation; realization of the essential virtues. The religious framework is also necessary, but it can never modify anything at all of these primordial and universal elements.

Thus it is not a question, I repeat, of "going from meditation to invocation"; meditation is nothing other than the intellectual or mental aspect of the invocation; in short, it is the formulation—and if need be the repetition—of the intention. Moreover: invoking "mechanically" is not a bad thing; it is better than nothing, so long as the underlying intention be good, namely normal and legitimate. And no perfectionism: one must not force matters in order to be perfectly concentrated; this introduces into the invocation a false and bitter element, which is worse than distraction pure and simple. Heaven does not ask perfection of us, It asks for sincerity, thus the right intention. It is not a matter of torturing ourselves, it is a matter of practising the invocation with simplicity and perseverance; perseverance is everything.

27 March 1983 · THE VIRTUES

The doctrinal reflections in your letter are perfectly satisfactory, thus there is no need for me to bring them up again; at most, there remains but one secondary point to be clarified, although

it is a question of formulation or opportunity rather than of anything involving the main content. When you say that for a Christian the acquisition of virtues is the imitation of Christ and the
Virgin, this is only too obvious in the sense that the human manifestations of the Logos necessarily possess every possible virtue;
but this is not exact in practice—strictly speaking—or from an
operative point of view, because here one must start with the
nature of things, namely with the primordial perfection of man;
having grasped what the nature and the modes of this perfection
are, one will obviously recognize them in specific human examples. Concretely speaking, nobility of character is acquired—insofar as it must be acquired—by the understanding of the essential virtues and by the elimination of the vices corresponding to
them; to assimilate a quality is above all to overcome a defect. It
is the return to our original theomorphism, for man is by definition "made in the image of God"; the *Avatāra* is "man as such",
while also being, inevitably so, "a given man".

Avataric beings, quite clearly, cannot evince any fault; but
they do not necessarily manifest every virtue in an explicit and
readily discernable manner. It goes without saying that the universal depiction of virtues coincides with the moral portrait of
a specific *Avatāra*, or of any *Avatāra*; in that sense, the virtuous
Christian cannot do otherwise than "imitate" Christ and the Virgin. But, once again, this cannot be *a priori* a question of want-
ing to imitate a given prototype; what matters is to know above
all what man is, what his specific nature and his reason for being
are, what his perfections are; otherwise there is a risk of lapsing
into what is arbitrary and fragmentary, if not into a sentimental,
or even hypocritical, mimesis; in short, into a sublimism which
is ultimately inoperative.

All told, the ontological origin of the qualities, in the microcosm as well as in the macrocosm, is the principial Quaternary, whose best-known symbolic expressions are the directions
of space and the alchemical poles: North and South, East and
West; Cold and Heat, Dryness and Humidity. And consequently: Purity and Goodness, Strength and Beauty; Incorruptibility
and Magnanimity, Courage and Nobility; Poverty and Charity,
Fervour and Humility; Patience and Generosity, Vigilance and

Gratitude; as well as other modes, not to mention their indefinite subdivisions.

27 March 1983 · ESOTERISM, CHRISTIANITY, ISLAM

Esoterism, being universal, always takes the nature of things as its starting point, the perception of which derives from the mystery of Intellection, hence from the "immanent Revelation"; whereas exoterism, being particular, takes a given phenomenon or symbol as its starting point, the perception of which derives from the mystery of Revelation, hence from "theophanic Intellection"; theophanic Intellection comes from the outside—with respect to the human subject—whereas Intellection properly speaking comes from within.

The tendency of authentic esoterism is to bring the "accidental" back to the "substantial", hence to simplify religious formalism in terms of what we would call the "esoteric schema", and not to complicate this outline in terms of religious formalism, or even of confessional "nationalism". Esoterism is discernment and serenity.

By "esoteric schema" I mean the triad of the three constitutive elements of the Path: I. Discernment between the Real and non-real, or between the Absolute and the contingent, the relative, or again, between the Essential and the secondary; II. the ensuing Concentration—which is invocatory—on the Real; III. moral Conformity to the Real.

In other words: Intelligence, Will, Soul. That is to say: I. the principial, universal and primordial—hence immanent or "consubstantial"—content of the Intelligence is metaphysical Truth, with its ramifications; II. the highest and profoundest content of the Will is the spiritual Act, the Remembrance of God, the Invocation; III. and likewise the highest and profoundest content of the Soul is Virtue, beauty of character; for "beauty is the splendour of the Real". In Sanskrit terms—and taking no account here of the aspects of subtleness and complexity of these terms—one could say that the three constitutive elements of the esoteric outline, or of esoterism as such, are the following: I. Discernment between *Ātmā* and *Māyā*; II. Concentration on *Ātmā*; III. moral Conformity to *Ātmā*. We could even go further—and this is moreover an integral part of our perspective—and add: aesthetic Conformity; or liturgical Conformity, which amounts to the same.

Furthermore, and still using Hindu terminology, I shall say that Islam is based on this truth: "*Māyā* is non-reality, *Ātmā* alone is Reality." And that Christianity, for its part, is based on this truth: "*Ātmā* became *Māyā* in order that *Māyā* might become *Ātmā*." Christianity offers us the salvific Manifestation of the Principle; Islam in turn offers us salvific Truth—Truth which is salvific because it is that of the Principle. On the one hand, the transcendent Real saves by its Truth; on the other hand, it saves by its Manifestation; but this difference in mode and perspective, or approach, does not affect the immutable esoteric triad, which moreover always underlies every religion.

From the viewpoint of Transcendence, *Māyā* is opposed—or appears to be opposed—to *Ātmā*; but from the viewpoint of immanence, it prolongs *Ātmā*; this is the symbolism of the Holy Virgin. While Eve personifies *Māyā* as such—as distinct from *Ātmā*—Mary is *Ātmā* as *Māyā*; thus, she transmits *Ātmā* in *Māyā*, and she engenders *Ātmā* in *Māyā*; and, still in *Māyā*, she attracts towards *Ātmā*.

29 March 1983 · ESOTERISM, EXOTERISM, CHRISTIAN ESOTERISM

What distinguishes man from the animals is I. the objectivity of his Intelligence, II. the freedom of his Will, and III. the compassion of his Soul; now esoterism intends to realize the essence of these theomorphic qualities by the fact I. that it is founded upon pure and total Truth; II. that man is the freest he can possibly be in the "Remembrance of God", the concentration on the Real; III. that the esoteric spirit is neither fanatical nor aggressive—though without being pacifist, however, or being tolerant towards intrinsic error—and that it thus realizes a compassion that reaches the depths of souls, thus without condemning anyone for reasons of form or husk.

Exoterism, for its part, is what it must be. But one must not lose sight of the fact that religion as such is aimed only at the moral man, not the intellectual man; the "psychic", not the "pneumatic", in the broadest sense of these terms; if it were aimed at the intellectual man, it would be inefficacious for the average man, whom it is intended to save, precisely. The sentimental, individualist and anthropomorphic voluntarism of religion is a function of divine Mercy; but this is certainly no reason to wish to reduce esoterism to this perspective—to "confessionalize" it while intending to benefit from its intellectuality and universality. Also, we accept from religion only its symbolism—dogmatic and ritual—and its so to speak sacramental graces, but not verbatim theology, which too often—though inevitably—reflects only preoccupations with psychological, moral and social opportunity, on the eschatological level, of course; one should not forget that saints have contradicted other saints, and that the Churches diverge.

The major question which can arise for a metaphysician situated in the Christian religious space, is that of knowing how to practise esoterism—the universal path of the "nature of things"—while participating sacramentally in Christic symbolism and the graces it confers. The answer is threefold, and it is the following: firstly, one must be conscious of the key Idea of Christianity, which I have formulated above, paraphrasing a well-known Patristic saying that I have often quoted in my books ["God became man in order that man might become God". *Ed.*]; secondly, one must be conscious of the quintessential meaning of the basic, not secondary, religious practices; thirdly, one must actualize union with the transcendent Real by means of a Name or a Formula taken from the Gospel. First of all, there is the double name *Jesu Maria*, which expresses and actualizes God's saving Will under the double aspect of rigour and gentleness, or perhaps more precisely virility and femininity, if one can use this symbolism; and there are then the following Formulas, each of which has a shorter and a longer form: *Pater noster qui es in caelis (sanctificetur Nomen tuum); Domine Jesu Christe (miserere nobis); Ave Maria gratia plena (Dominus tecum).*

Having come to the heart of the problem, I should stop, since I cannot say it better. Nonetheless, there is a question yet to resolve: that of obligatory religious practice. Catholicism—the authentic kind, as I am not speaking of the other—requires the following practices: 1. attendance at Mass every Sunday; 2. confession, at least once a year; 3. Communion, at least once a year, preferably at Easter. That is, one must—and I now resume the two Sanskrit terms for simplicity's sake—1. attend the rite that actualizes the principle that "*Ātmā* becomes *Māyā* in order that *Māyā* might become *Ātmā*"; 2. by confessing, purify ourselves of our tendency—due to the Fall—towards *Māyā*, I mean lower, centrifugal *Māyā*; 3. by receiving Communion, assimilate *Ātmā* ("in *Māyā*", of course, but it is essentially *Ātmā*). By these means of grace, methodical invocation benefits from a particular super-natural aid, even though in principle it is sufficient in itself; in principle, but not necessarily in fact, since to say the least, not everyone is a "pneumatic" in the strong sense of the word. Be this as it may, it is important to know that in principle, we bear the sacraments in ourselves; Meister Eckhart insists on this in his manner.

I repeat that in esoterism one must simplify and not com-plicate things; "substantialize" and not "accidentalize". "Pray without ceasing", said St Paul; and the quintessence of prayer is invocation.

I well realize that in this letter I have said many things that must be obvious for you, but I thought I could—or must—recall them "for good measure", given that the practical relationships between esoterism and the Christian religion seem to pose some problems in your mind; at least, your letter gives this impression.

7 September 1983 · THE SPIRITUAL MASTER

The role of the spiritual master, or if need be of his representa-tive, consists in defining the nature of the obstacles and of indi-cating the remedies; this requires intuition as well as experience; inspiration as well as sanctity, at whatever degree.

7 September 1983 · ABSOLUTE AND RELATIVE ESOTERISM

Esoterism is: 1. the quintessential object of the intelligence, Truth; 2. the quintessential object of the will, the Good; 3. the quintessential object of love, Beauty. Specifically: 1. discernment between the Real and the Non-Real, or between the Absolute and the Relative, *Ātmā* and *Māyā*; including the prefiguration of the Relative in the Absolute, and the reflection of the Absolute in the Relative; 2. concentration (in principle perfect and persevering) on the Real; however, an adequate intention prevails over perfection; 3. moral conformity to the Real, to discernment, to concentration.

In Christianity: "God became man in order that man might become God"; that is: the Absolute projected itself into the Relative in order that the Relative might be reintegrated into the Absolute; and this to whatever degree, since *"in my Father's house are many mansions"*.

Esoterism consists of: a Doctrine, a Method, a Morality. The Truth, the Way, Virtue; thus Comprehension, Concentration and Conformity. The first element is pure metaphysics, thus the discernment (*in divinis* as on all cosmic levels: macrocosm and microcosm) between the Absolute and the Relative, *Ātmā* and *Māyā*. The second element is jaculatory prayer that has become methodical: invocation. The third element is virtue: beauty of soul; intrinsic and spiritual—not only extrinsic and social—morality. Nobility of character; there is no wisdom without beauty.

All of this constitutes essential esoterism. But there is also a secondary esoterism that consists of seeking the deep meanings—metaphysical or mystical—in the various symbols in religion; one too often thinks that this is esoterism as such, but it is nothing of the sort; one can perfectly well be an esoterist without bothering with these questions, which moreover always run the risk of luring us into the restrictive nets of theology. Moreover, the essential meanings of scriptural, ritual, liturgical and other symbols are revealed of their own accord over time, *Deo volente*; at least in part, as this field is limitless.

Essential esoterism does not depend on our profound interpretation of a given dogma or sacrament; but our prior knowledge of universal principles may afford us the profound meanings. *A priori*, let it suffice for us to know that every symbol contains a meaning that refers directly or indirectly to the distinction between the Real and the unreal (or the "less real"). To love God and our neighbour is to love *Ātmā* as such, then *Māyā* in *Ātmā* or *Ātmā* in *Māyā*; Communion is possible being assimilating necessary Being, and thereby assimilating itself to the latter.

The Absolute (necessary Being) became contingency (possible being) in order that the latter might return to the former. *Et Verbum caro factum est.*

Integral (not just partial) esoterism is secret because it is too precious, and because it is dangerous; these are the "pearls" Christ spoke of, although this saying has a more outward application *a priori*. Esoterism is dangerous because it transcends religious formalism, intellectually and in principle even operatively; yet the equilibrium and well-being of the social order depend on this formalism.

That is: man bears within himself, as potentiality or virtuality, Revelation and the means of grace—sacraments and rites—and in principle he can dispense with these external supports; some of the saints of the early Church were obliged to dispense with them. When man, with Heaven's help, has been able to surmount the "outer" and fallen man, and thus released the "inner" and primordial man, he himself has become "his own Law". The Prophet—the legislating Logos (*Avatāra*)—is immanent in man; he is the "Heart".

The essence of every religion and all spirituality is *oratio et jejunium*: consciousness-concentration, on one hand positive and inclusive, and on the other, negative and exclusive; on one hand, divine Symbol, and on the other, abstention from everything that is contrary to it, either *de jure* or only *de facto*. *Ātmā* and *Māyā* in the microcosm, viewed as alchemical poles.

Thus the "Prayer of the Heart" or the "Remembrance of God" contains, in principle or in fact, the whole of religion and the whole of the path.

6 January 1984 · ESOTERISM, JESUS CHRIST
to Jean Borella

You are right, there is not just a "relative esoterism"; a "relative exoterism" is also a possibility, and that is the case of general Christianity, precisely; Islamic exoterism, for its part, is absolute, or rather total, as is Jewish exoterism. One finds with a Meister Eckhart and an Ibn 'Arabī, and no doubt with a few others, elements of a "total esoterism"—one could also say of "pure esoterism"—but the most clear-cut example of such an esoterism is Shankarāchārya, and no doubt also certain Greeks of the Pythagoras, Plato, or Plotinus type. Some Sufis make great efforts to persuade us—or to persuade themselves—that Islamic exoterism is esoterism, but this thesis is in reality untenable; it belongs to the domain of piety pure and simple. I do not know if the Kabbalists do the same, *mutatis mutandis*, but it is in any case plausible that they would. No doubt every symbol can lend itself to an esoteric interpretation, but that is not the point here.

If we start with the idea that esoterism is fundamentally the discernment between the Absolute and the contingent, the Real and the unreal, we can say that Christ personifies this discernment, and that our participation with Christ is our integration into transcendent Truth, just as, conversely, our metaphysical discernment encompasses us to some degree into the nature of Christ. As for Islam: if we start from the idea that the object or the content of esoterism is the Absolute, we can say that Allah is this Absolute, or the Absolute as such. But what I want to highlight above all here is this Christian mystery: that Christ is not merely "manifestation" but also "discernment" of the Absolute or of the Real; this specification is esoterically crucial, because discernment is something direct, whereas the manifestation is indirect. [...]

PS. Christ, as the "Wisdom of the Father", is the Knowledge God has of Himself; this is captured likewise by the Sufi expression: "knower by Allah" [*'ārif bi-Llāh. Ed.*].

25 July 1984 · THE PNEUMATIC, THE GNOSTIC, ORIENTAL ART

In the expression "choosing a path", when applied to a case such as Guénon's, there is something inadequate, awkward, ill-sounding; for Guénon was intrinsically a "pneumatic"—of a "gnostic" or "jnanic" type—and in such a case the question of a "path" does not arise, or at least it changes meaning to such an extent that the very expression lends itself to confusion. The pneumatic is in a way the "incarnation" of a spiritual archetype, which means that he is born with a state of knowledge that for others would be the goal, precisely, and not the point of departure; the pneumatic does not "advance" towards something "other than himself", he remains where he is in order to become fully himself—namely his archetype—by progressively eliminating veils or shells, impediments contracted by the ambience, possibly also by heredity. He eliminates these by means of ritual supports—"sacraments" if one wishes—without forgetting meditation and prayer; but his situation is nonetheless completely different from that of ordinary men, even if they be prodigiously gifted. On the other hand, one must know that the born gnostic is, by nature, more or less independent, not only with regard to the "letter", but also with regard to the "law"; which however does not simplify his relationship with his surroundings, either psychologically or socially.

The quality of being a pneumatic—or a born gnostic—comprises not only modes, but also degrees: on the one hand there is the difference between the *jnāni* and the *bhakta*, and on the other hand there are differences of plenitude or scope in the manifestation of the archetype.

The pneumatic is situated, by his very nature, beneath the vertical and intemporal axis—here there is neither a "before" nor an "after"—so that the archetype which he personifies or "incarnates", and which is his true "himself" or "oneself", can at any moment pierce through the contingent individual envelope: whence, in some pneumatics—not in all—certain spiritual expressions that may appear excessive and provoke scandal; but it is then the archetype that speaks through the envelope; it is thus really "himself" who is speaking. The true gnostic attributes no "state" to himself, for he is without ambition and without ostentation; he has rather the tendency—by "instinct of self-preservation"—to conceal his nature, all the more so since he is in any case aware of the "cosmic play" (*līlā*) and since it is difficult for him to take seriously the seriousness of profane and worldly people; that is to say, of "horizontal"—not "vertical"—people, who live blissfully unaware, and who do not live up to the vocation of man.

What the gnostic seeks by nature, from the point of view of "realization", is much less a "path" than a "setting"; a traditional, sacramental, and liturgical framework that will allow him to be more and more authentically "himself", that is, a given archetype of the celestial "iconostasis". And this makes me think of the sacred art of India and the Far East, which shows in a super-naturally evocative way the celestial models of earthly spirituali-ty; that, moreover, is the purpose of this art which is at once rig-orous and musical, and founded upon the principle of *darshan*, of the visual and intuitive assimilation of the symbol-sacrament. This symbol, moreover, does not pertain solely to art, it materi-alizes also—and *a priori*—in animate and inanimate nature, for in all beauty there is a liberating, and ultimately salvific, element, which permits us this esoteric paraphrase: "He who hath eyes to see, let him see!"

25 July 1984 · DIVINE INSPIRATION, THEOPHANY, ESOTERISM

Each of the monotheistic Scriptures manifests an *upāya*, a reli-gious perspective—particular and characteristic by definition—and average hermeneutics is affected by it; such is not the case for the fundamental formulations—or the fundamental sym-bols—of religions which in themselves are not limitative in any way. In Islam, the *Shahādah* for example—"the most precious thing that I have brought to the world", the Prophet said—ex-presses integral metaphysical truth in a most direct and limpid way; in Hindu terms, I would say that it is at once an *Upanishad* and a *mantra*; and the second *Shahādah* is the complement of the first, which is to say that to the mystery of transcendence is joined the mystery of immanence. In Christianity, the patristic formula of salvific reciprocity is a priceless jewel: "God became man that man might become God"; this is a revelation of the highest magnitude, at the same level as Scripture; this may seem surprising, but it is a "paracletic" possibility, examples of which can be found—very rarely, it is true—in all traditional worlds. The sentence *Anā'l-Ḥaqq* of Al-Hallāj is a case of this kind, it is so to speak the Sufi equivalent of the Vedic *Aham Brahmāsmi*; Al-Hallāj himself affirmed this possibility of post-Koranic sayings situated at the level of the Koran, for which other Sufis did not forgive him, at least not in his time.

But there are not only formulas, there are also human the-ophanies. Christ, as universal symbol and from the point of view of esoteric application, represents first of all the Logos in itself and then the immanent Intellect which at once enlightens and

79

liberates; the Holy Virgin personifies the soul in a state of sanctifying grace, or this grace itself. There is no theophany that is
not prefigured in the very constitution of the human being, for
the human being is "made in the image of God"; now esoterism
aims at actualizing the divine content which God has placed in
this mirror of Himself that is man. Meister Eckhart spoke of
immanent sacraments; analogous natural or "congenial" things
may serve as supports for this, he said, in the same way as the
sacraments in the proper sense of the word.

Hence one must distinguish between an esoterism more or
less broadly founded upon a given theology and deriving from
the speculations which traditional sources offer us *de facto*—and
it goes without saying that these doctrines or insights may be of
the greatest interest—and another esoterism resulting from the
truly fundamental elements of religion and also, for that very
reason, from the simple nature of things; the two dimensions
may be combined, of course, and in fact they often are; but there
is a question of emphasis here, and it is evidently to the second
dimension that our perspective pertains *a priori*.

15 September 1984 · THE CHRISTIAN ESOTERIC PATH

Thus, having become aware of the doctrine—metaphysics, cosmology, eschatology—you wish to put it into practice, as far as
possible, and on the formal basis of Christianity; in other words,
you aspire to an esoteric Christian path. You know that pure
metaphysics is 1. essential, 2. primordial and 3. universal: being
essential, it is independent of all religious or confessional formulation; being primordial, it is the truth that existed before all
dogmatic formalism; being universal, it encompasses all intrinsically orthodox symbolism, and consequently may be combined
with every religious language. Next comes method, which is
quintessentially prayer, in the broadest as well as deepest sense;
the practice of the Hesychasts and the life of the "Russian pilgrim" [*The Way of a Pilgrim*, anonymous work. *Ed.*] are examples
of this prayer in a Christian setting. And all this requires, in an
imperative manner, the fundamental virtues on the one hand
and on the other, extrinsically, a corresponding comportment,
hence one that is in conformity with the doctrine and the way.

Metaphysics is not a religion, but it gives a profound and universal meaning to the ideas and the phenomena of every religion: thus, it teaches *a priori* the distinction between the Absolute and the relative, *Ātmā* and *Māyā*, the Principle and manifestation; now the phenomenon of Christ—or the metaphysical truth that determines this phenomenon—means that "God became man in order that man might become God", according to a famous patristic formula, which however must not be taken literally, for man as such cannot "become God"; but this is not the place to explain this reservation, which in any case I have done in my books. "God became man": *Ātmā* became *Māyā*; as a result, Christ is a bridge from *Māyā* to *Ātmā*, and consequently—and this is the mystery of the *Avatāra*—his name contains a salvific power; the same is true for the name of the Holy Virgin, for she too is an avataric phenomenon, in the sense that she incarnates the feminine aspect of the Logos.

Jaculatory prayer is altogether fundamental, it has a truly eucharistic function; but man also has need of individual and ordinary prayer: from time to time—whenever one feels the need—one must speak to God and ask Him for help; one may do so through a celestial intermediary, the Holy Virgin for instance.

Before entering a path of prayer—before undertaking to invoke God thrice daily and, to the extent possible, at every available moment—one has to promise Heaven to persevere in this path until death; this is the equivalent of monastic vows. As for the classic vows of "poverty", "chastity", and "obedience", they have, aside from their literal meaning which concerns monks, a spiritual import which concerns every man.

When one devotes oneself to a spiritual practice, it is important to have the right intention; one must not have intentions that are beneath the reason for the existence of the practice. God accepts that we invoke Him for several reasons, and for these alone: firstly, He accepts that we invoke Him to save our soul, and this is the intention of fear; then He accepts that we invoke Him because we love the celestial atmosphere, so to speak, and this is the intention of love—"I love because I love", as St Bernard said; finally, He accepts the intention of gnosis, which is founded upon the metaphysical evidence of the Real or of the

Absolute. But God will never accept the intention of obtaining perceptible graces, or of having experiences, or of making an experiment; or of realizing a given virtue or some other eminent state; or of becoming this or that, and so on. And when man experiences a spiritual state or a grace, or if he has a vision or an audition, he must never desire that it happen again, and above all he must never base his spiritual life upon such a phenomenon or imagine that this phenomenon confers some eminence upon him. The only thing that matters is that we practise that which brings us closer to God, by observing the conditions required by this practice; we do not have God's measures and we do not need to ask ourselves what we are. Life is a dream, and to think of God is to awaken; it is to be already in Heaven, even here below.

15 March 1985 · MORALITY AND AESTHETICS

Guénon did not want to be either a moralist or an aesthete; however, as far as I am concerned, I want to be both a moralist and an aesthete, and even fundamentally so; because I cannot conceive of any metaphysical wisdom or operative science outside those two qualities. Needless to say, I am referring to intrinsic, and not merely social, morality, to integral and not merely profane aesthetics; in short, one cannot without impunity be a metaphysician without being at the same time a moralist and an aesthete in the profound meaning of those terms; moreover, this is proved by all the traditional civilizations, whose atmosphere is made of virtue and beauty.

5 August 1985 · BAPTISM, THE FALL OF ADAM

Returning to the question of the definition of the sacraments: the theological explanation of baptism is metaphysically insufficient because the notions of "freedom" and "sin" are not enough to account fully for the "Fall"; for the Fall was cosmologically necessary, and it is precisely its providential complement—the Redemption—that proves this; *felix culpa*, as St Augustine would say! We would need to avail ourselves here of the Vedantic ideas of *māyā* and of *avidyā*, of "illusion" and "nescience"; sin is but a consequence of these two factors. I mention this example to indicate that religious definitions are not always satisfactory in all respects—their symbolism notwithstanding—and that one sometimes has no choice but to superimpose on them definitions which are less limited, and not determined by particular salvational perspectives.

28 September 1985 · PENITENTIAL PATH AND GNOSTIC PATH, THE GRACES, THE CURÉ D'ARS

I have always liked the Curé d'Ars—I read an account of his life some forty years ago by the Abbé Trochu—but without losing sight of the following factors: this saint's path is that of a penitential *bhakti* which, by definition, resorts to the will and sentiment, but not to intelligence; this means that metaphysical arguments play no role in this path, whereas in gnostic esoterism, on the contrary, ideas are keys of paramount importance; it is owing to the efficacity of the metaphysical concepts that a disciple of Shaykh Al-'Alawī told me: "It is not I who have left the world, it is the world that has left me". In Christian mysticism—especially Catholic—one begins by "leaving the world"; in esoteric sapience, one begins by understanding what it is; now "there is no lustral water like unto Knowledge" [*Bhagavadgītā* 4:38. *Ed.*]; nothing so disarms seductive *Māyā* as the knowledge we have of it, both around us and within us. The beginning of all gnosis and all liberation is indeed our understanding of what the relationship between *Ātmā* and *Māyā* is; now this doctrine—and its corresponding alchemy—remain outside the bhaktic perspectives, especially those that are voluntarist and penitential. These perspectives, which at the same time are fundamentally suspicious of anything that for them resembles quietism, likewise underestimate the sacramental grace of the Divine Name; they place the entire burden on the side of man and ignore by design—with a few exceptions—that God can put Himself in the place of our weakness.

And yet, sanctity is sanctity, and Paradise is Paradise, whatever the path may have been of him who has attained them. [...]

The Curé d'Ars, to whom you turned, came to your assistance; but are you certain that the beneficent presence you have felt since that moment does not come from the Holy Virgin? For the Curé d'Ars always placed himself under Mary's mantle, if one may say. I am not at all sure that an ordinary saint can grant an earthly person a permanent presence, whereas this is something that the Blessed Virgin can do, and she even does so readily towards those who place their trust in her; as the Curé d'Ars did, precisely.

At all events, our spiritual life should not depend on any sensible grace; it is fine to feel a celestial presence, but this has nothing to do with our path; our path is active, not passive, and it is based on ideas and practices, not on experiences. We should not be overly interested in whether our states of soul are agreeable or not; we can certainly accept sensible graces with respect and gratitude, but what matters in the eyes of God is what we do and not what we experience. For there are only two absolute certitudes: metaphysical certitude, which constitutes the *raison d'être* of our path, and the certitude of our spiritual duty. [...] God alone is God, and we must attach ourselves to Him; this is the meaning of life, and above all, it is the *raison d'être* of the human state.

12 November 1985 · OVERCOMING PASSIVITY

In your nature there is a certain passivity, against which you must absolutely react; you owe it to Heaven, to yourself and to your family. With prayer—thus with God's help—everything is possible; even "the things which are impossible with men", according to the Gospel. You have no other choice, as you have only one life; and this is what I would say to all men.

6 December 1985 · TRADITIONAL ART, PRAYER

Thus you do not limit yourself to studying ancient manuscripts, you even relive their origin; this reminds me of something Coomaraswamy said, namely that traditional art imitates not nature but its modes of operation, and even more so, its archetypes; the modes of operation being in function of the latter, in a certain way.

In your November letter, you allude to prayer as conversation with Heaven; this aspect, overly neglected by most believers, though prefigured by the Psalms, is of fundamental importance; for all sectors of our immortal soul must participate in the path towards God, which is the *raison d'être* of our creation. "God became man in order that man might become God", according to St Irenaeus; the expression "become God" obviously having a symbolical, not a literal, sense; but the profound intention— both subtle and complex—authorizes the audacity of the formulation, in any case. In a word, we must go to God with all that we are—*ex toto corde tuo et ex tota anima tua*; God knows the mystery of man better than we do.

On one hand, one is alone before God, and this solitude is an aspect of our nature; on the other hand, one stands before God with the help of a celestial being—the Blessed Virgin—and this, too, corresponds to a fundamental aspect of human nature.

9 December 1985 · THE TERNARY TRUTH-PATH-VIRTUE

All that matters for us are these three factors: the Truth, the Path, and Virtue. God will hold us to account on these three points; He will not hold us to account about the modern world, nor His motives for having allowed such or such an evil.

Hence, metaphysical Truth; with all of the discernments which derive from this and which our encounter with phenomena requires. Then, the Path: namely prayer in general and the invocation in particular. And consequently, Virtue too: that is to say the absence of all of the defects that demean and mar the soul. And that is all. Nothing and no one, in the modern world, prevents you from understanding and accepting metaphysical Truth, from distinguishing what is real from what is false, and right from wrong; nothing and no one prevents you from invoking God every day; and nothing prevents you from being virtuous.

There is no question of living, in our times, as men lived in the Middle Ages. First of all, this is impossible to do, and then, there is no reason for doing so. It is out of the question that Truth— or God—could ask of us something unreasonable or impossible. Were someone to say to me that the Truth, the Path, and

Virtue cannot be followed in the modern world, I would respond that there is no reason that one could not do so, and that there are thousands and even millions of men who do so. Moreover, spirituality—of whatever degree—makes no distinction between ancient man and modern man, because it applies, not to a "given group of men", but to "men as such"; that is to say, it concerns the invariable factors defining man or human nature. In this respect—which alone matters—there is no distinction to be made between men of the time of the Council of Nicea and those of the time of the pseudo-Council of Vatican II. Likewise, two plus two have always equalled four, in the time of the Apostles as in our time. That is all that matters.

9 December 1985 · RELIGIOUS ORTHODOXY

You say in your letter that Islam, Hinduism, and Buddhism today no longer benefit from the orthodoxy of their early days; but yes, they do! The orthodoxy of the religions of today is that of a thousand years ago, two thousand years ago, or more. The Catholicism of the time of Pius XII was just as orthodox as that of the Apostolic times; a sacrament administered in 1958 was just as valid as a sacrament administered in the year 38. Religious degeneration has absolutely nothing to do with the question of orthodoxy.

There is no need for Catholicism to return to the perfection of early Christianity; that would moreover be impossible to do, given the degeneration of humanity. But it should and could return to the orthodoxy of thirty years ago; this would be easy to do. The degeneration of the world corresponds unquestionably to a certain divine Will, but this does not mean that we ourselves must degenerate! One might as well say that the existence of sin proves that God wishes it and therefore that man must sin. Degeneration is never, as you insinuate, an effect of divine Mercy; what is an effect of Mercy is such or such an adaptation of the Path to our weakness, but this is done according to Truth and not error.

9 December 1985 · SPIRITUAL REALIZATION

You speak in your letter of your "attempts at realization"; such a thing does not exist, "realization" cannot be the object of "attempts". For there is no such thing as "attempts" in spiritual life, and "realization" depends on God, not on us; for us, there is only the method based on the doctrine; the rest depends on Heaven. In any case, our first concern has to be to save our soul; one can, of course, practise that which logically may lead to some kind of "realization", but we do so without worrying about the results, because we cannot force anything; and we cannot have sufficiently concrete notions about this kind of thing *a priori*.

29 January 1986 · OBSTINACY

One must beware of false certitudes about men, things, and situations, because there is a classic pitfall here, well known in mystical theology. The subjective phenomenon of certitude can be an illusion—all the more pernicious in that the stakes are greater—and as for the proofs one alleges, they can be a matter of interpretation, or of "projection" as one would say in psychology; they can be refuted by other proofs, which for their part are real, but which one ignores or wants to ignore.

Stubborn perseverance in a radically false opinion concerning a person who is a superior human being or concerning something sacred is always a sign, if not of fundamental satanism, at least of a satanic inspiration. St John of the Cross insists on this: the devil is fond of inculcating in people predisposed certitudes that are unshakeable but diametrically opposed to the truth; the earmarks of satanism are precisely this diametrical falseness and this obstinacy in error. And I can assure you that I have a great deal of experience in this, by dint of circumstances and most unwillingly.

9 May 1986 · JACULATORY PRAYER
to Pastor B.

I would have liked to wait, before writing you, to have all my strength back, but the days go by and there is a tiredness that does not leave me; it is due no doubt to my advanced age and perhaps also the vagaries of the climate; I am close now to my eightieth year and I am beginning to feel it. But it is in any case a pleasure for me to give you at least a sign of life.

We too were happy to have your visit, and the occasion we had of having you partake a little of the near paradisal ambience that we have found here, by the grace of God.

You speak to me in your letter of the meetings for the invocation of the Prayer of Jesus; this is most gratifying, and I am glad also to learn that you were able to create an ambience that suits this holy practice. Thank you for sending me the liturgical outline of your gatherings; praise be to God.

What matters in jaculatory prayer is not—or it is less—what we say, it is above all how we say it. When we address ourselves to the Unique, we must be total; in fact Christ said this, referring to the formula of the Torah: to love God with all that we are. The oneness of the Sovereign Good demands metaphysically the totality of the heart.

6 September 1986 · EXTERIORITY AND INTERIORITY

Man is *pontifex* by definition, which means that he lives in two completely different dimensions; this is the Eckhartian distinction between the outer man and the inner man. First of all, we stand before God, and this situation has something absolute about it; then, we live in the world of phenomena, and this situation—woven of relativities—is determined by the preceding one. The result of this incommensurability is that when we look towards God—when we invoke Him—all the noise of earthly *māyā* is shut out; it is thus sufficient that we know that everything is in God's hands; our forgetting of the world equals trust in God. A Koranic sentence teaches us to "Say *Allāh*! and leave them to their vain discourse"; this "vain discourse" is our thoughts and the worldly matters that provoke them. The best way to master life's problems is to forget them in the face of God, while putting them in His hands; this forgetting, I repeat, is synonymous with trust. Life is complicated, but we must simplify it by means of the absolute element I have just mentioned; we must not give way to the vertigo of phenomena. We must realize an equilibrium between the outer and the inner, the horizontal and the vertical; this equilibrium is man's vocation. *Et in terra pax hominibus bonae voluntatis.*

27 October 1987 · CHRISTIAN ESOTERISM, RENÉ GUÉNON

I did receive your letter from the month of July and I am glad to learn that my books were in some way enlightening to you; I am all the more glad given that you are a priest. It is very true: Truth finds its extension in Beauty, hence also in Virtue; it is this dimension that the Holy Virgin embodies.

Always mindful of separating esoterism sharply from exoterism, Guénon could not accept that the sacraments, which are *de facto* religious rites, could have *de jure* an initiatic character; yet this results from their forms and is proven by their theological definitions. I shall add, in passing, that there was never a break between Guénon and myself, contrary to the popular version of the story; the divergences are nonetheless altogether real. If esoterism is as important an element as Guénon maintains—and rightly so!—it is not possible that Christ could not have, or would not have wanted, to guarantee *a priori* its preservation; in fact, Christian esoterism is to be found less in the initiatic rites that would have been added than in the interpretation—concrete as well as abstract—of the general rites, which are sacraments, precisely. "God became man in order that man might become God": this is an elliptical formula meaning that "*Ātmā* reflected itself in *Māyā* in order that *Māyā* could be reintegrated into *Ātmā*."

These few lines with all my best wishes—the little picture of Chartres is truly beautiful.

31 March 1988 · CHARACTER

When one notices in a person defects of character, or even vices, one should not be surprised even if the parents happen to be normal or virtuous, for if there are saints whose parents were bad people, the reverse must also be possible, namely that there be bad people whose parents were saints. A person's traits of character have two possible sources: either the individual substance—the origin of which no one knows—or heredity; when a character cannot be explained by heredity, then this means that it is entirely specific to the individual. For a child is not just the product of his parents; he comprises something new that comes from himself, otherwise there would never be exceptional men, and a quality or a defect would always belong to the entire paternal or maternal line, all the way up back to the ancestors and back to Cain and Abel. The core of the problem, metaphysically speaking, is All-Possibility; evil cannot not exist since the world is not God; "for it must needs be that offences come", but there is also the parable of the prodigal son. All that we can do in such cases is to pray for the person who has gone astray; this is what St Monica did, the mother of St Augustine; you could also pray for your grandchildren.

What matters for us is to practise resignation on the one hand and trust on the other: resignation to the Will of God and trust in his Mercy.

Summer 1988 · THE ORIGIN OF THE SOUL

The individual substance, which "transmigrates", arises from the potentialities of divine All-Possibility and has nothing to do with genes, which transmit hereditary configurations; these configurations are added to the individual's substance. They do not start to be actualized until the moment when the substance enters the body, around the third month of pregnancy; this combination constitutes the soul. It is perfectly useless to do research on the origin of the empirical soul; it is due to All-Possibility on one hand, and heredity on the other, that the individual is what he is.

1995 · CONTEMPLATIVE LIFE

Strictly speaking, contemplative life is not a question of "vocation", it is imposed on all; to believe one lacks the "vocation" for it is to deliberately choose error, lukewarmness. All the saints were contemplatives; those who were at the same time very active could only be so because they were saints, precisely. Everyone should begin in silence, contemplation, prayer; if God then wishes to ask something else of us, this will present itself of its own accord; it could never be the object of a doubt. Everything is uncertain, except the necessity of silence and contemplation. What God wants is our soul. In the world, there is no other "path"; the so-called "active path" is nothing but dissipation and flight before God. This flight is hypocritically called "responsibility".

The "renewal" in the Church is quite simply a concession made to the world, so there is no point in asking ourselves if we can "get used to it" or not; an error is an error.

Unknown date nᵒ 1 · THE TRUE ESOTERIST

PS. Still on the subject of religious speculations, in connection with the esoteric perspective: the metaphysician (authentic) or the esoterist (integral, not partial) considers everything from the aspect 1. of the metaphysical distinction between the Absolute and the relative; 2. of sincere, profound, quasi-permanent concentration on the Absolute.

Thus, in the face of some religious circumstance, some religious fact or some historical, mythological, symbolical, ritual or other phenomenon, he will ask: what does this mean in relation to the distinction between the relative and the Absolute; or in relation to spiritual concentration? Or again: in relation to transcendence or immanence? And finally: in relation to the soul's conformity, or our participation in divine Beauty ("Be ye perfect, as your Father in Heaven is perfect"); thus in relation to intrinsic virtue, to fundamental virtues?

The true esoterist will not enclose himself in the phenomenal religious order; things are without interest in themselves, that is, outside the connections we have just outlined; the vertical takes precedence over the horizontal. For example, it is not a question of exploring a given incident in the life of Christ or the Virgin, historically, psychologically and ever anew; it suffices to grasp their metaphysical and mystical meanings, always supposing one really feels called to examine them in depth; most often, such incidents retrace aspects or states of the soul's nearness or distance in the face of God—if they have no other word-for-word meaning. Moreover, one can have the vocation to wish to understand a given religious phenomenon, but one is not obliged to understand everything; one must grasp the essential and bear the fact that there are things one does not understand in depth; not that they are out of reach by their nature, but it is neither possible nor desirable that man know everything, or think about everything; he should thus hold *a priori* to the essential.

Unknown date n° 2 · FAITH, INTELLECTION, CERTITUDE

R.C. writes: "Concerning the traditional rites of the Church, we can accept them with the 'certitude of faith'. Such a certitude is greater than 'theological' and 'mystical' certitudes, as it is the highest of all certitudes—it derives from God Himself."

This amounts to saying, firstly, that metaphysical certitude is not the most elevated of certitudes; and secondly, that it does not derive from God! First of all, there is no difference between theological certitude and the certitude of faith; theology only defines, analyses or makes explicit what faith imposes on us; if one is certain of a theological thesis, it is because one has faith, unless it is a minor thesis addressed only to reason.

Furthermore: the certitude of faith is a divine Grace received passively, whereas metaphysical certitude arises from a divine Immanence operating actively; this allows Meister Eckhart to declare that the pure Intellect is "uncreated and uncreatable". And in the same way: "The Sufi is not created".

The mystics sometimes suffered cruelly from "temptations against faith"; but nobody has ever suffered temptations against metaphysical certitude.

According to degree, religious faith can be lost, or it cannot be lost; the faith of a simple believer does not necessarily have the same quality—to say the least—as the faith of a St Thomas Aquinas or a St Bernard.

To say that only faith comes from God, and not metaphysical intellection, is a very grave error, deriving from the exoteric confusion between the Intellect and reason, intellection and reasoning; according to this classic error, only Revelation and faith are "supernatural", whereas intellection and metaphysical certitude—confused with reason—are "natural". Hence the rejection of gnosis by theology, that is, by exoterism.

Certainly, man must make a volitive and sentimental effort to open himself to the divine gift of faith; nevertheless, this gift is received passively, otherwise it would not be a grace. Inversely, from man's side there is something passive about intellection, since the individual is not the Intellect, although the latter is immanent in the soul; immanent, but inaccessible to the ordinary mind, and volitive and sentimental in its substance.

Obviously there can be an element of intellection in faith, and inversely, if one thinks of the complexity of the human soul, but this takes nothing away from the rigour of the principial positions.

The theologians speak of the "obscure merit of faith": this merit is "obscure" because one believes in something one does not see, in conformity with what Christ said to St Thomas. But this merit does not constitute faith in itself, since the latter is a grace and a gift from God. The merit in intellection is the absence of the passional element in the intelligence; this absence does not constitute intellection, but it conditions and favourizes it.

The inferiority of faith in relation to intellection is proven by the fact that the object of faith is one particular religious symbolism and not another—a given faith excludes and combats another given faith—while the object of intellection is truth as such, which is one and universal. One can lose faith in favour of another faith; this is what is called a "conversion". But one cannot lose metaphysical certitude in favour of another metaphysical certitude, for this certitude is one, like fundamental truth itself.

One could object that the supreme content of faith, the Divinity, coincides with the supreme content of intellection, the Absolute; but this is not so, for the simple reason that theology's object is the hypostatic aspect of the Absolute and not the Absolute itself; theology—thus religious faith—does not, by definition, have the notion of universal Relativity, of *Māyā*.

The esoterist must forearm himself—if need be—against the temptation of letting himself be influenced by a given theology; to overestimate it with respect to tradition and by religious solidarity. For the sacred has degrees, as truth itself does. And "there is no right superior to that of truth".

To come back to the initial quotation: to say, on the subject of traditional Catholic rites—thus before the "Council"—that we have a "certitude of faith" is a weak and reversible argument. If we know for certain that the old rites are valid, it is because we still know how to think; it is because we have theological, canonical and historical reasons to accept this; it is because our intelligence is not perverted by modernism; as for the "certitude of faith", this is quite another question which does not have to intervene in this controversy.

Unknown date n° 3 · HAMLET

The story of Hamlet is the drama of a man who lives in two dimensions and who is so to speak torn between them, namely the ordinary human vision of things and the vision of the cosmos in its totality. Hamlet is at once a chivalrous, sensitive soul and a metaphysical and contemplative intelligence; in other words, and it is this that characterizes him, he does not know how to concretely reconcile "action" and "contemplation", the exigencies of human sensibility and the consciousness of the vanity of all things. This is what explains his famous "hesitation" and also his profound pessimism; he wants to act, but at the same time he sees himself from above, as an actor, he sees his human role in all its contingency and all its futility; he knows that he cannot change either men or the world.

Hamlet should act and would like to act, but it is as if he has two souls, that of a prince who would like to act with justice—not base vengeance—and that of a contemplative who finds himself hypnotized by Solomonian wisdom: "Vanity of vanities... What profit hath a man of all his labour which he taketh under the sun?...The thing that hath been, it is that which shall be; and that which is done is that which shall be done: and there is no new thing under the sun".

This is in any case one important aspect of Shakespeare's play.

Unknown date n° 4 · WARNING TO A DISCIPLE

You say that one of your problems is "a very powerful inner call to establish myself in the intellectual dimension of the path", a call you attribute to the preponderance in yourself "of elements that relate to it", that is, to the intellectual dimension. There is the kernel of your problems: this ambitious and illusory intellectualism; if it were not illusory, you would have no problem. So begin by forgetting your "inner call" and practise the path as it presents itself to you, without being in the least preoccupied by your nature. You cannot know *a priori* what you are in reality; you will know it *a posteriori*, when you have lost all interest in this question. The very length of your letter proves that your problems are artificial, thus illegitimate; for one does not need to write a twelve-page letter to outline real problems.

You think far too much, in an artificial manner that is both bookish and psychological. You speak of "tracing a regulated and coherent line of action for yourself" in function of the discrimination of the "real nature of certain inclinations and predispositions" of your soul, and so on. That is the last thing you need!

Through your reading, you have accumulated a mass of traditional data, methodical as well as doctrinal, but you do not know how to handle this data, because of a lack of spiritual science or even simply discernment of phenomena. Thus you should not seek to "operate" with this data, which is in fact unusable; you must forget it or put it in parentheses, and begin again from zero with the means offered by the Path.

You also tell me of the motives for your desire to travel. There is individualism here, narcissism, even pride; these motives are ridiculous. I am not against travel, I am against the motives. You want to go travelling in order "not to doubt yourself indefinitely" and "to affirm with pride" your "own criterion"; if this is the case, stay at home. What sort of man ceases to doubt himself just because he goes travelling, or who needs to travel in order to cease doubting himself? And who aspires to affirm his "own criterion"—what's more, "with pride"? And in this state of mind, you still dare to practise the invocation?

You say you have a certain taste for teaching; I assure you that this taste is perfectly illegitimate. You also speak of a "more and more perfect theoretical elaboration"; you would be wasting your time, given your tendency to complication, subjectivization and dilettantism. No, you do not "vehicle" truth and it is not for you to "proclaim" it; you have everything to learn. It would certainly be harmful for you to persist in such temptations. Forget who you are, what you want to be or do, and practise the invocation with the themes, like the least gifted of disciples. Before finding oneself, one must lose oneself. It is God who will decide who we are.

The Path is something objective, not subjective, in the sense that it imposes on us a Norm that exists outside us—although it acts on our subjectivity—and with regard to which the question of knowing whether we are "saturnine", "venusian" or something else does not even arise, any more than that of our ethnicity for example, on condition that we are mentally sound. Let us not ask what we are; let us ask what God is: the Absolute, the Infinite, the Sovereign Good.

Unknown date n° 5 · GOD DETERMINES MAN

Metaphysical certitude is not God. Man must always count, not only on God who determines him and on Whom everything depends, but also on the divine Will which concerns human, earthly and cosmic facts in a particular manner. Thus man depends on the Divinity in two ways: firstly, inasmuch as he is man, manifestation and creature, and secondly, inasmuch as he acts; and man must devote himself to God in two respects, first that of existence and second, that of action. To be through God and for God; to want what He wants; to annihilate oneself in the root and in the fruits. Only in this way is man fully man; and it is only by being fully man that he can "realize God". "Deification" is for man, not for the human animal.

Unknown date n° 6 · THE SAINT AND THE WORLD

The world is what it is; it is for us to transform it inwardly into gold. The world as such does not concern us; only its reflection in ourselves has importance. The saints are the beings who have realized this; they expected nothing from the world, and they were without bitterness. They drew everything from themselves, through God and for God.

A Hesychast has said that at the moment man pronounces the Name of God with perfect concentration—or perfect abandonment—nothing distinguishes him from a saint. The saint is the man who has been able to "anchor" this attitude. God does not ask this of us, but each of us must give what he can.

Letters to Muslim Correspondents
Devoted to the Sufi Path

29 April 1940 · LAUGHTER AND WEEPING

As for laughter, I am not at all convinced of what you say about its origin, nor of the definition you give of it. I know that laughter plays no role at all in either Sufism or among the Kabbalists; that on the contrary, it is sadness and tears which have a positive meaning in these two initiatic traditions, and are mentioned everywhere, denied only by intellectual serenity itself, sometimes also by joy, but never by laughter; that the Sufi Al-Kattānī compared laughter to a hideous old woman; that the Sufi Al-Qushairī said: "He who knows sadness advances further on the path of Allah in a month than he who is devoid of sadness advances in years"; that it is said of Christ that no one ever saw him laugh; that something analogous is said of Dante; that it is not said of any prophet or saint that he excelled in laughter. But none of this should have anything absolutely exclusive about it, which would be impossible even in principle; there are also passages where spiritual people have laughed, and in particular I know a Taoist text regarding this, but it is an exceptional possibility, for since laughter is a relative loss of equilibrium, much more than tears, the spiritual man does not laugh, or rather, he does not make a practice of laughter.

1 May 1940 · LAUGHTER, PRIMORDIAL MAN

I am adding a few more words to my preceding letter, so as to better clarify a few things. No doubt it is unnecessary for me to stress the following: if laughter and weeping are characteristic of man, it is obviously not in the way of a superiority, for neither of these manifestations of the soul characterizes man differently than does the mental faculty, which itself is only a specific, thus distinctive, characteristic, while not serving as a term of comparison, as Guénon demonstrated. As for primordial man, I do not think that he either laughed or wept, his psychism being neither as developed, nor therefore as exteriorized as that of "fallen" man; primordial man was much closer to the state of *prājna* or rather of *samādhi*, which is to say that everything in him was absorbed in a kind of state of beatific undifferentiation; laughter is but a kind of fallen and vulgar fragment of this beatitude, intensified due to outwardness; whence also the physical manifestation of laughter.

I have never thought of criticizing spontaneous and unassuming gaiety, so long that it remain compatible with dignity; such gaiety is a question of temperament; thus, in itself, it is something neutral. But once gaiety is established as a matter of principle, I condemn it, because it then ceases being unassuming; it loses its spontaneity and becomes pretentious; it opens the door to foolishness, while including a kind of self-sufficiency which, although more or less unconscious, is nonetheless paralyzing with respect to spirituality. I reproach you less for liking clowns, whom I dislike, than for setting up laughter as a principle. Far be it from me to criticize your gaiety, as long as it does not harm your path.

21 December 1947 · THE ART OF WRITING

I have read your article, and I must cause you disappointment again. You do not have the vocation to write; it is certainly not your mission. Perhaps things will be different later on. You do not control thought, it is thought that controls you. You "think too much", and that is your business; but the reader has neither interest nor desire to follow you in your inner problems, which you clothe with metaphysical ratiocinations. It would perhaps be a good discipline for you in the meantime to translate, very simply, not Ibn ʿArabī, but texts such as Ghazālī's treatise on the divine Names, or the life of the Prophet by Yus. b. Ismail an-Nabhani, or some book of this kind. I do not have the time to explain myself at length on this subject; I can say only one thing for now, that the shortcomings of your last two articles are conspicuous, and their root cause is a psychic disproportion, due to an overly one-sided development; in a word, you are not yet sufficiently yourself to be able to serve as a receptacle for metaphysical inspiration.

17 January 1950 · HAPPINESS AND SANCTITY, THE FAST

The worldly or imperfect man journeys through life as if on a long road; if he is a believer, he sees God above him in the far distance, and also at the end of this road. However the spiritual man stands in God, and life passes before him like a stream. [...]

Happiness is where holiness is. Holiness is like an opening towards Heaven; it is being recollected in the Unique. Every man is holy when he thinks of God, if he is thinking of nothing else. [...]

Fasting is like a sacred garment that reminds us that we are cut off from the world and that we find ourselves on the side of God.

22 October 1950 · SPIRITUAL FUNCTIONS

If a man in my position is mistaken about a central question, this error must be prefigured in his nature, that is to say, there must be in him, not only an intellectual lack, but above all a passional element; according to traditional heresiology, heresy is above all a question of passion. If there is no lack of intellectuality, nor any psychic passion, there is no chance that a man will make a mistake in the exercise of his spiritual function, for tradition offers by definition certain guarantees. Thus one must be extremely prudent before affirming that a way of acting—especially in a chaotic world like our own—is contrary to a spiritual function, and especially, that it is contrary to the Divine Will.

19 March 1951 · AN ARTICLE ABOUT RENÉ GUÉNON

I wrote an article on Guénon, which is due for the special issue dedicated to him, this summer [*Études Traditionnelles. Ed.*]. The article, bearing the title "His Work", defines this as being: 1. intellectual, 2. universal, 3. traditional, 4. theoretical; and it indicates that the content of this work is: 1. metaphysical doctrine, 2. traditional principles, 3. symbolism, 4. the critique of the modern world. The article ends with these words: "The theoretician as such effaces himself, by definition, behind the doctrine; nothing could be more unjust than to reproach him for this, and to expect another argument from him than that of the doctrinal truth. Therefore it strikes us as pointless to speak of the person of Guénon, and we shall limit ourselves to noting the impression of self-effacement and simplicity that he made upon us during all of our meetings. The man seemed to be unaware of his genius, as his genius, conversely, seemed to be unaware of the man."

6 May 1951 · A TRIAL

I regret having spoken to you again about these Parisian woes. I would like to be the bearer of some beautiful news. But beautiful things are within us, they are eternal. We cannot be ungrateful. One must not forget that ancient sages blessed the end times because of the particular graces and simplifications that can be obtained in them. We must not complain.

Every event is an opening towards the Truth. Allah plays with the soul as with a veil now concealing Him and now revealing Him.

1951 · TRIALS

The spiritual path encompasses all events in life; there is nothing that is entirely beyond its purview. Life's trials are not disturbances empty of meaning, but aspects either of ourselves or of Reality, thus necessary and inevitable elements of the path. To make them fruitful, we must accept them as coming from God: with gratitude and praise. Only then can man hope to understand the meaning of the trial fully, or hope to be delivered from it, God willing, if it is a question of an apparently insoluble situation. Insofar as an unavoidable ambience imposes them on us, even distractions must be accepted, not as obstacles or annoyances that have come by chance, and about which we must complain, but as trials sent by God; we must integrate them into our spiritual life and turn them to account. A true spirituality does not claim to be situated, like a luxury object, on the margin of life's indignations, for it will not envisage life in a completely egoistic and profane manner; every event is good in that it comes from God, and every evil as such comes from human na-

ture; this means that for the contemplative, facts cannot fail to
have a spiritual meaning.

4 October 1951 · FLORENCE AND SIENA

After your departure, we spent several beautiful days in Florence with Titus Burckhardt and his wife. Two things struck us
the most: the Tuscan churches in black and white stone, which
resemble mosques, and the so-called "primitive" paintings, the
most beautiful of which are in Siena, and represent one of the
most perfect of arts. We also visited Pisa and Pistoia.

15 March 1955 · ADAM

An orthodox interpretation of the Koran is never false, of course,
but it can be artificially constrained and weak; for instance,
there are commentaries that give the same meaning to different
words, which obviously does not explain what the differences
are and even less the juxtaposition of certain terms. You quote
to me two explanations of the verse in sura *al-Tīn*[1], neither of
which accounts for the essential meaning of this verse. Instead
of presenting applications as definitions, would it not be more
normal and simpler to understand the verse cited in its immediate and universal meaning, which concerns man as such? Man
can sin, something that an animal cannot do, nor an angel; this
is enough to explain the verse. As for Adam, since he had to
experience the human possibility within the scope of his own
prophetic possibility, it was necessary within this framework
that he be for an instant as "low" as possible, although since this
framework was "lofty", there can only be a distant analogy here
with the case of ordinary man; keeping this reservation in mind,
the idea of a "fall" must be acceptable even for a Muslim, if he is
a metaphysician. God's Mercy towards Adam did not reestablish
the earthly Paradise. *Wa Llāhu a'lam.*

---

[1] This evidently refers to verse 5. — Verse 4: *Surely we created man of the
best stature*; Verse 5: *then we reduced him to the lowest of the low*; Verse 6: *save
those who believe and do good works, and theirs is a reward unfailing. Ed.*

26 January 1955 · THE FALL OF ADAM

As to the expression "*asfala sāfilīn*" ["to the lowest of the low".
Ed.] in the sura *al-Tīn*, the word "fall" is perhaps too Christian,
but what you have quoted to me confirms this interpretation.
The extreme decay of Adam, in his old age, would have no meaning were it not for the Fall, for in Paradise Adam was immortal;
old age and death are marks of the Adamic Fall, in every man.
That is why the sura goes on to say: *illa l-ladhina āmanū...* ["save
those who believe...". *Ed.*], which would be meaningless if it
were only a matter of old age. The degeneration of the human
species is another consequence of the Fall; it cannot be dissoci-
ated from it.

28 January 1956 · FAITH, INVOCATION

A very important element in the invocation is faith. Faith is the
consciousness of the concrete and immediately tangible character of a saving truth. Faith engenders the desire to invoke much;
one loves being close to what one knows has an irreplaceable
value. A negative incentive for our faith is the consciousness of
our wretchedness; a man who does not know that he is drowning cannot have the reflex to cling to a rope; it is therefore a
good thing to know that every man who does not go towards
Beatitude goes towards suffering, and that the invocation is the
simplest way, if one may say so, to save one's soul. The simplicity
of this spiritual means is not facility and vulgarity, for it ultimately involves all that we are; but whatever might be the greatness or nobleness of any spirituality, the aspect of simplicity or
even of facility exists, as does grace; moreover, nothing is possible without divine assistance. A Hindu or a Buddhist would say
that the simple means are within our reach only by virtue of our
good *karma*.

Many a failure can be explained, all told, by a lack of faith
and a lack of fear, within a general milieu in which faith as well
as fear appear ludicrous; it suffices for passion, inexperience,
and unintelligence to become involved, and then the devil too,
who cannot but take advantage of such a golden opportunity,
he who always exploits the weaknesses of men. In a traditional

world, in which everything is homogeneous and shares a solidarity of purpose, there are temptations which are inconceivable; "traditional forms" are not presented as merchandise in a shop window, and daily life is not a struggle in a bog of trivialities. Now we must recognize that we do not live in a world governed by tradition, and awareness of this fact spares us from being surprised by certain things.

28 January 1956 · ESOTERIZED EXOTERISM

Concerning the question of the "formal" and the "informal", or the "letter" (which may kill) and the "spirit" (which is life-giving), I would like to point out that there is always, or nearly always, an intermediary region between exoterism and esoterism, a *barzakh*, that appears both as an esoterized exoterism and an exoterized esoterism; Christianity is nothing else, whence its paradoxical character; as for Islam, we find this *barzakh* in the ritualism of an Al-Ghazālī and in popular Sufism, but also throughout the collective forms of *Taṣawwuf.* Between exoterism and esoterism there always exists a ritualist and moral *karma-yoga*; now the latter, by the very fact of its individualistic nature—for action and merit necessarily belong to the individual— is opposed to the metaphysical perspective as well as to the way of the saving Name. The rationalizing individualism of Muslim piety is as unmetaphysical as the sentimental individualism of Christians. There is also, in any esoterism—inasmuch as this point of view is affirmed in a direct manner—a marked tendency towards a transcendence of forms, on the doctrinal plane (where every formulation becomes an *upāya*, an "unavoidable artifice") as well as on the methodical level (where concentration and its direct supports absorb most of the exterior rites); to deny this tendency is to go against the nature of things.

The whole emphasis must be placed on metaphysical truth and the Divine Name; this is a "religion" that runs through all traditional forms as the weft thread runs through the cloth. Starting from a source of doctrinal, and therefore intellectual, evidence, one must realize faith and find, in the Name and by it, inner certitude, that which is our very being.

31 January 1956 · SPIRITUAL LIFE

Your error is to be beset by the idea that everything depends on your efforts; you forget the virtue of the *dhikr*, the grace resulting from the Name—or the *Shahādah*—quite apart from your merits. Japanese Buddhism has developed this aspect of the question very well, and it is a great pity that you cannot read the texts referring to this. What matters in our spiritual life is first of all metaphysics, which discerns the Real from the unreal while admitting that "each thing is *Ātmā*", and then the invocation, which brings the Real into us, or rather which absorbs us into the Real. One must invoke with faith. The Name is Himself. Whoever remains in the Name could never be lost. Our passional nature may protest at first—either out of bitterness or out of boredom—but it cannot indefinitely resist the all-powerful Name; sooner or later, it will submit. Bitterness, sadness, boredom, doubt—all of that is ourselves, or rather it is that something in ourselves that we must overcome. We must put the Name in place of ourselves. We are incapable of being perfect, but the Name is all perfection; it is enough that it be perfect in us. If we lack in virtue and efforts, we must have faith, while abstaining from evil. The basis of faith, for us, is metaphysical truth. I have explained the basis of the way of the Divine Name in a book which will be sent to you as soon as it is published; but it would also be worth your while to read oriental texts, such as Rāmakrishna, Rāmdās, Mā Ānanda Moyī, Shivānanda.

It is unfortunate that you are so isolated, but there is nothing to be done about this. One cause of your troubles is that, like most modern men, you have neither fear of God nor love for Him; and yet, every man must die. If we consider the sufferings of *samsāra*, and if at the same time we know that all that we love or could love is to be found infinitely in God, and in Him alone, then it is easy for us to break free from the laziness of our nature and live in the Divine Name, which is both Wisdom and Mercy.

7 March 1956 · LOVE AND FEAR ON THE PATH

By "fear" must be understood all that brings us closer to God by negative means, whether it be physical pain, some moral distress, the contemplation of the star-studded heavens, or a meditation on Rigour; all this belongs to the domain of "fear", of *makhāfah*, of *qabḍ*. On the other hand, all that brings us closer to God—hence to the *dhikr*—in a positive or agreeable way, is of the domain of "love", of *maḥabbah*, of *baṣt*. The central idea of "fear" is the Last Judgment; the central idea of "love" is Beatitude, Paradise, Deliverance.

"Love" contains an element of trust, just as "fear" contains an element of distrust: distrust towards ourselves, trust in God. "Truly, my Mercy cometh before my Wrath" [hadith *qudsī. Ed.*]: "love" must therefore prevail over "fear"; it is in a sense "more real", but "love" is imperfect without "fear", for man does not cease to be man. The criterion of the correct attitude outside "fear" is the continuity of "love". "Love" burns "fear" as fire burns wood, but "love" needs "fear" in order to be able to burn. Pure "love" is beyond this opposition, but it is also beyond man as such; man does not "possess" it, he plunges into it and loses himself therein. "Fear" is then the world that remains outside "love", whereas "love" is God.

"Love" is to accomplish the *dhikr*; "fear" is not to omit it.

14 November 1956 · EARLY ISLAM

It is not clear to me whether the Islam of the first years comprised anything more than a *bhakti*; it is quite possible that *jnāna* did not manifest itself before a certain moment, perhaps during the Hegira[2], or a little earlier. It is said that the Prophet revealed in the cave, during the flight, the mysteries of the Divine Name to Abū Bakr.

5 January 1957 · WHY INVOKE?

As to the question "why invoke?" the profoundest response would no doubt be: "because I exist", for Existence is in a certain way the Word of God, by which He names Himself. God pronounces his Name to manifest Himself—to "create"—in the

---

[2] *Translator's note.* Hegira or "migration" is the flight of Muhammad from Mecca to Medina in the year 622.

direction of "nothingness", and the relative being pronounces this Name to "be", in other words to "become once again what he is" in the direction of Reality.

The idea of "duty" is very useful, humanly speaking, for the world needs the invocation. What matters is not our personal worth, nor the graces God discloses to us, but the fact of the manifestation of the Name. Moreover, we have no worth save by this Name. We are incapable of doing any good by ourselves; all that we do is conjectural, except the Name, the agent of which, precisely, is God; we lend ourselves thus to the divine act.

Japanese Buddhists have rightly stressed the fact that the invocation is not meant to produce joy; this lack of joy is ourselves; all the better if grace pierces this wall; but this is something independent from the immediate efficacy and the final validity of our orison. You are right to say that the ego wishes to seize everything, even grace. I think that books on Japanese *Jōdo-Shinshū* would provide you with insights on this subject.

1 August 1957 · MAN, THE SUPREME NAME
to Titus Burckhardt

The body is a fabric of sensations and instincts. The ego is a fabric of images and desires. All this is part of the current of forms, which is not our true Self. The supreme Name is the expression and the receptacle of our veritable Self; it is not really a part of the current of forms; in it we are perfectly Ourselves. It is the "form of the informal"—or of "the Supra-Formal"—and "manifestation of the Non-Manifested". Shankara has said: "Discern between the ephemeral and the Real, repeat the holy Name of God and thus calm the agitated mind".

June 1958 · OLD AGE

There are many men who do not age well, because they drag behind them the psychology of a bygone time. If one must bury oneself a little at fifty, one must do so even more at seventy. It is as if one were to conclude, on a personal basis, a new pact with God. What is absolutely imperative is to be contented with one's condition.

Every age has its advantages: from a certain point of view, elderly people are to be envied; their state simplifies many things; all they need to do is to live in God until the end; they can be sure that God does not ask more of them. Traditionally, old age is a blessing. [...]

Often, during prayer, grace comes at the moment when one resigns oneself happily to dryness. If something is painful for you, give thanks to God, this is the best way to come out of it.

17 December 1960 · THE HUMAN CONDITION, DIVINE MERCY

Your difficulties stem from the fact that you are not aware of the gravity of the human condition; and you are not aware of this because nothing in your habitual surroundings—the world in which we live—suggests it, to say the least. It is finally a question of imagination; I am not saying that you are directly responsible for this; but you are in any case its victim, and you are not alone in being so. The articles I am presently writing—"Man in the Universe" and "The Cross of Space and Time in Koranic Onomatology"—can give you many an answer [articles reproduced in *Light on the Ancient Worlds* and *Form and Substance in the Religions*. *Ed.*]. However, all in all these answers are already contained in the themes of meditation.

Let us take the theme that can be reduced to the ternary "distress-trust-Mercy". What does this mean? It means that the infinite Divine Mercy, which is miraculously contained in the Name of God, saves us to the degree of our trust, and that our trust springs from the depth of our distress; without an awareness of our distress, no trust is possible, and without trust, no Mercy. We must therefore know that we are fallen from original perfection, that we are incapable of saving ourselves, and that God alone can save us; knowing this, we could despair, logically speaking; but this is where trust comes into play, for we know through Revelation that God wants to save us and that His Mercy is infinite. Trust, or, what amounts to the same, faith, is thus determined, "above" by our knowledge of Divine Mercy, and "below" by our awareness of human wretchedness.

Most people believe that one goes to Paradise because one follows the rites of a religion and one has neither murdered, nor stolen, and so on; however, only the saints and the sages go straight to Heaven, and even so they go only because Mercy dissolves their imperfections, not because they are perfect. When you are walking on the street, you believe that "I"—S.H.—"am here", "on this street", "now"—you do not see, I assume, the metaphysical and eschatological abysses surrounding you. In the Middle Ages, the whole civilization was structured in a way that one could at least "sense" what one's cosmic situation was; nowadays, one lives in a kind of misleading "extraterritoriality"; we live in opaque back rooms that mask reality. However, God touches us everywhere, there is no vacant space nor any respite. He is "the First" and "the Last" and "the Outward" and "the Inward" [Koran 57:3. *Ed.*], man is like the point of intersection of the "divine dimensions".

You must detach your life from the awareness of the multiple and reduce it to a "geometrical point" before God. You have but one life, and this life is not just anything; it is everything, for you, and it owes its greatness to its divine origin and its divine goal. The human condition is something great because its foundation is God; the modern error is to believe that we are small, that is to say that we are biological accidents; that we are entitled to lukewarmness; that we are free to be small, lukewarm, mediocre. In reality, we are condemned to greatness, if I may say, and we find this greatness in spiritual smallness before the divine Greatness. It is God who is Great, but we must open ourselves up to this Greatness knowing that there is only God, that we are bound to Him, that we cannot escape Him; knowing that, we must resign ourselves to our human and personal condition—to the fact that the sacred is inescapable—and we must rest in trust.

31 May 1963 · HENRI CORBIN AND FRITHJOF SCHUON
to Seyyed Hossein Nasr

Concerning Professor Corbin, here is the problem: he is a scholar, I am a contemplative. On what plane can we meet? Believing that I am interested in books and read much, and that I like to speak as academics do, whereas in reality I love contemplation and not books, he would be disappointed when he saw me. I have much to offer disciples; I have nothing to offer a scholar such as him. I suppose that he is mistaken about me, that he does not realize the degree to which I am different, not just from other Westerners, but also, in an entirely general way, from other men.

1964 · HERE AND NOW

Whatever the forms may be, the essential thing is always to discern the Eternal from the impermanent, and to attach oneself to the first, thus reducing the world to a blessed point—a centre where God touches us—and life to a single beatific instant: the moment when we think of God, when we are with Him.

22 June 1964 · MODERN SCIENCE

[...] still on the plane of physical facts: it is only in part that modern science is wrong; conversely, it is totally wrong as to higher planes and with regard to its principles. It is wrong in its negations and in the false principles deriving from them, and then in the false hypotheses ensuing from all of that, and finally in the monstrous effects it produces as a result of its Promethean premise. But modern science is right about many physical points and even about certain psychological points, and moreover it is impossible that this would not be so, given the law of compensations; it is impossible that modern men could not be right on points where ancient men were wrong; this is even part of the mechanism of decline.

Also, one must not forget that Ptolemaic astronomy was not a sacred science. What is decisive in favour of the Ancients, or of traditional men in general, is that they are right about all the spiritually essential points; in fact even on the physical plane, they know an infinite number of things to which modern men are oblivious.

12 December 1964 · THE SPIRITUAL HEART

There is some diversity of interpretation about the question of the spiritual heart. Most traditions do not specify anything as to its relationship with the physical heart; thus it is *a priori* accepted that the two hearts coincide operatively. The Maharshi apparently said that the subtle heart is to be found on the right; the Japanese situate it in the solar plexus; often it is simply identified with the breast. In fact, the spiritual heart is where the awareness of the profoundest inwardness or selfhood is subjectively situated. With regard to myself, when grace erupts particularly in the heart, the impression of it is felt in the physical heart; otherwise, grace is pectoral, it dilates the breast.

1 June 1965 · THE WORLD AND THE EGO, HAPPINESS

Two things eat away at man, the "world" and the "self": the "world" disperses and dismembers, and the "self" imprisons and crushes; now there is in our depth, beyond the world and the ego, a beatitude containing all possible types of happiness—in a golden and timeless "now"—which is at once blissful Centre and blissful Dilation.

It is a joy to grow old, believe me; for spirituality is not a question of choice or vocation; it is the only thing left for us to do, given that we are human beings. Human beings are hells wandering like blind men in a paradise: happiness is everywhere, it is in the very substance of our existence; the universe is woven of Bliss.

You should find the means of working less and seek peacefulness in virgin nature and in solitude. Never seek peace or consolation among men, all the more, I repeat, as we have no choice; we must in any case detach ourselves. God awaits us, there is no other outcome. Faith and trust: everything lies in these two attitudes! We are made for happiness, but we must find it where it is.

7 November 1965 · SPIRITUAL COMPANY, THE SPIRITUAL MAN

I recently spoke to the disciples about the question of *satsanga*, namely of the traditional obligation of frequenting only men having *sattvic* tendencies and avoiding the others; now given that I lived in an anti-traditional world, and not having any money, I had to frequent men with *tamasic* tendencies throughout my youth; it was a life in hell. But ultimately it was a useful trial, which moreover gives me the right to speak about this problem. I said that believers who are obliged to frequent unbelievers are martyrs, and that faults of theirs resulting from this abnormal situation are forgiven them in advance, provided they are ashamed of them. In my youth, I needed to be alone so as to become myself, but I could not afford the luxury of solitude; thus I was often dragged into situations I abhorred, and I was ashamed of existing until Heaven took pity on me. But for several years I still suffered from inner wounds that were closed only when I was adopted into the Lakota tribe. [...]

Most men believe they are "now" in this street, then in this house, and so on, and they believe in any case that they are on earth among an indefinite number of phenomena and situations; but the spiritual man dwells in the Divine Name, which binds him to "Allah's Rope", and around him there is only the wheel of *Samsāra*. The spiritual man is not altogether here, nor there, he is not either before or afterwards, he is always in the Centre and in the blessed Now of God.

11 January 1966 · SPIRITUAL LIFE

A.H. should also be told that we have our whole life for the path and we must pass through many temptations; our inner states are not criteria, and we must not be attached to them. There are things in the world and in life that are certain and others that are uncertain; we must attach ourselves to those that are certain. It is certain that *lā ilāha illā Llāh*; similarly, *al-Ākhira* is something certain. And in life, the only certitude is death; then the meeting with God; then our Eternity. Apart from these metaphysical and eschatological certitudes, there is another great certitude for us, right here: it is the certitude of the *dhikr*. Life is an instant, and this instant is now; if it contains the *dhikr*, all is well; what we are now, we shall always be, if we do not depart from this "now" of *dhikru-Llāh*.

15 June 1967 · BEING ONESELF

This is the guiding thread for the soul: not to be external things, but to be oneself; not the ego determined and hardened by external things, but in the sole remembrance of God.

26 December 1967 · FRITHJOF SCHUON SPEAKS OF HIS HEALTH

I am writing to you very briefly because I have been ill and I am not yet fully recovered. I think it is not just physical; in the world I am living in, there are too many elements that compress me. To this may be added the incommensurability in the soul between the human support and the divine Content; one cannot prevent there being a contraction sometimes—but "verily with hardship cometh ease" [Koran 94:5. *Ed.*].

Sometimes there is the accumulation of little things that make me ill, little trivial documents, meaningless letters, books to look at—I am speaking of things without value—and so on. But none of this counts, the grace of invocation is incalculable.

7 January 1968 · OLD AGE, INVOCATION

I recall having spoken to you once about certain temptations or trials of the soul that may arise when one grows old; this is not to say that such things are entirely inevitable, but in any case, there is a good chance that the forces of illusion—lower *Māyā*—will try to hold back the soul that is tending to escape it through spiritual work. Before the soul is truly conquered, it sometimes tends to revolt in one way or another, if only by a sort of dryness or lethargy. That is when one must say to oneself, with the Koran: "Say *Allāh*! and leave them to their vain discourse".

Human nature tends to lose sight of the tremendous happiness represented by the possession of the Name. What bliss to be born as man, and being man, to have obtained the *dhikr*! Even if one had failed at everything in life, if in this very moment one has the grace to invoke the Supreme Name, one's whole life is won, nothing is lost; every life, even a dissipated one, is worth being lived if its outcome, in this very moment when we think of it, is the possibility of pronouncing the Name with faith. I am writing you this for the simple reason that I have just spoken of it to someone; I often have occasion to insist on gratitude.

February 1968 · INVOCATION, FEAR OF GOD, HAPPINESS

Life is a dream, and we must cross this dream; now, we cross it on the vessel of the *dhikr*, and in this vessel one does not dream;

only in the Divine Name are we wholly awake, without know-ing it. The Prophet said that God has cursed all things except the remembrance of Allah; you can see what this intentionally lapidary and absolute formula implies. One must cling to the Name, or to the *Shahādah*, as to a lifeline. All men are drowning, eschatologically speaking; therefore they have no choice: they must save themselves. Life has no other meaning.

In *Taṣawwuf*, one must always begin a new life, so as to main-tain grace and not be lost. Man is weak, but Allah is Strength, and with Him everything is possible, even things that seem im-possible. You have often spoken to me of your weakness; if you do not feel that you are able to love God, you must at least fear Him: "Fear of God is the beginning of wisdom". Allah is merci-ful, but He is also formidable; and it is impossible to understand his Mercy if one does not understand his Wrath. One must never think oneself too intelligent; our intelligence is nothing with re-gard to the Absolute. If God has given us the gift of intelligence, it must be combined with a childlike simplicity and purity; God abhors pretension and self-assurance. Thus, whatever opinion we may have of ourselves, only one thing is absolutely certain: it is that "*lā ilāha illā Llāh*". And it is certain that—in keeping with that very same supreme certitude—we must die and appear before Allah. All the rest is meaningless.

It is never pointless to tell a *faqīr*: begin a new life, this very day; and if you do not wish to do it for yourself—although in reality you have no choice—do it for those around you because you owe them happiness. The only way to be happy is to make those who depend on us happy; to make them happy in God and by Him.

16 October 1968 · TRUST IN GOD

If you were surprised for a moment by this harshness of Heav-en towards you, you see now that Heaven was not harsh at all; at most, it was so by leaving you to struggle painfully in your illusion. But do not regret this; it was certainly for your good, since the soul sometimes needs to be tilled. Other people pass through crises, you had to pass through these anxieties; to each his turn. As you read these lines, you must thank Heaven, as Jonah did when he emerged from the whale.

The thoughts that assailed you in *khalwah* did not come from the good side, believe me; such things happen in *khalwah* precisely because certain powers want to disturb us at the moment when we turn towards God. How can you believe that this fine visit to England could end on such a discordant note, and what is more, that this was your fault, whereas your intentions are irreproachable, to say the least? And it is for this very reason that you ought to have said to yourself that it is impossible that I would be angry. In a word, the only thing you have to reproach yourself for is a lack of trust; this suffices to explain that Heaven would have allowed this trial. *Tawakkul* is one of the most precious treasures, and one of the virtues most difficult to practice in this lowly world, where the absurdity of the ambience is so easily combined with the absurdity of the soul. Always think of this: "Say *Allāh*! and leave them to their vain discourse".

14 April 1970 · INVOCATION AND SINCERITY

I said recently during a prayer gathering that a man should practise the orison (*dhikr*) as if he were alone in the world and as if he had but one hour left to live. Indeed, this symbolic situation includes all the conditions for sincerity.

26 June 1970 · RENÉ GUÉNON'S OPUS

The work of Guénon comprises two dimensions: I defined the first in an article in *Études Traditionnelles* [July-November 1951. *Ed.*], republished without my permission by the review *Planète* in its issue on Guénon. It is the strictly intellectual aspect of his work: metaphysical doctrine, traditional orthodoxy, esoterism as a principle, criticism of the modern world. If we leave aside certain questionable opinions, this dimension is masterful and essential.

But there is also another dimension: "supreme centre" and "king of the world", Western esoterism, hence Order of the Temple and Freemasonry, nature of mysticism and the Christian sacraments, "ascending and descending realization", etc.;

here I must formulate the most explicit of reservations. And if a "continuator of Guénon's work" is supposed to base himself on this combination of concepts and opinions, I could never be such a continuator. My attitude—regarding what distinguishes me from Guénon—results clearly from my writings.

9 September 1970 · JESUS AND MUHAMMAD
to Martin Lings

Concerning the case of A.K., the main question is not whether the Prophet is "the best of creatures", which we acknowledge without difficulty in an intrinsic and not comparative sense, but whether Christ is humanly and spiritually inferior to him, something that we shall never acknowledge, and which the most narrow of Asharisms does not ask us to accept.

There is something of a compensation between Jesus and Muhammad: with the former, it is the mode of manifestation that is superior; with the latter, it is the message, in the sense that this message is more directly metaphysical and universal, and because of this it is complete, having a *shari'ah* and a *haqīqah*. But even when formulated in this manner, the question is not made completely clear, for on the one hand the Muhammadan manifestation contains an underlying quality—or a substance—that transcends its formal mode, and on the other hand the Christic message expresses in its way all essential truth and indicates all of its earthly applications. Strictly speaking, an *Avatāra* should always be envisaged according to his own mode and not according to other avataric modes; but in the case of the Semitic religions, such comparisons cannot always be completely avoided, unfortunately, all the more as certain misunderstandings and shortcomings of imagination oblige us to make them.

27 November 1970 · UNIVERSALISM AND EXCLUSIVISM

This exoterist passion is a very strange thing in a man like A.K.; there is a large amount of inadequate imagination here, for instance the total incapacity to put himself in the place of a Christian or a Buddhist. Reference is made to the authority of Muslim saints; very well, but what becomes of the hundreds of non-Muslim saints? What does the wisdom of a Shankara or a Kōbō-Daishi signify in the eyes of God? I have always been surprised at the lack of imagination, spiritual sensitivity and rational perspicacity of those who lock themselves fanatically in a single religion, in an epoch such as ours where civilizations touch and where, for those who have a minimum of culture, foreign religions are more than simplistic abstractions.

All told, one would like to ask A.K.: why do you think that your religion is more real than another, or that it alone is real? Because your religion declares it so? But the other religions do the same for themselves. Because you were born in it? But other men are born in other religions. Because the arguments of your religion are better than those of other religious systems? Wrong: the arguments of any religion are acceptable and irrefutable from their own point of view, without being convincing outside it. The intrinsic truth of Islam is something we notice from the vantage point of metaphysics, thus on the basis of the *Religio Perennis*, not by virtue of Muslim argumentation; but that which enables us to accept Islam is precisely that which enables us to accept other religions likewise, or rather that which obliges us to do so.

12 January 1971 · POETRY

Poetry is the "language of the gods"; and "*noblesse oblige*"; what I mean by this is that the poet has certain responsibilities. In poetry, the musicality of things, or their cosmic essentiality, erupts onto the plane of language; and this process requires grandeur, hence also authenticity, both of the image and of the sentiment. The poet spontaneously has the intuition of the underlying musicality of phenomena; under the pressure of an image or an emotion—this emotion, moreover, being naturally combined with concordant images—the poet expresses an archetypal beauty; without this pressure, there is no poetry, which implies that true poetry always has an aspect of inner necessity, whence its irreplaceable perfume. Therefore, there has to be the subjective and objective grandeur of the point of departure or the content, then the profound musicality of the soul and the language; now that of language must be drawn from its own resources, and this is the entire formal art of poetry. Dante had not only grandeur, he also knew how, on the one hand, to infuse this grandeur into language and, on the other, to wield language so as to render it adequate to his inner vision. When Shakespeare describes some situation or other following the strains of a popular song, he usually succeeds in presenting its quintessence and thereby bringing appearances back to their cosmic musicality, whence a liberating feeling that is characteristic of all true poetry.

Translations of Oriental poems provide only the meaning, not the cladding; thus an essential element of musicality is lost, so that literal translations—for instance the English—of ʿAṭṭār or Rūmī cannot be said to be paradigms of poetic art. This brings to mind—since the form is just about the same—"rhythmic prose", or "poetry in prose"; in most cases, this is not poetry at all, but imaginative chattering punctuated by stops intended to be "poetic"; in fact, this type of literature is almost always too gratuitous, and too "philosophical" as well, and certainly too small-minded. It is the style of Whitman and Eliot, which is conversational; with Tagore, there is a truly poetic element that intervenes—he does not stoop to chat with the reader.

There is the beauty of the content and that of the language; in the Bible—the Books of David and Solomon for instance—the beauty of the content is such that it remains intact when translated; but when Dante takes advantage of the musical resources of the Italian language to make some kind of description, the beauty, or the musicality, is obviously lost in translation, unless an Italian linguistic quality can be incidentally replaced by an analogous quality in the translator's tongue.

I am rather averse to poetry because hardly anyone knows how to do it—spiritual motives notwithstanding—and also because most true poets are the dupes of their talent and get lost in prolixity instead of letting the muse take over, all the more as the muse is sometimes very parsimonious. Now allowing the muse a free hand is no small thing! This implies that there be an inward pressure that tolerates no wavering vagueness, nor any verbosity, and this pressure must result from some degree of grandeur or another; whence the "musical crystallinity" of poetry, the convincing power of its inward necessity. There is no beauty without grandeur; these two qualities must be in the soul of the poet as well as in the form he is capable of giving to language. Gem of perfection and vibration of infinitude!

A great merit of poetic art is knowing how to combine illimitation—the musical or vibratory element—with formal rigour, that is to say, how to convey a perfume of infinitude through a gem and its strict interplay of facets; this is what makes for all the evocative power of good sonnets. When the formal framework, which is one of poetry's greatest distinctions, fades into a vaguely rhythmic prose, the content risks leaking into a shapeless puddle determined by subjectivity alone; the polarity between the gem and the music is lost, and there is the danger of prolixity. Beauty favours not only the melodious and delicate element, it also favours the sculptural and powerful element; the magic of the sonnets of a Dante, a Michelangelo and a Shakespeare owes much to this complementarity.

There are not only gemlike poems, there are also diluvial poems, epic poems; the rigour of the form, in this genre, lies in the structural element, whether it is classical hexameter or the *terza rima* of the Divine Comedy. One can put an indefinite quantity of images, thoughts and feelings in this stream, but even here there are architectural limits, as is proven precisely by the subdivisions in Dante's poem. I would add that epic poetry has rights that cannot be assigned to lyric poetry.

16 June 1971 · WORK

I hope that S.M. is satisfied with his new work; he must in any case make an effort to be so. With good will and imagination one can find a *modus vivendi* everywhere; one has these two qualities in the measure that one has faith.

3 August 1971 · WHEN FACED WITH INJUSTICE
to Michel Valsan

To be affected only by the injustices aimed at truth, not those aimed at us: that is fine, but the truth authorizes us, and even obliges us, to draw the conclusions that we must, all the more since our rights and those of the truth can coincide, in the very measure in which we situate ourselves outside the profane order. It would be different were the injustice but an impersonal and blind force, and were we but individuals prey to our passions. Conversely, it goes without saying that we must accept injustice inasmuch as it is destiny, for in that case it comes from God and cannot be unjust, but this is a new dimension that exists independently from the plane where the injustice is what it is. I would even say that we are entitled to self-defence in the very measure in which we accept everything from God. Finally, to claim our legitimate right can be not only a matter of truth, but even of charity; I have always been astonished at these *malāmatiyah* who set a bad example so as to be purer before Allah, as if they provided thereby some kind of service to other men. *wa Llāhu a'lam.*

10 January 1972 · SANCTITY, VISIONS, HUMILITY

There is no sanctity without a great victory over the soul. It is not enough to "live" by the spirit; one must also have "died" by it. One needs to know how to "jump over one's own shadow"; very few succeed in doing this perfectly. And yet, our natural gifts and our supernatural gifts are nothing without this.

There is a great teaching to be found in a criterion that is well known in theology: if a man has a celestial vision, and if this vision is authentic, the man will have become noticeably better from it; if he has not become noticeably better from it, according to objective criteria, then it is because the vision was false. Sanctity does not have only intrinsic characteristics that may be beyond all verification, it comprises also—and by the same token—extrinsic signs. [...]

The humble man is not sensitive to a slight humiliation on the part of a [spiritual] brother—of an elder brother especially—and he is even prepared to humble himself in order to approach others. "When the servant takes ten steps in the direction of his Lord, his Lord rises from his throne and takes one hundred steps in the direction of his servant" [hadith]; it may even be that the servant will take but one step, and that the Lord will take one thousand; now if this is how God acts, how much more should we be ready to sacrifice a smidgen of our pride! And the humble man is all the less concerned with his little claims to preeminence in that he is all the more mindful of not forgetting his smallness before God; would he want God to manifest Himself to him only according to his incommensurability and under his aspect of Majesty?

8 February 1972 · MUHAMMAD

How could you have the idea that the Prophet is a *Bodhisattva*, and that Alī and Abū Bakr are *Pratyeka Buddhas*? I see that you have lost sight of the meanings of these Buddhist terms. The Prophet, being the founder of a religion, is a *Samyaksam-Buddha*; Alī and Abū Bakr, being apostles, are *Bodhisattvas*; neither of them could be a *Pratyeka Buddha*. One can see a *Pratyeka Buddha* in Uways al-Qaranī—or in our times and in India, in Shrī Rāmana Maharshi—but not in an apostle who would have had to have some disciples. Furthermore, not every spiritual man can represent everything; it is not a question here of capacity, but of providential manifestation. Christ embodied supreme wisdom— it could not be otherwise—but he addressed sinners and did not manifest the spiritual mode of a Bādarāyana, author of the *Brahma-Sūtra*. *wa Llāhu aʿlam.*

29 March 1972 · THE QUATERNARY NAME-HEART-INVOCATION-POVERTY

In integral or "sincere" *Tawḥīd* there are four principles: the Truth which determines everything; the Heart which assimilates and "becomes that which it is", and which represents *a priori* the Intention, Faith, and *a posteriori* Union; the realizational Activity based on the two preceding principles; Virtue, namely spiritual Poverty, which is also based on the Truth and the Heart, or on unitive Faith. These four principles, which correspond analogically to the four streams of Paradise, are at once conditions and criteria of the Path: in the "Remembrance of God" there is necessarily the Truth, then Faith or the Subject, then operative Activity, and finally detaching Virtue, Poverty in view of the One, the *vacare Deo*. Now the Truth is the Name (*Ism*); Faith is the Heart (*Qalb*); Activity is the Invocation (*Dhikr*); Virtue is

Poverty (*Faqr*). Poverty, which encompasses all the fundamental and indispensable virtues, is essentially to resist all unhealthy curiosity, to say the least; it is to remain from now on in this antechamber of Paradise that the *Dhikr* represents; it is "Peace in the Void"; it is to remain like a child in his little garden, without wondering what is happening outside.

29 March 1972 · FRITHJOF SCHUON DISCUSSES HIS PAINTINGS

My paintings represent the Holy Virgin in the form of the Sulamith of the Song of Songs and at the same time in that of the Hindu and Buddhist *Shakti*; this is how her particular form could be explained retrospectively, that is to say inasmuch as one may have need of traditional arguments or points of reference.

31 October 1972 · SUSCEPTIBILITY

When one is exceptionally gifted in a spiritual sense, it can happen that one's human reality is not on the level of these gifts, and this discrepancy manifests itself paradoxically and painfully in certain circumstances, which then constitute a real trial; now one must accept the repercussions and consequences of this disharmony without being surprised by it, and above all avoid being offended or too easily wounded by it. In the spiritual life, one must "jump over one's own shadow", for the person that we are in reality, that we are in our substance—by the grace of God—is someone that we rarely are *a priori*. There is someone in ourselves that must be delivered from ourselves; that is why, from the point of view of susceptibility, we must look at ourselves from the outside as it were, as if the habitual "I" were a stranger. The whole question is knowing "who" we are, that is to say: who is "ourselves". In other words, the spiritual man is condemned to overcome himself, and much more so perhaps than he can conceive of beforehand; it is appropriate therefore not to be too sensitive about a "oneself" that is not yet sufficiently defined. All of this may be obvious, but spiritual teachings are woven of evident truths, precisely.

31 October 1972 · THE JINNS

You allude in your letter to the question of the jinn, saying that you did not interpret from my words that they are "absolutely negative", something which in fact was never in my thoughts, for I know very well that the jinn are "various parties", as the Koran says. What I positively condemn are not the jinn as such, but contacts with them, at least for our friends; because there were always saintly men who had the gift and the vocation to occupy themselves with these creatures. When one does not have either this gift or this vocation—which is in any case very rare—how can one discern *a priori*, either between the good and the bad jinn, or—among the good—between those that will in the end harm us out of ignorance or narrowness of outlook, and those who will not harm us? First of all—but no, I do not want to re-peat again all that I said to you directly. I only want to empha-size that, in the present case, the question of knowing whether the jinn are good or bad does not apply, practically speaking, or does not arise at the outset; the problem lies elsewhere. All told, I think that the best among the jinn, even if they sometimes pro-tect men, children for instance, do not seek to enter into contact with human beings.

21 November 1972 · POETRY

You know the importance I attach in poetry to the balance be-tween vigour and beauty, power and gentleness; now the ele-ment of vigour is in some measure guaranteed by the classical rhythms, the decameter notably, and also, by the architecture of the sonnet. I like rhythmic prose if its content is such that the equilibrium in question is provided by the text itself, as is the case for the Psalms, but I am not at all in favour of the poetic genre that employs rhymes with no regard for prosody; although there are some rare exceptions here, for instance in a naïve genre of popular poetry.

I do not encourage anyone to write poems and I suppose that your poetic cycle has now come to a close; but if ever the muse should prompt you to exteriorize something of this kind, I think that it would be important for you to oblige yourself to follow the rules of English prosody [the correspondent is English. *Ed.*]—which is that of all Germanic tongues—and to do so within the framework, for example, of the sonnet, or even preferably so, be it only to neutralize certain less than architectural tendencies in your nature. That is to say, you slip easily, in poetry, into a conversational tone—descriptive or introspective, depending on the case—or you have a lyrically playful side that, while not in itself blameworthy at all, nonetheless requires—or makes it desirable to have—the rigorous framework of prosodic or poetic architecture.

I am myself a born poet, and yet I have not written any poems for many long years; the exception are the little Arabic poems you know, which belong to a totally different order.

10 March 1973 · CANONICAL PRAYER, THE GREATER PILGRIMAGE

In prayer, to bow or to prostrate, is virtually "Disappearance" or "Extinction" (*fanā'*), at two different degrees; to sit upright or to stand up, is "Reintegration" or "Permanence" (*baqā'*), also at two different degrees. [...]

In broad outline, I would say this, from the perspective of *taṣawwuf*: the visit to Mount Arafat enables the pilgrim to partake of the *barakah* of the Prophet—*'alayhi l-ṣalātu wa l-salām*; it is as if one took part in his contemplation, or as if one were listening to his most recent sermon; it is a meeting with his spiritual presence. The stoning of the *jamarāt* means, mystically speaking, the rejection of what is evil in our own soul (*an-nafs al-ammārah*); it is our own evil that we are stoning, which indicates, precisely, that it is not truly ourselves. The sacrifice of the animal requires no special explanation; it is sacrifice as such, which is an act of gratitude towards Allah. The Kaaba is our own heart, receptacle of the Divine Presence (*Ḥuḍūr*); the *ṭawāf* is the *tawbah*, it is to withdraw from the world or from outwardness, in order to remain within the Divine Centre (*maqām ilāhī*); consequently, the *ṭawāf* is the centripetal movement, the "inward life". To kiss the Black Stone is to kiss the Divine Presence; it is a fragment of Paradise. As to the ritual race between the hills of Ṣafā and Marwah, it refers to trust in God (*tawakkul*), since it repeats Hājar's race in the desert; analogously, to drink the water of Zemzem is to drink of Mercy (*Raḥmah*). The inside of the Kaaba is the Spiritual Secret (*al-sirr*); here one is beyond all forms. *wa Llāhu a'lam.*

19 July 1974 · CORRECT ATTITUDE

Indeed, the past is a matter of complete indifference, all the more as it is materially impossible, in certain cases, to verify to what degree we were right or wrong. It is not because we were right in the past that we are pleasing to God; it is because, right now, we give ourselves to Him in prayer and forget the past, be it good or bad.

And what matters is that God welcome us into Beatitude, not that He introduce us into a given Paradise rather than into another. "Deliverance" (*Moksha*) or the "Paradise of the Essence" (*Jannat adh-Dhāt*) is for the great sages; be that as it may, every soul that is saved is in a certain manner "delivered". If we can hope to be saved—and we can, by practising prayer while abstaining from evil—the question of knowing where God will place us should be the least of our concerns.

Forget S.M., but do not judge him, for you could be mistaken about a given point, and in that case your error would harm your spiritual life. Once again, this is in any case of no interest, for God will not ask you what others have done.

Metaphysics is a boundless domain, and one must not want to understand everything; first of all, because not every man can understand everything and because one must be resigned to the possibility of having limitations, and, secondly, because the basic metaphysical truths are sufficient and in prayer we possess all that we need.

20 November 1974 · THE SOUL'S FLUCTUATIONS

I also insist on the idea that the *dhikr* is a prolongation of Paradise; and I shall add that in the *dhikr* we are in communion with all those we love.

The soul is situated in time, and all that exists in duration is subject to phases; consequently, there are highs and lows in the life of the soul. But the *faqīr* is not the dupe of these fluctuations, he beholds them from the outside as it were without identifying himself with them; he remains unshakeable on the basis of the immutable Reality: *lā ilāha illā Llāh*. One must remain unshakeable, not in a stiff manner, but with gentleness; one must become a single person instead of being split into two in keeping with natural phases or depending on what circumstances draw from us; in short, one must "become what one is", that is to say we must, by the intelligence, the *dhikr*, and prayer, extract our true nature, the one God has willed for us. To be happy one needs faith, but one needs also health of character, and that is *faqr*; we must be one, as the Truth is one.

12 December 1974 · THE DIVINE NAME, FAITH

It is written in the Koran: "God suffices to us, and excellent is the Protector". If we proceed from the idea that God is really present in His Name—since the divine Cause must be present and active in the divine effect—we must also know that we have a sufficient refuge in the divine Name at every moment, and that it is even an earthly prolongation of Paradise. The divine Name is the sword of Alexander which cuts through the Gordian knot of our soul; it contains all the answers to our incertitudes and all the remedies for our wounds, even if we are not aware of these answers and do not feel these remedies.

Faith is everything; that is, the unconditional "yes" in our inner depths to the supreme Name. If we are weak, It is our strength; in a way It is even our virtue and our faith, on the sole condition that our intention is good and that consequently we abstain, as far as we know, from everything that is contrary to the divine Will, or from all that distances us from God in fact. Our soul may be ailing, but it is enough that we put the supreme Name so to speak in its place; we can ask ourselves if we are good enough and we can doubt it, but we have the certitude that the Name is good and that in It we cannot be bad, provided our will is good. "Protect God in thy heart and He shall protect thee in the world"; this saying of the Prophet is one of the best viatica.

29 January 1975 · SPIRITUAL DEATH
to Martin Lings

In the cases of S.T. and of N.D., I did not pray just for a cure, because I foresaw all too clearly that the Will of God might be otherwise—for their own good. [...]

There cannot be a definitive and hence unvarying equilibrium between God and man; God alone is immutable. Now He sometimes breaks an equilibrium so as to replace it with a new equilibrium, which causes the *faqīr* to pass through a kind of death: the *faqīr* still knows that *lā ilāha illā Llāh*, but he no longer knows who he himself is. Consequently, he must find a new identity in terms of the only certitude that remains to him, which is precisely that *lā ilāha illā Llāh*; during such nights, there is no longer anything but Truth and Faith, and in virtue of these, Patience and Trust; these enable us to overcome all losses of balance. A perfect equilibrium between the vertical (*ṣalāt*) and the horizontal (*salām*) dimensions needs to be realized. Now with most men, the horizontal dimension takes precedence over the vertical, the spiritual life becomes too human, too individual, too earth-bound and too comfortable; we must therefore begin again, more or less from zero, and be reborn yet again. In the supreme Name, there is all of *Raḥmah*, and in *Raḥmah*, which is inexhaustible, nothing is ever lost to us—quite the contrary, for in it is contained all that we are capable of loving. Whosoever dies for *Raḥmah*—in the *dhikr* which, being inwardness, is darkness in relation to the brightness of the outward or the world—whosoever dies for *Raḥmah* is reborn through *Raḥmah*; for "I am black, but beautiful" [*Song of Songs*, I:5. *Ed.*].

12 March 1975 · FRITHJOF SCHUON'S WRITTEN MESSAGE

In all that I write—you noticed this very well—the traditional information is but the cladding for truths that I have to communicate and which, it goes without saying, do not come from books; and apart from the content, I seek on the one hand to teach readers how to think, and on the other hand to transmit to them a character or a mentality or, one might say, a soul.

19 August 1975 · SINCERITY, CYNICISM, HYPOCRISY, PRIDE,
VIRTUE, PERFECTION, THE SPIRITUAL MAN

[...] One obviously needs, along with metaphysics, teachings
that integrate the human into the spiritual, that is to say, encom-
pass all of man and not his intelligence alone.

I would like to draw your attention to the danger of the
modern "cult of sincerity" that is in the air and that we breathe
through our social contacts; obviously, this cult of sincerity
is nothing more than individualism, more or less cynical and,
moreover, with a democratic tone. There is always some danger
of contamination when one lives in a decadent world, unless one
has unflinching lucidity and adamantine vigilance.

Cynicism and hypocrisy are two forms of pride; moreover,
cynicism is the caricature of sincerity or frankness, whereas hypocrisy is the caricature of virtue or discipline. Cynics believe
that sincerity consists in displaying defects and passions, and
that to hide them is hypocrisy; they do not exercise self-domination let alone seek to transcend themselves; and the fact that
they take their defect to be a virtue proves their pride, precisely.
Hypocrites, on the contrary, believe that to display virtuous attitudes is to be virtuous; their vice consists, not in manifesting the
forms of virtue—for this is a rule incumbent upon all—but in believing that this manifestation is virtue; above all, their vice consists in mimicking virtues with a view to being admired, which
is pride since it is individualism. Pride is to overestimate oneself
and to underestimate others; this is what the cynic does, as well
as the hypocrite, crudely or subtly depending on the case.

The virtuous man hides his defects for the following reasons:
first, because he does not recognize any right to their existence
and, after each lapse, hopes that this lapse will be the last; one
really cannot reproach someone for hiding his defects when en-
deavouring not to sin and to behave correctly. Another reason
is conformation to the norm: to get rid of a defect, one must not
only have the intention to get rid of it for the sake of God and
not for the sake of pleasing men, but also enter actively into the
mould of perfection; and if it is obvious that one does not do
this to please men, it is no less obvious that one must also do
this—apart from the intrinsically spiritual intention—so as not

to cause scandal and not to set a bad example to others; this is a charity that God requires of us, since the love of God requires the love of one's neighbour.

When so-called sincerity breaks the framework of traditional—or intrinsically normal—rules of behaviour, it betrays its prideful nature by that very fact; for such rules are venerable, and we do not have the right to scorn them by placing our subjectivity above them. It is true that saints may sometimes break these rules, but they do so from above, not from below: they do so in virtue of a divine truth, not some human sentiment. Be that as it may, if traditional man effaces himself behind a rule of behaviour, this is certainly not out of hypocrisy, it is out of humility and charity; out of humility, because he recognizes that the traditional rule is right and that it is better than he is; out of charity, because he does not want to expose others to the scandal of his defects, quite the contrary: he wants to manifest a healthy norm, even if he is not yet personally at its level.

The noble man is he who exercises self-domination, and who loves to do so; the vile man is he who does not exercise self-domination, and who loathes to do so. The spiritual man is he who transcends himself, and who loves to do so; the worldly man remains horizontal and loathes the vertical dimension. And this is important: it is not possible to submit to a demanding ideal—nor to seek to transcend oneself in view of God—without carrying in the soul what psychoanalysts term "complexes"; this amounts to saying that there are "complexes" that are normal for a spiritual man or even for a merely decent man, and that, conversely, the absence of "complexes" is not necessarily a virtue, to say the least. No doubt primordial man, or deified man, no longer has complexes, but it is not enough to be without complexes to be a deified man or a primordial man!

The root of all real sincerity is sincerity towards God, not towards our own good pleasure; in other words, it is not enough to believe in God, one must also draw all the necessary conclusions in our inner and outer behaviour; and when one aspires to a perfection—since God is perfect and wants us to be perfect—one seeks to resemble it even before having realized this perfection, and in order to realize it.

He who submits to the inner and outer norms, he therefore who endeavours to follow the way of perfection, or that of ridding oneself of imperfections—he it is who knows full well that among those who do not make such an effort there are some who are better than he is from the point of view of natural qualities; but being gifted with intelligence, otherwise he would not be a man, he cannot fail to know that from the point of view of metaphysical truth and spiritual effort, he is necessarily better than worldly people, whether he likes it or not, and that an effort in view of God is worth infinitely more than a merely natural quality that is not put to any spiritual use. Meanwhile, worldly people are always looking for accomplices in their dissipation and their ruin, and this is why spiritual men try to keep their distance from them to the extent possible, unless they have an apostolic mission; but in that case, spiritual men will be most mindful not to imitate the bad behaviour of the worldly, thus not to go against what they preach. [...]

PS. I do not know if I stated clearly enough that the content of sincerity is our tendency towards God and consequently our conformity to the rules required by this tendency, and not our nature purely and simply with all of its defects. And hypocrisy consists not in adopting a superior behaviour in view of realizing it, but in adopting it with the intention of appearing to be more than what one is. If the mere fact of adopting a model behaviour was hypocrisy, it would be impossible to strive for the good.

14 July 1976 · ACCEPTING POSTULANTS, READING SOULS

In the Muslim countries, at least before the intervention of the modernist influence, men who wished to enter a *ṭarīqah* were subjected to all kinds of tests, sometimes for very long periods; the *shaykh* observed them, which was easy for him since the postulants lived in the *zāwiyah* as servants of the community; everyone, not just the *shaykh*, could observe them and censure them. And all this proves that neither the *shaykh* nor his entourage were supposed to know the neophyte's worth at first glance; there were sometimes cases of immediate intuition, of course, but it was not the rule, even for the prophets.

For the Prophet—*ṣalla Llāhu ʿalayhi wa sallam*—was deceived more than once, by the *munāfiqūn* for example, or by the Jews of Medina and elsewhere. And I shall say this: many men are in hell because they unjustly suspected honest men; but not a single honest man is in hell because he let himself be deceived. [...]

It happened to me more than once that I saw into the depths of a soul, I mean at first glance, but this, I repeat, cannot be habitual; it would not even be bearable. Moreover, if one does not penetrate souls from the outset, it is often through lack of interest, or a desire for psychic health, for one wants to live in one's own world, not anyone else's; and one wants peace. Be this as it may, it happens that God reveals the depth of a character to us, or on the contrary that He wants us to have an experience, and in this latter case He leaves us to feel our way. [...]

When a man has traits of a Brahman or a Kshatriya along with a vile character, he is a pariah. The pariah is ambiguous, unpredictable, unintelligible and deceptive; he can do everything and nothing; he is a comedian who has no centre; he is a born medium.

P. looks like a discarded circus clown; besides, he has shown this character or talent on two occasions. He is energetic and insignificant, moralist and immoral, modest and proud, intellectual and rudimentary. There is something in his gaze like a broken mirror; something empty and heteroclite, a little stupid and a little mad.

One should distinguish between sincerity itself, which encompasses and engages the whole man, and a fragmentary, sentimental, passional sincerity, which is only a psychological phenomenon and commits him to nothing.

2 October 1976 · DETACHMENT, FAITH

"Say *Allāh*! and leave them to their vain discourse." This Koranic sentence applies first of all to the enemies of God; but then it applies to our own thoughts also, and likewise to events in the world.

What matters for us is not that such and such a thing occurs, but that we attach ourselves firmly to God; we are not answerable for events in the world, nor for the actions of men. God will not hold us to account for what others have said or done; and we do not even need to understand why they said or did it. Perhaps a particular person is good, perhaps he is bad; perhaps we know it, perhaps we do not. All this is indifferent, provided that we attach ourselves firmly to the certitude of divine Reality and divine Mercy. We cannot do more than faithfully remain close to God and wait for death. Each of us will have to die alone, whether he has been happy or unhappy. Only he who dies in God is happy.

What surrounds us is *Māyā*, *Samsāra*, *Līlā*, *Karma*; in the centre we are free; the centre is not our ego, it is prayer, invocation, God. We must not wish to force the world to be other than what it can be or wants to be. If God is favourably disposed to us, all is well; and the proof that He is favourable to us is in prayer: in our freedom to attach ourselves to God.

At heart, everyone knows what has just been said. However, knowing it is not faith. We should remember this: in the spiritual life, once learning has been acquired, everything depends on faith. Faith—the unconditional "yes" to God, to His holy Will, to the blissful hereafter—faith is capable of making us happy from the centre, independently of external things. Faith and gratitude; patience and trust; these are everything.

6 July 1977 · ON THE SUBJECT OF A VISION

The spiritual event you describe to me in your letter is authentic. This is why you are right not to talk to anyone about this, except to your wife, and possibly to an intimate friend if you think that it may be of help to him.

You ask me if this event requires a particular attitude on your part. Yes and no. When a spiritual experience is authentic and profound, it leaves a trace in us; now one must be faithful to this trace. He who has benefited from such a grace knows exactly what he must and must not do; he can no longer be exactly the same man as before. He must not seek to do extraordinary things; from the point of view of the spiritual method and social comportment, nothing changes, unless there was something improper in this comportment. What Heaven wants of us is our soul; it beckons us therefore to inwardness. "The kingdom of

God is within you," Jesus said. "I am black, but beautiful," says the Song of Songs, and this saying is attributed to the Holy Virgin; once again, this is about contemplative inwardness.

A major spiritual event, comprising a kind of vision, cuts us off in a certain way from the world; it is as if we were living henceforth in a kind of invisible sanctuary already belonging to the hereafter; or as if we were in a little garden that is already celestial, and whose happiness is no longer terrestrial. If we have the impression that we are unfaithful to the vision, we must make a prayer to the celestial Personage who has come to meet us. [...]

PS. Heaven does not ask more of us than the *dhikr*, and this requires *faqr*. If we have problems, they are resolved in the *dhikr*. In the *dhikr*—if our intention is good—we are perfect, because the *dhikr* is perfect. It is as if Heaven lent us its perfection. All of our infidelities are as if burned away by the *dhikr*, which presupposes that we have the intention of being faithful. There is no *dhikr* without *faqr*, because there is no valid act without a sincere intention. Now the spiritual graces—such as celestial apparitions—wish to intensify our *faqr* and facilitate our *dhikr*: *faqr* is "I am black" and *dhikr* is "I am beautiful."

28 September 1977 · THE DISORDERS OF THE SOUL

Regarding the problem of the state of your soul: "to sense an illness is no longer to have it," Lao-Tzu would say; in other words: our awareness of an ailment provides us *ipso facto* with the means to overcome it; the remedy lies in our very awareness of the ailment. Apart from intelligence, which allows us to discern the causes of our faults, there is prayer, by means of which we ask for Heaven's help; and there is the invocation that acts in an indirect but absolute fashion.

I think that you have had a difficult youth and that you have in you a heredity which does not facilitate matters; you are no doubt cruelly traumatized. There must be in you a deep and secret wound, of which you are not even conscious, and for which you compensate—as if to hide it from yourself—with paradoxical attitudes. But all of this is relative, whereas the invocation is absolute: whatever the causes may be of your inward contrasts,

136

they will not be able to resist the grace of the invocation indefinitely, because this grace is supernatural whereas they are natural.

One must combine the rigour of discernment—applied above all to ourselves—with the gentleness of trust; that is everything. One never has the right to despair; every man must undergo personal experiences, however painful; that is why we are on earth.

17 June 1978 · GNOSTICISM, PATHS OF LOVE AND KNOWLEDGE, EXOTERISM'S RIGHTS

[...] This gives the false impression that Gnosticism would be a heresy in itself, whereas there was also a Gnosticism that was, in itself, orthodox, for instance with Origen and Clement of Alexandria. [...]

To say that "the Way of Love is itself an indirect mode of Knowledge" is misleading, despite the word "indirect". All that one can say is that *bhakti* contains an indirect element of *jnāna* in the form of dogmatic and speculative theology; this element is intellectual speculation as such, it is not in the object of this speculation, which is limited, otherwise it would not be *bhakti*, precisely.

[...] for there are formulations in Meister Eckhart that the most well-meaning exoterist cannot accept. Likewise in the case of Ibn 'Arabī, I often have to justify the exoterist opponents; for exoterism exists legitimately and therefore has its rights.

7 August 1979 · INTELLECTION AND REVELATION

You ask me if I wanted to say in one of my books "that intelligence cannot discern truth without referring either to esoterism, on the one hand, or to the Revelation and its commentators on the other, beginning with Sayyidina Muhammad". This is what I wanted to say: in principle, pure intelligence—the intellect—can know all that is knowable; it can, in principle, know it by itself, without the intervention of some external teaching. But in fact, it is very likely that even the most gifted mind cannot draw all of metaphysics from itself; if a Shankara had grown up in total ignorance, if he had never heard of the *Vedas*, *Ātmā*, and

Māyā, can one affirm with certainty that he could have drawn those notions from himself? Revelation, Vedic or other, exists not only to communicate key ideas, but also, and above all, to awaken or actualize in us a fund of latent knowledge that we bear within ourselves. You say: "But the Muslim philosophers, like their predecessors in Greece, talked about many things mentioned neither by the Prophet nor by the early luminaries of Islam…" Obviously, since the Prophet—or the Koran—provided only the initial impetus; the Greek philosophers also needed certain traditional motivators. Each man has parents, and parents always have ideas; what I have in mind here is Antiquity. The impulsion—Koranic and Hellenist for the Arabs—once given, metaphysical and mystical authors can have completely original ideas, either by inspiration, or simply by reflection.

7 August 1979 · SHANKARĀCHĀRYA AND THE BUDDHA

You allude in your letter to the painful invectives of Shankara against the Buddha. Now what is at stake here is not the intrinsic reality of the Buddha, it is an extrinsic aspect, that of the destructor of Brahmanism; in fact, there was the risk that Buddhism would totally overwhelm the world of the Vedas and castes. Already well before our time, Hindus fully grasped the distinction I have just mentioned, and I have good reasons for believing that in our times all Hindus venerate the Buddha without thereby disavowing Shankara. In his time, Shankara was like the medium of the rebirth of Hinduism; it is as if the Brahmanical gods had armed him with a sword. There is more than one example of a spiritually positive reality becoming, in another spiritual and traditional perspective, the symbol of a negative and hostile reality, but this does not affect the intrinsic truth; it can even take place within the very same tradition; Shiism is an extreme example of this. In our Western world, I could mention the demonization of the gods of Antiquity by Christianity and, within Christianity itself, the antagonistic interpretations of St Thomas Aquinas and St Gregory Palamas, each being orthodox or heretic, good or bad, depending on the confessional bias.

18 September 1979 · ESOTERISM AND EXOTERISM, KNOWLEDGE,
ISLAM

to Michel Chodkiewicz

All that you say at the beginning of your letter on the relationship between exoterism and esoterism is perfectly plausible, and
I never meant to contest that esoterism *de facto* is necessarily
different from esoterism *de jure*, be it only at the level of traditional language, but in that case the specificity remains neutral and has nothing restrictive about it; all I am reproaching is
an over-accentuation of the exoteric element—or rather of the
exoteric attitude—in esoterism. Apart from that, I would say
that "chemically pure" esoterism does exist well and truly, and
that it manifests itself sporadically in the midst of any civilization; this is simply metaphysics—and its initiatic implications
or consequences—presented in a manner that is free, not from
a given religious symbolism, but from the sentimentalities of a
given theologico-moral system; it is not true that man is unable
to express the highest truths without having to enclose himself
in what Guénon terms the "religious point of view". To say that
pure esoterism is found only in supreme knowledge amounts
to affirming that there is no purely metaphysical, and hence
extra-theological, doctrine, namely a doctrine unfettered from
the "sentimental attachment to an idea" which, according to
Guénon, characterizes the "religious point of view" and "religions". Certainly, sentiment is something natural, and a positive
thing—as a mode of adequation and assimilation—so long as it
does not usurp the function of intelligence; but I really do not
see why adhering to the doctrinal and ritual symbolism of Islam
would compel an emotionality other than that required by the
sense of the sacred and the love of God. Agreed, "the *sharī 'ah* is
itself a *ḥaqīqah*", as Ibn 'Arabī says, but on the express condition
that by *sharī 'ah* is meant the pure symbolism of sacred forms,
and not the narrow, superficial concerns of theology and the piety corresponding to it.

Knowledge is at once inexpressible and expressible; to deny
the second term would amount to saying that no metaphysical
doctrine is possible, that the only possible doctrines would be
theological speculations, hence those marked by a "passional"

139

element and consequently "not disinterested", as Guénon might say. That the most rigorously metaphysical doctrine is not supreme knowledge as such, no one will contest, but this could not mean that short of this doctrine there are only speculations of a confessional type, or let us say metaphysical speculations that are more or less subject to the directives of theology and the psychology resulting therefrom. The theological limitations for which I reproach some Sufis are not reducible to the natural and therefore general limitations of human language, otherwise any possible language would be theological; in short, to reproach a Shankara for the limitations inherent to language, of which he has to make use on pain of not being able to express anything at all, would amount to reproaching a man for being a man.

Someone who is purely and simply an exoterist has no choice but to accept, on pain of heresy, some providential errors or half-truths; he will accept them within the penumbra cast by a fundamental and compensatory truth. These canonical errors are never gratuitous, they are functional or, in other words, their point is to ward off dangers that are likely or certain to happen given the collective nature of the human recipient; in that sense, they are indirectly and symbolically "truths", at least *de facto*. Be that as it may, "there is no right superior to that of truth"; this amounts to saying that an esoterist is never obliged before God to accept points of view he knows are false, were it even a canonical point of view; I mean: to accept them as regards their falseness, for he can obviously accept them as regards their symbolism and function, although this reduces everything to a question of terminology. A religion is an *upāya*, a "salvific mirage" or a "divine means"; however no religion can do without some defect or other, and an esoterist cannot overlook this; the proof of this defect or this error, one might say, being precisely the quasi-canonical obligation to revile the religion of one's neighbour. [...]

If someone asks me how I account for the "disparities" and "dissonances" in the writings of so many Sufis, my answer is: I account for them in part because Sufis do not know what the limitation, and thus the relativity, of the Islamic *upāya* is—Islam being for them a "fact" and not a "perspective"—and above all because of their hereditary solidarity with the inevitably exoterist psychology of the general ambience. Of course, one has the right to speak of the relativity of an *upāya* only on condition of seeing its absoluteness; but at the level of gnosis the converse is also true. Be that as it may, if some Sufis have the right to criticize Messengers other than Muhammad—and they have no qualms about doing so, in view of the Prophet's merits—I do not see why I would not, in principle, have the same right—and with all the more reason—to criticize some Sufis, who are not situated canonically beyond all possible criticism, as on the contrary should be the case with all Messengers, precisely; if a given Sufi has the right to say that the Prophet is superior to the other Messengers—including Christ, naturally—and that he is so in an absolute way; and that the love of God, among those others and therefore in Christ's case too, is less perfect than the Prophet's love of Him; and that the other Messengers—including, as always, Christ—were not raised to the rank of "friend" of God, as the Prophet was—Abraham being so at a lesser level—hence, if a given Sufi has the right to assert all of this, then I certainly have the right, and have it even beyond the mere logic of things, to consider that the authority of a given Sufi is relative and that nothing obliges me to approve of his position or to follow him. It is obvious that Islam, like every religion, sees in its Founder the Logos as such, and in the other Messengers aspects or functions of the Logos, and that each of the greatest Messengers possesses a distinctive trait that stands out in terms of this perspective; but in that case the arguments must be conclusive. To say, at the level of the Founders of religions, that this one had a "love of God" that was more perfect than that of another, or that more than another—or more than all of the others—he was the "friend" of God, makes no sense, and cannot make any sense, given the supreme level under consideration, precisely. Although the symbolism is legitimate, the argumentation is sentimental, petty and ridiculous; if it is already ill-sounding coming from the pen of a theologian, it is much more so coming from the pen of an esoterist.

Muslims are traditionally mindful of the fact that in Christianity, as well as in Judaism, the collective human receptacle was ultimately not at the level of the Message received; now one has to be exceedingly naïve to believe that this situation would not be in any degree analogous in Islam, and this despite the advantage of the "terminality" specific to the Islamic Message; that is to say, despite the fact that one of the reasons for Islam is precisely to avoid the mistakes—if one may say—of the two preceding *upāyas* or rather that of the respective collectivities. And here is the point I wish to make: what in Hinduism so famously favours the purity—or the rigour—of the esoteric element is essentially the caste system; in the absence of this system, esoterism becomes far too consolidated with an average collective mentality that is not proportioned to the requirements of a disinterested perspective, or put differently, that is not free from all confessional narcissism; to be wholly objective is to die a little. These few remarks provide the key for many a paradox found in monotheistic esoterisms, though I believe it is enough to simply point out here the overall nature of the problem.

17 January 1980 · THE ISLAMIC MENTALITY

Each religion has its perfume; each religious collectivity has its own mentality; authentic Muslims have the Islamic mentality and no other, and this mentality is that of the Caliph Omar, of Saladin, of the Emir Abd al-Qādir, of Shāmil, to mention only a few particularly outstanding names; it is composed, not only of piety and courage, but also—and essentially—of nobility and generosity; it excludes all moral ugliness. I mentioned Saladin: he was faced with the crusaders, which was not a trifle; the crusaders, who had pitilessly massacred the whole population of Jerusalem; nevertheless he was always chivalrous, impartial and generous; he never stooped to a systematic, mean hatred. One definitely cannot say as much of certain present-day Muslim leaders who, while meticulously practising the prescriptions of the Sunna, no longer have the Islamic mentality, and this is a sign of our time. Together with the disappearance of nobility of character, there is also a strange rarefaction of the intelligence, even in people who arrogate to themselves the right to speak in the name of God.

7 February 1980 · AMBIENT ABSURDITY

One of the hardest things to bear is human absurdity; to accept it on the basis of its ontological necessity is part of Islam. There are people who think it is virtuous not to see evil and to pretend that black is white, which is the very negation of intelligence; in reality, one has to discern exactly between good and evil while resigning oneself, not to evil as such, but to the metaphysically unavoidable existence of evil. All of this is clear as day, but if I write about this it is because the sight of evil makes one suffer and it is already a degree of holiness to know how to combine implacable discernment with inviolable serenity; although this serenity, I might add, does not exclude holy wrath.

24 December 1980 · FAITH

What is lacking in many disciples—but this is quite human—is the sense of the concrete on the spiritual plane; and the sense of the concrete, it must be said, is something altogether different from the sense of the sublime; the first has its demands whereas the second costs nothing. It is all very well to have doctrinal knowledge, but one must also have faith; and faith is a kind of mystery. It is, moreover, largely a question of imagination: one must transfer imaginativeness into the domain of the "one thing necessary", and this is why there are the themes of meditation which, by their concrete character and their tireless repetition, act slowly but surely like an autosuggestion pointed towards Heaven; the sacramental nature of the Supreme Name does the rest, on the basis of normal conditions, of course. Personal prayer is also important because it contributes to developing sincerity and creating a kind of intimacy with God or, in short, conferring faith on us. "Faith that moves mountains": indeed, the human soul is like an opaque and ponderous mountain which obstructs the way towards immanent Beatitude; but in reality it is but a mist. *Vincit omnia Veritas.*

3 August 1981 · FRITHJOF SCHUON'S EMIGRATION TO THE
UNITED STATES
to Jean-Louis Michon

There is a world that now lies behind me which fashioned my
imaginative soul, and it is that of Lac Léman [Switzerland] with
its prolongations toward the Valais, resulting from my travel
habits; and there is a new world that is now mine, but which lies
"before me" given its newness, precisely, that is to say a world
that has not yet become wholly incorporated into my soul [the
author emigrated to the American Midwest in 1980. *Ed.*]; however, this new world is infinitely close to my nature, so that in
meeting it I am meeting a deep layer in my being. Be that as
it may, I spent almost all my life in towns; and here I am now
suddenly placed in virgin nature, which is marvellous and places
me from the outset in the sacred, but it is also something that a
certain part of my soul has not yet fully assimilated; what I mean
to say is that the total and irreversible character of this situation
is inevitably something new for me, or at least was so till quite
recently. In my experience, and moreover this is self-evident,
there is no happiness without a consecration that springs from
within, from our relationship with God; I was happy in Lausanne owing to my invocation, for it is the invocation that gilded,
so to speak, everything that could make me happy on the plane
of natural things. And it is ultimately the invocation that allows
me to incorporate the beauties surrounding my soul here, and
this—I can affirm it—without having to go through the horizontal detour determined by habit; what we behold on the basis of
the invocation and with the eyes of the invocation is something
we possess entirely; inward beauty is thus a part of ourselves. In
the invocation, and in its atmosphere, there is neither before nor
after, neither old nor new, and this is an experience which in the
end no disciple can escape; quite fortunately so.

4 December 1981 · EVIL, THE KORAN

What we term evil—not due to a bias but because it really is
an evil on its plane of manifestation—has its ontological root
in All-Possibility, inasmuch as All-Possibility requires the mani-

festation, on the one hand, of a portion of the good that is presented in a contrasting fashion and, on the other, the absence
of the good that, according to Ibn 'Arabī, is "non-existence".
Now quite obviously All-Possibility is an aspect of the Sovereign
Good, and so is universal Radiation. "Possibility of the impossible", or "existence of the non-existent" resulting from the Infinite, and by definition within relativity: this is the answer to the
problem, inasmuch as it can be expressed. [...]

Koranic language does not shy away from the boldest elliptical expressions, for example when one finds in the text that
"God leadeth into error whom He willeth"; but God reestab-
lishes equilibrium *a priori* in defining Himself as *Raḥmān* and
Raḥīm; and the other Names.

January 1982 · INVERNESS

The blessed region of Inverness, near Bloomington, has the
meaning of a spiritual message, it is *dār es-salām*: the peace of
the vast sky and the plain stretching out under its light, and the
peace of the silent forest; an image that conveys two realities of
the contemplative soul: blissful expansion and blissful inwardness. For peace has two manifestations, one that dilates blissfully and one that encloses blissfully: on one hand, the beatitude
of the limitless, luminous sky that blesses the green countryside
and encompasses it in its immensity; and on the other hand, the
beatitude of the mysterious forest, evocative of a sacred presence; happiness of the liberating expanse, and happiness of the
protective shelter or sanctuary. The first quality corresponds to
serenity, which transcends and extinguishes all that is petty, and
this is also evoked by the natural beatitude that is breathing, the
dilation and liberation of the breast that drinks from the cup of
the limitless. The second quality—the one that encloses—corresponds to contemplation, withdrawal to the centre, repose on
the threshold of inner infinitude.

The spiritual quality of generosity and elevation, or serenity, is founded upon the certitude of the one transcendent, divine Reality, yet it also implies, fundamentally, resignation to
the Will of God; and the quality of contemplation or depth is
founded upon the consciousness of the immanent divine Pres-

145

ence, yet it also implies faith in God's Mercy. For the ungrateful, accusatory, petty man cannot escape his narrowness, he cannot go beyond himself and look at himself from above; similarly, the faint-hearted, indecisive man, or the ambitious, hardened man, cannot have access to the sacred centre.

The name "Inverness" originally refers to the meeting of a river with the sea; it is the soul's return to its eternal homeland.

17 March 1982 · OLD AGE

Thank you for having spoken to me of S.D. in your letter. He was one of those men who know how to age well, who know how to take advantage of the phenomenon of ageing so that what is at first only a natural process ends up transmitting a supernatural element. This is the miracle of invocation, in a man who opposes no obstacle to it, who on the contrary opens the door of his heart wide for it.

26 May 1982 · TRUTH AND REALITY

By "Truth"—with a capital T—two things are meant: doctrinal—thus mental and theoretical—Truth, and realized Truth, thus "Reality". When one says that our point of departure is Truth, and not such and such a form, one is perfectly correct; and it goes without saying that one means doctrinal Truth "with a capital T" since it is a majesty like concrete Truth, that is, like the Reality it reflects. The difference between doctrinal Truth—which is sacred in function of its prototype—and Truth-Reality corresponds to the difference between the circle and the sphere, thus between planimetry and three-dimensional geometry.

Of course, divine Reality is neither *Vedānta* nor *Taṣawwuf*. But both *Vedānta* and *Taṣawwuf* manifest divine Reality on the plane of human intelligence, and they are sacred and venerable—and absolute on their level—due to this transcendent origin.

13 October 1982 · PROTESTANTISM

I am answering your questions on Protestantism; the first one concerns this confession's orthodoxy. Protestantism is intrinsically orthodox because its dogmas are metaphysically sufficient—explicitly and implicitly—and because its means suffice for salvation; I am, of course, speaking of authentic and not liberal Protestantism. As for the question of its formal homogeneity, it is true that the Protestant movement gave rise to three groups: the Lutherans, the Calvinists, and the Anglicans; other groups are connected to these, or do not merit being taken into consideration; Zwingli, for example, is intrinsically heterodox, and the little sects, such as the Salvation Army, are without interest. Each of these great groups possesses a formal homogeneity that is at least sufficient. It should not be forgotten that ancient Christianity—Catholicism, Orthodoxy, the Abyssinian Church, the Eastern Churches—is not homogeneous since, precisely, it is split, but each of the Churches possesses the necessary homogeneity.

You then ask me "to what part of the phenomenon of Protestantism do the positive remarks of our Master refer"; well, to the three great groups mentioned, but above all to Lutheranism. Luther is so to speak the soul of Protestantism.

Third question: I did not say that "Protestantism is like Amidism", but I did say that its fundamental thesis derives from the same spiritual archetype as *Jodo*; now this archetype does not in itself imply the invocatory mode, any more than the invocatory mode implies the archetype from which *Jodo* and Protestantism derive; but it does imply constant prayer, which pious Protestants do in fact practise.

Fourth question: Protestantism is "a lesser way in Christianity" since, as I said in my article, the scope of the Eucharist is lessened, and it excludes the monastic path. But it is a sufficient path, and it rejoins the principal level of Catholicism in the esoterism of a Boehme, a Tersteegen, and others; in short, among the Lutheran theosophists.

It is noteworthy that King Henry VIII, who was always a Catholic, is not the founder of the Anglican Church properly speaking; it is after his death that Lutheran and Calvinist elements were introduced into the Church of England. Quite paradoxically, Anglicanism protected England against Baroque art and left it a certain medieval climate, especially in the small towns and in the countryside.

6 February 1984 · OLD AGE

I was very surprised—but the emotion was even greater than the surprise—upon receiving your letter. I often wondered what had become of you, and finally I attributed your silence to the harsh trials of your health; now, I dare hope—and your handwriting seems to indicate this—that your state has greatly improved. Growing old is something quite relative—I know this from experience—because there are phases in which one seems to grow younger; this is not something that one necessarily aspires to, but it is a fact, and it is often a kind of reward for those who are not afraid of growing older. Be that as it may, one must centre oneself in the Immutable, right in the midst of the terrestrial *Māyā* that surrounds us and wishes to ravish our centre from us; from this point of view, age is a grace, because it renders many things easier, provided we can understand it. Resignation and trust: these two words contain everything, humanly speaking, metaphysical certitudes aside. Resignation to what cannot be avoided, and trust in Mercy; we need but open ourselves to it. This is the *raison d'être* of human existence.

25 February 1984 · THE ESOTERIC EXEGESIS OF THE SCRIPTURES

I dislike an esoterism that consists in squeezing Scripture like a lemon; I shall be told that Scripture is there for that purpose, to which I reply that everything has limits and it is not for nothing that God gave us the intellect which "bloweth where it listeth". Faced with the spectacle of a certain "hermeneutic" jungle, I would prefer not to know how to read, and invoke the Great Spirit on the summit of a mountain.

16 December 1984 · FAITH AND INVOCATION

Do not say: "I invoke God—or pray—but I am not sure that He is listening to me." For the very fact of invoking God implies the fact that He is listening to me—this is in the very nature of his Name—and this certitude is part of faith.

Assuredly, one must address oneself to God with faith; and faith entails the right intention. One must not invoke God with an intention unworthy of the invocation: that is to say, one must not invoke Him in view of some earthly goal, nor invoke Him to be able to tell oneself that one is saintly; but one can invoke Him either because one feels miserable and without help, or because one loves the fragrance of his Presence and Peace, or again because God is That which is. It is also important to know that when we pronounce the Divine Name with sincerity, God sees everything that we are in need of; the invocation contains all possible prayers that we might have, including our gratitude.

One must not wait for the Divine Name to give us serenity; on the contrary we ourselves must offer it serenity; for to have serenity is to have faith, and to have faith is to have serenity. Before the Name can give us a happiness of some kind—if it wishes to give this to us—one must know that it is itself happiness, and that consequently, the invocation is happiness; this is part of faith.

Moreover, happiness consists not only in receiving, it consists also, and essentially, in giving!

The *dhikr* is a gift: it is a gift of our soul to God, and a gift of the Presence of God to the world. To give the world to God, and to give God to the world.

28 March 1985 · INTELLIGENCE AND OBJECTIVITY OF THOUGHT

All too many people are considered "intelligent" because they are excellent at thinking, as long as their thinking moves in the grooves of their sentimental wishes and prejudices, as well as in the grooves of their outward advantages; but as soon as this is no longer the case, they can no longer think; I do not call such people "intelligent", even if they be brilliant philosophers. That is why I wrote somewhere: "To be objective is to die a little." With all of this I wish to say: what one ought to observe above all in the perfect man—apart from the absence of vices—is the capacity to be able to think independently of any feelings or wishes. And to ascribe sentimental or interested prejudices to such a man is the surest sign of a deep-seated imperfection; for in his imagination the inferior man—however gifted he may be—transfers his own inferiorities into the soul of the other, thus he sees the other as he should see himself, which precisely, he is incapable of doing; this incapacity is the very touchstone of his inferiority. In certain cases this infirmity of the soul and the mind is curable, in others not; it is curable if it is superficial, i.e. stemming from external circumstances, but not if it lies in the soul's substance. But I must add here that there is nothing ab-solute in the world—God alone is absolute—and that with God and through God things are possible that seem impossible for man.

Now he who really loves God is also able to think; for the love of God—the knowledge of God—admits of no limitations that would affect thinking. The incapacity to think is always conso-nant with pride; for the veritably humble man is always inclined to look at himself from outside and from above; he wants to belong to God, not to himself!

8 November 1985 · OVERCOMING A TRIAL

Since your wife alluded to trials, I shall remind her that there are four great arguments that help us to overcome them, which are: firstly, the *Shahādah*, which enounces the absolute primacy of divine Reality; secondly, holy resignation to the will of God (*mā shā'a Llāh*); thirdly, trust in divine Mercy (*Allāhu karīm*); and fourthly, gratitude, which prevents us from losing sight of all the good things God has given us and continues to give us (*al-ḥamdu li Llāhi wa al-shukru li Llāh*). Truth, resignation, trust, gratitude: this is a viaticum that we cannot do without and that no one can ravish from us. Our spiritual relationship with the Supreme Truth presupposes or requires our human relationship with God.

26 May 1987 · THE *SHAHĀDAH*

If the *Shahādah*, a revealed and *a posteriori* traditional truth, is absolutely true—as it is by definition—it cannot intrinsically—or esoterically—exclude another revealed and thereby traditional truth, such as avatarism; otherwise either the *Shahādah* or the doctrine of the *Avatāra* would have to be false, *quod absit*.

If I see some object, a pebble for example, I can say *lā ilāha illā Llāh*, thinking: God alone is real, therefore this pebble is unreal; God alone possesses Reality. This is the perspective of transcendence or "abstraction", *tanzīh*. But from a quite different viewpoint, I can also think: from the moment that this pebble exists—thus that it is real—its existence or its reality can only be that of God; given that *lā ilāha illā Llāh*, precisely. This is the perspective of immanence or "resemblance", *tashbīh*.

Or let us take another example: if I see a beautiful creature, I can think, in conformity with the *Shahādah*: God alone is beautiful, thus this creature is not beautiful; God alone possesses Beauty: *lā jamīla illā Llāh*. This is the perspective of transcendence, *tanzīh*. But I can also think: from the moment that this creature is beautiful and that every positive quality necessarily belongs to absolute Being—*al-Wujūd al-muṭlaq*—its empirically incontestable beauty can only be that of God. This is the perspective of immanence or "resemblance", *tashbīh*, of which one Koranic expression is the affirmation that "Allah is the light of the heavens and the earth"; the classic expression of *tanzīh* being, "No thing is like Him". This is a flagrant contradiction if one does not accept the existence of the two parallel, complementary perspectives, the transcendentist and the immanentist; in other words, if one does not accept esoterism with all its modes and degrees of vision and interpretation.

Similarly for the phenomenon of the *Avatāra*; *a priori*, the *Shahādah* means: God alone is divine, thus the *Avatāra* cannot be divine; consequently, there is no *Avatāra*. But, basing ourselves on the incontestable phenomenon of a given degree of human participation in the divine Nature—a possibility that is a metaphysical necessity—we can also think that from the moment the *Avatāra* is divine, his divinity can only be that of God; in which case the word *illā*, which is exclusive *a priori*, assumes an inclusive meaning, but always to God's advantage; *ad majorem Dei gloriam*.

Here we have a play of relationships—well-known in *Taṣawwuf*—resulting from the nature of *Ātmā* and *Māyā*.

22 October 1987 · THE TWO DIMENSIONS OF ESOTERISM

As I have pointed out more than once, there are two dimensions in esoterism: there is one that prolongs exoterism and another that is opposed to it, or that seems to oppose it, and such is the

case of spiritual music in Islam. How great the distance is between the attitude of the Companion who stopped up his ears
so as not to hear a flute, and the dervishes who, several centuries
later, introduced the flute into their sessions of the *dhikr*!

13 November 1987 · BRANCHES OF THE PRIMORDIAL TRADITION

The North American Indian world—like the archaic religions
of Siberia and the Far East—belongs to Mongolian shamanism,
and this is a branch of the Primordial Tradition—the *Sanātana
Dharma*—whose other branch is Hinduism, to which the religions of the Germans, the Celts, the Greeks and the Romans are
related, as is well-known.

Unknown date n° 7 · THE GREEK PHILOSOPHERS

You ask yourself how those such as Plato, Socrates, Pythagoras,
Plotinus were able to attain their [spiritual] degrees although
they do not seem to you to have that exoterism whose necessity I
underlined. First of all, it is not true that they lacked exoterism.
They lived in a traditional setting which, however degenerate
one supposes it to have been, nonetheless included an exoteric,
thus "religious", framework (rites, ceremonies, beliefs, morals);
furthermore, spiritual geniuses of their scope were no doubt
able to resuscitate the original purity of these exoteric forms for
themselves; anyway, if one wished to accept that one cannot even
speak of degenerate exoterism for a Plato, for example (which
is not my opinion), one should not forget that the necessity of
the exoteric ambience is not a rule without exception; these were
exceptional men, connected with both the category of *afrād*
("solitary ones" not subject to the Pole or Legislator of their
time) and that of minor prophets, in the sense that they stamped
an entire civilization with their spiritual hallmark. Be this as
it may, I remind you that all these men were not only philosophers, but also "believers", "practicians", an aspect that modern
historians persist in neglecting.

Unknown date n° 8 · THE SOUL, PSYCHOLOGY

Basically there is only one Subject, the divine Self, *Ātmā*. But it diversifies, refracts and multiplies in the midst of Relativity, which is a dimension of the unique Subject; hence the diversity and multiplicity of relative subjects. The divine Self is Being or Power, Consciousness and Beatitude; *Sat, Chit* and *Ānanda*. Similarly its microcosmic reflection, the human soul: it is made of will, intelligence and sensibility, which amounts to saying that it is made for the Good, the Truth and Happiness.

The intelligence is made for discerning between the Real and the contingent, or between the Substance and the accident. The will is made for drawing the consequences of this on the plane of our very existence, realizing an adaptation of our entire being to the Real; this is the foundation of the spiritual methods. Sensibility is made for finding one's happiness in this adaptation or realization, which amounts to saying that it is made for the Real.

The truly human, not animal, content of our intelligence is the Real; it is this which constitutes the sufficient reason of human intelligence, which would not exist without it. This is why only this intelligence is capable of what is absolute; it alone is total. The content and sufficient reason of the human, not animal, will is the realization of the Real; it is in proportion to this possibility that only human will is free. The content and the *raison d'être* of the sensibility, or affectivity, of the human genre is the love of God, thus happiness in the things that converge upon the absolute and infinite Real. Man cannot find perfect, stable happiness except in God.

But the human soul is fallen; it has lost its primordial perfection, that of the earthly Paradise or the Golden Age. Consequently there is something in the soul that must be destroyed; one must "hate one's life", said Christ; and likewise the mystics: "Hate thy soul". However, there is another dimension in the soul that is neutral, ambiguous and available, namely passional energy; this must be channelled and interiorized, it must be put into the service of God. It must contribute to spiritual realization. And there is a third element in the soul that is fundamental and so to speak uncreated, and this is the pure Intellect; this must be saved in order to become entirely what it is. "What you are—this is what you must become," says an Upanishad.

Consequently, the spiritual path implies: on one hand and above all, discernment between the Real and the illusory, attachment of the will to the Real, the happiness of the soul in the Real; and on the other hand and in function of the above, the destruction of the soul's tenebrous elements, then the interiorization of the soul's ardent elements, and finally the liberation of the luminous elements, which constitute the quintessence of the immortal soul.

To reply to your question, essentially psychology needs to take all these factors into account, or it is nothing; which amounts to saying that there is no valid psychology outside metaphysics and spirituality.

Unknown date n° 9 · THE TERNARY INTELLIGENCE-WILL-CHARACTER

Man is made of intelligence, will and character; which renders him capable of knowledge, realization and nobility, and even obliges him thereto. Comprehension of the Real, concentration upon the Real, conformity to the Real: this is man's vocation. Truth, Way and Virtue; Doctrine, Method and Morality.

Clearly, these fundaments are in themselves independent of religious forms; the latter are diverse, whereas the former are invariable. They are necessary in an absolute manner, but cannot be improvised; they must be conferred by Heaven, thus in the context—and with the blessing—of a religious form.

Unknown date n° 10 · BITTERNESS, INJUSTICE, DESTINY

We have no right to bitterness, for what is unjust and hurtful on man's part is not so on God's part. If we undergo an injustice, this proves that there is an element in our nature—accidental or substantial—that deserves it. Every destiny is an aspect of our present nature. Essentially, sanctity implies the capacity to keep this in mind always and draw the consequences from it; which does not prevent man from defending his right with respect to other men, as necessary and within the limits imposed by virtue and faith.

Unknown date n° 11 · DISTRACTION AND CONCENTRATION

There are three ways to combat and overcome the thoughts that assail us: invocation, individual prayer and reflection. Invocation is the global method, for in the long run nothing can resist the divine Presence; contingencies—psychological or other—can do nothing against the Absolute. It seems to me that there is great consolation in this truth. Similarly in individual prayer, which allows us to speak to God as to a human being. As for reflection, it consists in looking at the causes of phenomena and in consequence seeing these in their just proportions and all their relativity.

You know all this in theory; but you ought to know it in a concrete way. We have need of four Treasures: the truth of the Absolute, invocation, patience and trust. You should be able to look at your psychological difficulties from outside, as if they did not concern you; one must be able to go outside oneself and look at one's ego as if it were a stranger. For in reality, the things that make us suffer are on the surface of our being, they are not ourselves. When one suffers from this genre of difficulties, one is a victim of an optical illusion; one does not realize the smallness of psychological contingencies. Even the things that one cannot in fact eliminate, that seem stronger than we are, are in reality weak and transitory; as long as they are there, we must bear them without doing them the honour of suffering from them, if I can express myself thus; for I repeat, in reality they are foreign to our substance.

I said that in the long run, nothing can resist the invocation, thus the supreme Name; I could also say that nothing can resist faith. The Name and faith constitute the invocation. Beside these pillars of spiritual life, our maladies are nothing. And when things seem to go beyond our strength, we must describe them to God in prayer; this contributes to exhausting them.

Letters to Hindu Correspondents
and Letters Concerned with Hinduism

to Arthur Osborne

First of all, I must say that I have never seen Shrī Rāmana; all I know about him is what I have gathered from the few books published or recommended by the ashram, or from M.I.; therefore it is only possible for me to draw conclusions to the extent that these books and accounts reflect the integral reality of the Maharshi. According to these testimonies, Shrī Rāmana was not initiated by a Guru, but obtained supreme illumination in a completely spontaneous manner in his youth. The traditional books of Sufism as well as those of Hinduism and Buddhism mention this possibility of a sudden realization without previous initiation, and you are certainly aware that in Islam these saintly men are designated by the term *afrād*, "isolated ones"; now if Shrī Rāmana really corresponds to the designation of the *afrād*, I must conclude that everything that is traditionally said of them concerns him, and this seems to be confirmed by the conversation related in your letter. If the Maharshi says that there is an initiation by silence—one could also say by the radiation of presence—he says it in the same way that he affirms that he is a guru, that is, in a universal and principial sense which does not coincide in every respect with what the treatises of initiatic science have in view; I must also add—without prejudicing the Maharshi's case—that the *afrād* may not know things of which they have no personal need; since they did not have to be initiated, they do not need to know what initiation means in the narrow, technical sense of the word; it is enough for them to know *Ātmā*, to know that "*Aham Brahmāsmi*"; therefore one can say of them that they speak in the manner of men of the *Satya-Yuga*—the epoch when initiation was not yet necessary—rather than in the manner of the spiritual instructors of the dark age [the *Kali-Yuga*, the present age. *Ed.*].

But there is another point I must mention: it may be that the cosmic law of compensation that intervenes at the end of every cycle—and consequently also at the end of the *Kali-Yuga*, or the entire *Mahā-Yuga*—affirms itself in the initiatic order by introducing certain concessions; this law of compensation was enunciated by the Prophet Muhammad in these terms: "At the beginning of Islam (or the *Mahā-Yuga*) he who omits a tenth of the Law (Koranic or dharmic) will be damned; but at the end, he who accomplishes a tenth of the Law will be saved". It is in conformity with this same cosmic compensation that, according to other inspired sayings, the flames of hell will cool at the end of its cycle of existence; or, concerning the caste system, one can also say that it does not apply today with the same rigour as in the past, except in the social order; the present state of the castes seems to retrace primordial non-differentiation, symbolically and to a certain degree, the intellectual differences between the castes being ever more diminished; the lower castes, which have become very numerous, represent an entire people and consequently include all human possibilities, whereas the higher castes, which have not multiplied in the same proportion, suffer from a decadence that is all the more significant since "the corruption of the best is the worst" (*corruptio optimi pessima*). According to M.I., Shrī Rāmana said one day that a *shūdra* may read the sacred Scriptures; such a thing, impossible in normal conditions, has become possible because of this law of compensation which in a certain sense—since "extremes meet"—replicates primordial non-differentiation. It is thus possible that initiatic transmission, too, may obey rules that are less rigorously defined than formerly, though without it being possible to theoretically delineate these simplifications or concessions to which the laws in question may hypothetically be subject.

Judging by what is said in the different accounts, Shrī Rāmana's spiritual knowledge seems to be essentially synthetic and principial and not analytical or scientific like that of a Guru in the technical sense of the word; thus it appears to me illogical and misplaced to ask the Maharshi questions raised by traditional initiatic science, that is, to oblige him to address subjects of which he has never spoken spontaneously, and which have no relation to the synthetic, simple mode of his radiation; a source of spiritual graces does not necessarily resemble a book. In the conversation reported in your letter, the questioner should have stopped after the sage's second reply, and meditated on it; the third question is as simplistic as it is incongruous, and similarly, the fourth constitutes a veritable violation of propriety, for one does not press a sage with questions when one does not understand his answers; one ought to have meditated at length on the first two answers before questioning him further; it was completely out of place to keep insisting, since at the beginning of the interview Shrī Rāmana did not consider it necessary to give detailed explanations.

5 May 1945 · RĀMANA MAHARSHI, CONCENTRATION

Some modern theoreticians of the "direct way" do not seem to ask themselves if it is psychologically possible to persevere a whole lifetime, by one's own means, in the mere concentration on the "Absolute Subject", nor if such efforts, assuming they were feasible, could end in a positive result; they forget that Christ said: "No man cometh to the Father but by me," and: "Without me ye can do nothing"; this means that only doctrine and the grace of the Word can render possible what is humanly impossible, that is to say, only revealed and orthodox doctrine can give spiritual concentration the required "quality", and only the initiatic means can enable this concentration to attain to its supreme goal.

But could it not be objected that simple concentration suffices by definition to reach the goal, and that it alone possesses the virtue of removing the obstacles separating the individual from Reality? Concentration possesses this virtue in principle, but in fact this is not how things are; otherwise all the methods of realization used for thousands of years, in India as elsewhere, would be merely complications devoid of meaning; the consecration rite of a *sannyāsī*, for instance, would be but a simulacrum lacking any sufficient reason.

In closing, I ought to make a comment on what some refer to as the "method of the Maharshi"; now such a method does not exist, for the simple reason that the Maharshi himself never followed any method. He owes his realization to a sudden enlightenment, and not to spiritual exercises; and since he never followed a method, he cannot teach one; his teaching through the question "who am I?" is much more the expression of his inner reality, or a principial and symbolic expression of any spiritual path, than a method that can be imitated in the absence of any other support. In no wise does this mean that the Maharshi has no radiation or that he does not transmit graces, but only that, having never had to follow a path himself, he could not have the mission of forming disciples, and this in fact is the reason why he refuses to accept any; to affirm that *mauna-dīkshā* constitutes in itself an integral path, instead of simply representing the essential aspect of every path, amounts to saying that the descent of the Holy Spirit on the Apostles constitutes a spiritual method. Let it not be objected that the Apostles, having had a quasi-sudden realization, as did the Companions of the Prophet also, could not therefore form disciples; the case of the Apostles and the Companions is altogether different, for not only did they receive an initiation, but also a method to be transmitted; this method, "simple" and "synthetic" at the beginning, became "differentiated" and more explicit, with the assistance of the Holy Spirit, as the origin and its flood of spiritual graces receded and it became necessary to adapt to increasingly precarious conditions; thus the position of a St John or a Sayyidna Alī is in no way comparable to that of a "later" saint, that is to say, someone who is not the direct disciple of a founder of a traditional form.

As for the Maharshi, he is clearly among those of whom Shrī Rāmakrishna says that they obtain realization without the aid of their will and in a sudden and spontaneous manner; these are the men Sufism knows under the name of *afrād*; they are the ones for whom the initiatic meaning of this saying of Christ applies: "they that be whole need not a physician"; now the existence of such men does not imply that initiatic rites, which exist in Hinduism as in any other tradition, are mere contrivances devoid of meaning; that these rites exist, means that they must correspond to some kind of reality and necessity. There really should be no problem here: if someone is a *fard*, then the initiatic question does not apply to him, and discussions on this subject are pointless for him; if he is not a *fard*, then he has no choice but that of a normal path transmitted by tradition, which is to say that—along with the help of the rectitude of his intention and of *barakah*—he needs to seek an orthodox *murshid*, and receive from him what this *murshid* himself had received from his *murshid*.

1949 · THE PATH OF KNOWLEDGE
to Atmānanda Krishna Menon (original letter in English)

Your disciple Pramānanda Nath has brought back your book *Ātmā-Darshan*. This same book had already been sent to me, and M.R. assured me that it is you yourself who had addressed it to me the first time; in this case, my thanks to you for it, and let me say that I read it with all the satisfaction of once more finding the absolute and sacred truths of eternal India.

You will have noticed that the writer of this letter is the former guru of Pramānanda Nath. The conversations I have had with him oblige me to make certain reflections which I think it opportune to submit to you, and which at the same time afford me the chance to develop some considerations which may give you a glimpse of our viewpoint concerning spiritual realization.

If I have properly understood certain explanations, all that is necessary in *jnāna-mārga* is on the one hand the certainty that "I" am neither the body nor the mind, but *Ātmā*, and on the other hand the presence of a Guru who has realized the Absolute; the human and intellectual value of the disciple do not count, nor does the tradition; only *jnāna* itself, and the presence of the Guru, have any importance.

Now as is the case with all precious things, *jnāna* can become a mortal poison, just as it can mean deliverance; it all depends on the individual nature of the disciple. To be able to realize *Ātmā*, this nature presupposes *a priori* a certain conformity with *Ātmā*. If the nature of the disciple is not prepared for *jnāna*, this method can have effects contrary to those normally to be expected: instead of being realized, identity with the Self will be replaced by a sort of fixed idea, a thought artificially grafted upon the mind; instead of leading to some degree of spiritual realization, this false attitude will be the source of an intellectual automatism, and of all sorts of vices, such as pride, pretentiousness, obstinacy, mental petrifaction, a certain dialectical monomania and a lack of sense of the sacred. It is thus imperative that before being abandoned by the "ego", the mind be purified, and this is the judgment of all sages in all times.

Thus in my view he who would follow the *jnāna-mārga* must first of all possess the general virtue of the man of good will, and secondly the particular intellectual qualification for *jnāna*. General virtue implies devotion with regard to *Brahman*, and by extension, with regard to mankind: justice, absence of egoism, charity in all its forms; for man as such—that is, as mind and body—is rigorously subject to *Brahman* to the degree that *Brahman* reveals Itself objectively and cosmically. The particular qualification for *jnāna* implies a contemplative intelligence capable of grasping metaphysical truths in all their depth, complexity and subtlety, and in consequence capable of perfectly discerning the value of things. He who lacks intellectual discernment, that is, he who is narrow-minded and illogical and thus incapable of accurately defining the nature of things on the cosmic plane, is not qualified to distinguish between the Real and the unreal; in other words, he who cannot tell Truth from error on the relative plane will not be able to tell Reality from unreality either.

Before going further I would like to answer a possible objection: one could indeed say that there are *jnānis* whose minds do not worship God and who confine themselves to realizing the idea that the mind, whatever it may do, is not the real "self". Now if there are *jnānis* who do not expressly worship God, it is because their minds are impregnated *a priori* with devotion, through having worshipped God in their youth, or having worshipped Him in former lives, or having inherited such minds from countless ancestors who worshipped God. Their minds are thus in a state of natural adoration. In any case, the greatest *jnānis*—such as Shrī Shankara or, in our time, Shrī Rāmana Maharshi—manifested a devotional attitude which in no way attached them to the mind. [devotional hymns by Shankarāchārya, Rāmana Maharshi and Rāmakrishna follow. *Ed.*]

As long as the mind exists—that is to say until death—it must worship the Divinity; without this attitude man will not be able to realize genuinely that he is not the mind. A mind that worships does not desire to be "I", any more than it opposes the truth that "I am not the mind, I am *Ātmā*". But a mind which does not bow down before the Godhead is an obstacle to liberation, and will replace this by an illusion of liberation; yet it would be better not to be liberated than to fancy oneself liberated. The fixed idea that "I am *Ātmā*" is not the same thing as the consciousness of being *Ātmā*; a madman who imagines himself to be God is not the same thing as a sage who knows that he is God.

In the same way, as regards the virtue required for all spiritual realization, I shall say this: the mind which has not been purified of the maladies of the worldly man and is not free from pride, passion and vileness of every kind does not allow the superposition of the idea "I am the mind" to be eliminated. The idea that "I am not the mind nor the body, but *Ātmā*", frees us from superpositions only on condition that the objectivations—that is, the body, the soul, the intelligence—realize *Ātmā* within the limits of their possibilities: the body by its purity, the soul by its devotion, and the intelligence by its discernment, its logic. If the body is impure through the tyranny of the passions, if the soul is impious by its contempt for God, and if the intelligence is obscured by pretentiousness and partiality, the idea that "I am neither this body nor this mind, but *Ātmā*", engenders the illusion—not the consciousness—of being *Ātmā*; and this illusion may engulf man in the torments of *samsāra*. Ignorance pure and simple is better than an illusion of knowing. The more elevated the content of the illusion, the more deadly it is.

Why have I written you all this? Because certain people deny all these things. According to them, it is enough to convince oneself, as it were by autosuggestion, that one is neither the body nor the mind. However, this truth is not realizable until body and mind have conformed on their plane to what I could call the "Divine Will"; one cannot attain *Ātmā* without God or in opposition to God. Only the "personal Divinity" allows those who adore Him to understand that He is not the absolute Reality.

Shrī Shankara, Shrī Rāmana Maharshi and you yourself are Hindus. The Hindus are the most contemplative people in the world; and for thousands of years you have been accustomed to seeing in yourselves what is divine. You say "I am *Ātmā*", "I am *Brahman*", just as your ancestors have done for thousands of years. Pure contemplation has forged the Hindu soul. It is often able to realize without difficulty what other souls come to realize only with difficulty. The case of Europeans—Christians and Jews—is quite different. The soul of their ancestors was far removed from the Hindu soul. The Jews did not live in contemplation, but in fear; their way was a *karma-yoga*. I am not in any way criticizing the Jewish religion, which is in conformity with the Hebrew mentality; I am only pointing out that it is radically different from the spirituality of the Hindus. Moreover, the same thing is true, though in a lesser degree, of the Christian religion, which is heir to Judaism. I am not claiming that a Jew or a Christian can never follow a Hindu *sādhanā*; I am saying that, if they follow it, they must take account of their own mental make-up— from a purely human point of view, not from the jnanic point of view which is above contingencies. They are neither Hindus nor Brahmins; *jnāna* is more dangerous for them than for men of the elite in your country. Being Europeans, they think too much, which gives them an appearance of intelligence; in reality, and in the majority of cases, their thinking is essentially passional, and lacking all contemplative serenity; the idea that "I am *Brahman*" may easily fill them with pride and contempt, because their ancestors have always thought "I am a mortal, a sinner"; and because their minds, unless they have been purified by rigorous disciplines, are not accustomed to bear jnanic formulas.

I am sure, very reverent Guru, that you know men, but I am not sure you know Europeans. Europeans are afflicted with a hidden individualism difficult for a Hindu to imagine; European civilization has been oriented for centuries towards the exaltation of man, of the individual—be it in a rationalist, sentimental or brutal manner—whereas Hindu civilization, which has never changed in its essence, has been oriented for thousands of years towards what lies beyond man and gives him his whole *raison d'être*.

7 October 1954 · SWĀMI RĀMDĀS, HARI PRASAD SHASTRI
to Titus Burckhardt (original letter in German)

We saw Swāmi Rāmdās in London on two occasions, first at Pallis's house and then at Patel's, a Hindu scholar. Our friends were still busy in the house when the Swāmi arrived with his entourage, so that I had to receive them by myself in the vestibule, after S.A. had opened the door to them. I conducted the Hindus to the living room, showed the Swāmi his place and began a conversation with him; our friends joined us one after another. At his request, we invoked the Name, and then the Hindus invoked the *Rāma-mantram*. Krishnabai, the celebrated Brahman, was present, as well as two beautiful Hindu women, and also the secretary and two or three other Hindus; they were accompanied by two Englishmen we did not know. We had invited our Christian friends, and the two Buddhists were there also, of course. Questions were asked, and the Swāmi answered with his marvellous eloquence; I said certain things also, and everything was written down. Sometimes the friends had to laugh, for example when I said towards the end, " Swāmi Rāmdās is like the Ganges: he is never tired!"

The next day I visited the Swāmi at Patel's house, with some friends; the Hindus behaved towards me as if I were a *swāmi*. If the day before Rāmdās had spoken to us with enthusiasm of the graces of the Name, this time he told us stories of saints, and events from his own life, such as when, one night in the jungle, he heard the roar of a tiger close by him. When we parted, the Hindus accompanied us as far as the garden bordering the street, a rose garden. Mr Patel had picked two, one for Swāmi and one for me, and we parted in this way, roses in our hands. The image of the Swāmi dressed in orange, in the company of Krishnabai and the other Hindus, greeting us as our car moved away, is unforgettable.

Yesterday I went with Pallis to see Pandit Hari Prasad Shastri, an old Brahman. He praised my writings on the *Vedānta* and told me that apart from Guénon's book, he had never read anything so correct on the *Vedānta*; and that my explanation of *Māyā* was the only good one he had ever found in a European work. After a conversation on the subject of the *Vedānta* and Hinduism, we spoke of Sufism; he then recited the sura *Al-Ikhlāṣ* and other passages from the Koran in perfect Arabic, comparing them to corresponding Sanskrit formulas.

1955 · REINCARNATION

If reincarnation were something as banal as it is in the minds of the average Easterner—who believes that the fish in a pond are reincarnated lamas (there is no point of being a lama if one is to be reborn as a fish!) or that a particular goat is a recently deceased English Lady (in the Maharshi's entourage)—then, if things actually were like this, there would be no explanation as to why beings such as Christ, Muhammad, Moses, and Abraham never said a word about it. Generally speaking, I think that there are in every tradition some "solidified", and hence crude, concepts, and this may be why an Asiatic sage said that only error is transmitted, not truth; for instance, the Muslim negation of the fact of the crucifixion is as astonishing as the Christian negation of the salvation of pre-Christian saints, not to mention the negation of "paganisms", and so on.

September 1955 · WE ARE ALL ONE
to Hari Prasad Shastri (original letter in English)

I feel that when I am invoking the Name of God, wherever I may be, I am with you; for in this state there are no longer spatial distances, and in the holy Names of the Infinite we are all one.

28 February 1956 · CONDOLENCES
to the widow of Hari Prasad Shastri

We know that death is not a real separation, that it is but an illusory and fleeting veil, and that in God souls meet, even here-below. We cannot be closer to those whom we love than by clinging to God, and losing ourselves in Him. It is in losing ourselves in Him that we find ourselves in Him again, along with those whom we love.

18 October 1957 · IN FAVOUR OF TRADITION
(original letter in English)

It is a great pleasure for me to learn through your kind letter of this splendid manifestation of traditional spirit, the Navaratri Pooja, and I am most grateful that you took the opportunity to present my three articles to H.H. the Jagadguru Shrī Shan-karāchārya [of Kanchipuram. *Ed.*]. I am very pleased to have this new contact with orthodox Hinduism. May our efforts in defense of Brahmanical India and the traditional spirit in general have the repercussions we hope for, with divine aid.

14 February 1960 · IMPORTANT BOOKS

Hindu books that all of our friends should possess and read are the following: the *Bhagavad-Gītā*; the *Yoga-Vāsishtha*, also called the *Mahārāmāyana*; the *Srīmad Bhāgavatam*. These books, which have exceptionally the value of an *Upanishad*, contain the very essence of the Doctrine, which is exposed by Shrī Krishna and—through the agency of Vasishtha—by Shrī Rāma.

15 March 1961 · MAHARISHI MAHESH YOGI

The affair of the Sādhu Mahesh shows once again how much Easterners have need of us, that is to say: how much they have need of 1. a rigorous doctrine and 2. the correct application of the doctrine to new circumstances. In general, they do not know how to go about such an application. The West needs the traditional East, but the East, for its part, needs the Easternized West; it is incapable of defending itself all alone.

The errors of the Mahesh Yogi movement are patently obvious. In reality, the goal of meditation is not to have access to "limitless energy, heightened efficiency of thought and action, and release from tensions and anxiety, peace of mind and happiness"! All such advantages have no spiritual value, because it is not happiness that matters, it is the motive of happiness and the nature of happiness. Of that—the sole important question—the Sādhu says nothing, and this is what condemns him.

If Mahesh Yogi has "discovered" a method of meditation—"profound" or not—this proves either that his method is worthless, or else that Mahesh Yogi is attributing to himself a glory not belonging to him. For every man who knows how to meditate necessarily has the sense that his meditation is a discovery, something that stands out from theories and precepts; "there are as many paths as there are human souls", the Sufis say, and Buddhism has a formula which is altogether analogous. The Sādhu in question is either a naïve person who believes he has "discovered" what all the masters before him knew, or an individualist who does not know how to resist such an "optical illusion", and who on the contrary desires it *a priori*.

Truth does not matter for him, nor tradition. He does not seek to save men, he seeks to soften their path to hell, just as psychoanalysis does. "Spiritual Regeneration" is a purely psychological matter, demanding nothing of us intellectually, morally, and traditionally.

False masters are dangerous because they are a mixture of good and evil; they seduce with the good.

A typical error is to believe that the rapid expansion of a modern sect—thanks to mechanical means—is comparable to the miraculous expansion of the religions.

24 April 1961 · INVOCATION AND ITS MODES

The quintessence of all tradition and all spirituality is discernment between the Real and the illusory and concentration on the Real. Everything is contained in this twofold definition. This is, in a more outward sense, the doctrine and the method; now there are many doctrines and many methods, but there is only one discernment between the Real and the illusory, the Absolute and the contingent, the Infinite and the finite, just as there is only one concentration on the Real, only one Union, only one Deliverance.

The most diverse traditions agree in this, that the best support for concentration and the best means to obtain Deliverance at the end of the *Kali-Yuga* is the invocation of a revealed Divine Name, and one that is destined by the Revelation itself for the *japa*. Consequently, when I speak of "concentration on the Real", I am thinking of *japa*.

One must enclose oneself in the Divine Name as in a shelter during a storm. One must also invoke it as if the Name were a miraculous sword during a battle, and thus vanquish the enemies we bear within ourselves. At other times, we must rest in the Divine Name and be perfectly content with it and give ourselves up to it with profound recollectedness, as if we were in a marvellously beautiful sanctuary full of blessings. And at other times, yet, we must cling to the Divine Name as if it were the rope cast to a drowning man; we must call God so that He hears us and so that He may save us; we must be aware of our distress and of God's infinite Mercy. Another manner in which *japa* can be practised is to concentrate on the idea that *Ātmā* alone is real, that neither the world nor we ourselves are real; then it is as if we no longer existed, and the Divine Name alone shines in us as if in a great void. Finally, we must unite to the Divine Name as if we were but one substance with it; we then have no more ego, it is the Name that takes the place of our heart; it is neither our body, nor our soul which are "us", but the Name; and we are "ourselves" not in this or that thought, nor in this or that act, but uniquely in the Divine Name, which is mysteriously identical to the Named, or in the sacred invocation, which unites us mysteriously to the Invoked.

Life is precious, for it allows us to attach ourselves to *Ātmā*; that is why we must be happy to live, and full of gratitude for our human condition.

1962 · GRACE
(original letter in English)

The question of Grace is the same in Christianity and Islam as in Hinduism, since the reality and necessity of Grace lie in the very nature of things.

We need Grace insofar as we are men capable of error and sin and bound by *karma*, not insofar as we are metaphysically *Ātmā*. The *mukta* no longer needs Grace in the ordinary sense, for he is himself Grace; he is above *karma*. The greatest misfortune is to believe oneself to be a *mukta* without being so; but this error never occurs where a man has purity of intention, and is consequently protected by Grace.

To realize *Ātmā*, we need the Grace of *Īshvara*, for as existing beings we are subject to *Īshvara*. There is no realization whatsoever without Grace.

To receive it, man must submit to certain conditions resulting from his very nature. First, he must submit to Tradition, for there is no possible Grace for the man who despises and violates it. Tradition may require very much or very little of us, according to our status and our vocation, or according to circumstances. Tradition is the framework of Grace.

There are three intrinsic conditions for Grace. The first is humility; this means: consciousness of our limitation as man in general, and also consciousness of our imperfection as this man in particular, this individual, this ego. Therefore we must be very careful not to overestimate ourselves and always be suspicious of the impulses of the soul.

The second condition is generosity: this does not mean to impute to others qualities which they lack, but it does mean not to deny qualities they really have, and to interpret their actions in a positive sense as far as possible. It is impossible not to be aware of the poisonous errors in the world around us, but it is sinful and harmful to impute errors or faults to men who are not guilty of them, or to impute, even to an evil or stupid man, intentions or faults he does not have. Since humility is absence of pride, so generosity is absence of egoism and wickedness in any form. Without humility and generosity, there can be no Grace. A *yoga* performed without humility and generosity leads to hell; it may offer us the illusion of high states, but it leads us downwards.

The third condition for Grace concerns truth: it is the love of truth, the absence of passional distortion in thinking, and therefore the absence of wishful thinking. This condition is very important for higher *sādhanās*; false thinking is incompatible with intellectual understanding and metaphysical realization.

One often speaks of the grace of the Guru; this grace is a traditional form of the Grace of God.

25 April 1962 · THE RĀMA-MANTRA

Indeed, transcending the symbol or the support is not of the domain of *bhakti*. But, given your metaphysical point of departure—your knowledge of *Vedānta*—the question does not apply to you. You are not concentrating on Swāmi Rāmdās and you know full well that *Rāma* is the Absolute, whatever the sacred sounds that you pronounce may be; what I mean to say is that *Shiva* and other Names are also God; you are aware that Rāmdās is Rāmdās and that the Absolute is the Absolute, and that a word

is a word. Hence there is no effort to be made in view of an objective transcending; it is the subject, it is you yourself that must
be transcended, and you do so virtually through the *mantram*
and in it. This is why you practise *japa*.

The grace of the positive revelation of *Māyā* occurs sooner
or later on the path. Besides, it is enough to perceive the beatific homogeneity of nature surrounding us; this is already something. We must not desire more than this.

As for the visualization of the Name, one must picture to oneself the unique syllable of *Rām*, in other words situate it in the
forehead. One must not meditate on each of the other words of
the *mantram* or visualize them.

One can invoke—without visualization, but concentrating on
the sound—in the breast, which represents the heart.

I am returning the letter of the Swāmi [Rāmdās] to you with
this letter. If you write to them, would you be so kind as to
transmit to the Swāmi and to Krishna Bai my *Namaskars* and my
Salām?

29 May 1964 · THE UNITY OF THE RELIGIONS, ECUMENISM

I must draw your attention to an important aspect of universality, or unity: the divergence between religions is due not only to
the incomprehension of men, it is also in the Revelations, thus
in the Divine Will, and that is why there is a difference between
exoterism and esoterism; the diverse dogmas contradict each
other, not only in the minds of theologians, but also—and *a priori*—in the Sacred Scriptures; yet God, in giving these Scriptures,
gives at the same time the keys for understanding their underlying unity. If all men were metaphysicians and contemplatives,
a single Revelation might suffice; but since that is not the way
things are, the Absolute must reveal Itself in different ways, and
the metaphysical viewpoints from which these Revelations derive—according to different needs for logical understanding and
different spiritual temperaments—cannot but contradict one another on the plane of forms, somewhat as geometrical figures
contradict each other so long as one has not grasped their spatial and symbolic homogeneity. God could not want that all men
understand Unity, since this understanding is contrary to the

nature of man in the "Dark Age". This is why I am against ecumenism, which is an impossibility and an absurdity pure and
simple. The great evil is not that men of different religions do
not understand each other, but that too many men—due to the
influence of the modern spirit—are no longer believers. If religious divergences become particularly painful in our times, this
is uniquely because, in the face of an unbelief that has become
more and more threatening, the divisions between believers
have become all the more acute, and also all the more dangerous. It is therefore urgent that: 1. men return to faith, whatever
be their religion, provided that it is intrinsically orthodox, and
in spite of dogmatic ostracisms; 2. that those who are capable
of understanding pure metaphysics, esoterism, and the internal
unity of religions, discover these truths and draw from them the
necessary inward and outward conclusions. And that is why I
write books.

There is moreover an unintelligent universalism, that of a
Vivekānanda and other pseudo-Hindu dreamers. Better to believe intelligently in one's own religion—while believing it to be
the only true one—than to believe stupidly in the validity of the
other doctrines and traditions; stupidly, that is to say on a sentimental basis devoid of any intellectual quality. The dreamers
I have in mind, moreover, understand nothing either of metaphysics or of spiritual life, so that their universalism amounts to
nothing.

22 June 1970 · CHRISTIAN SANCTUARIES IN INDIA, THE BLESSED
VIRGIN

K.I. writes that there are many Christian sanctuaries in India
which are visited by Hindus. This is not surprising; this is an
aspect of the Hindu spirit, based on the *Bhagavad-Gītā*: "Under
whatever form you worship me, said Krishna, it is always Me
that you are worshipping." If Hindus obtain graces in such places, these are Hindu graces; it is the Hindu Heaven that grants
the prayers through a Christian or other form. The Holy Virgin
is an exception, for she herself can grant a Hindu's prayer, if she
wishes to. [...]

The Holy Virgin is not the founder of a religion, thus her case is different from that of Christ; and since she is—in Hindu parlance—a plenary and direct incarnation of Shrī Lakshmī, or of the *Shakti* as such, therefore also of Saraswatī and Pārvatī, she can radiate beyond forms; it is thus conceivable that she grants the prayers of Hindus directly, given the typical attitude of Hindus which is based on the *Bhagavad-Gītā* and other sacred Texts.

13 July 1974 · GOOD AND EVIL

That Yogaswāmi was a *jīvan-mukta* is something that I am quite willing to admit in principle, but even so he did not possess an adequate, prudent and effective gift for doctrinal expression. Moreover, the translator has too often chosen "sayings" that mean nothing outside their context, to say the least; this is the case, for instance, of sayings affirming that there is no evil in the world, and that one must not criticize any evil nor preach any good. I answer that one must discern evil while knowing that in the essential substance of things there is no evil; moreover, evil has a necessary function in the cosmic economy, but this is yet another question. In short, one can and must preach the good, including and above all the truth, while knowing that the world is what it is and that the fatality of its nature will not change; for one preaches to abolish a "given evil" and not to abolish "evil" as such. I am writing all of this to tell you what I think, and not for the sake of the translator of *Songs and Sayings* by Yogaswāmi.

I do not know what to do, because it is not my role to evaluate a given book or a specific person, unless I take the initiative to do so for reasons of which I alone am judge, as in the cases of Shrī Rāmana Maharshi and of the Jagadguru of Conjeevaram [= Kanchipuram. *Ed.*]. I could say that, in both of these cases, I had a doctrinal interest in making a statement, in keeping with my mission.

17 February 1978 · LIBERATION IN THIS LIFE

You say in your letter that "the *jīvan-mukta* is so to speak absolute", so that there could be no "gradations between a *jīvan-mukta* of the *Krita-Yuga* and another from the *Kali-Yuga*"; and you add that you cannot conceive of a being "superior", for example, to Shrī Rāmana Maharshi. My answer is that this is easily conceivable when one knows all the elements of the problem; the question is to know where the gradations are situated. For it is necessary to distinguish *a priori* between the outer man and the inner man, as Meister Eckhart might say; outer man—on pain of not existing—belongs to the realm of cosmic phenomena, whereas inner man pertains to the supernatural immanence of the Self in the soul. In concrete terms, I shall say that Rāma and Krishna, as human phenomena—or as major *Avatāras*—are incomparably greater than any *jīvan-mukta* of our times for instance; Shankarāchārya too—as a minor *Avatāra*—is incomparably greater than any of his disciples who realized *moksha*; and no one is going to make me believe that any *jīvan-mukta* is as great as Christ.

This applies to the outer man, the man who is simply human, the cosmic phenomenon. But even from the point of view of the inner man, there is inequality, and this in parallel to equality: the Self is always the Self, certainly, but the human modality always remains the human modality and determines an indefinite number of variations with respect to the encounter between the human and the Divine. Hindu dialectic, which is always elliptical with regard to the human aspect of things, hardly accounts for this diversity; it only singles out "identity", which indeed is the sole decisive element. Sufism is more explicit in this regard: it emphasizes that "identity" is the paramountcy of the Divine Presence in our centre, and that the meeting between the Divine and the human takes place through an indefinite number of modes or combinations; otherwise identity would mean that man as such would be the Divine as such, which is impossible. I have dealt with these issues in *Logic and Transcendence*, in the chapter "The Servant and Union".

There is no need at all for the *jīvan-mukta* to be a perfect man constitutionally speaking; certainly, he is perfect as to his behaviour, but not necessarily as to his physical form nor as to his animic scope or his gifts; whereas primordial man possessed constitutional perfection in all respects, which is also and *a fortiori* the case for *Avatāras*, hence for all the founders of religions, and including the Virgin Mary. Christ expressed the incommensurability between the I and the Self by saying: "Why callest thou me good? There is none good but one, that is, God." When it is said that "the Yogī is *Brahma*", one should specify: "in a certain respect"; this is not done because one wishes to offer a principial definition and not a description. The question of the *jīvan-mukta* pertains largely to what is inexpressible, for the simple reason that it is not possible to mentally grasp the nature of the Self.

3 March 1978 · HATHA-YOGA

You tell me in your letter that you have practised Hatha-Yoga; now to practise it safely and with benefit, one must have an orthodox Hindu master, and to have access to a Hindu master, one must be Hindu by birth and belong to a higher caste; moreover, one must fulfil the ritual and moral conditions that Yoga requires. This means that Hindu methods are inaccessible to a non-Hindu, which the orthodox Brahmans know, of course, but which the incompetent Hindus who seek disciples in the West do not know—or do not want to know. All the same, certain elementary yogic exercises, practised with an intention that is simply physical, and without exaggeration, may be beneficial, quasi-incidentally and without there being any guarantee; but this is without interest from the spiritual viewpoint. Generally speaking, one must abstain from all improvisation or experimentation in spirituality; one must submit to the rules *a priori*, assuming that the method to which they belong is accessible to us; which is the case in principle for Islam and Buddhism, but not for Hinduism. [...]

PS. To be able to practise a spiritual method, one must be aware, concretely and not just theoretically, of the difference between the profane and the sacred; one must therefore fulfil all sorts of conditions, not only intellectual, but also psychological and moral. And nothing can be accomplished without Heaven's blessing.

19 May 1978 · A MALEFICENT PSYCHIC INFLUENCE, AUROBINDO

"To sense an illness is not to have it any more," Lao Tzu said. In other words, the remedy against an evil is in the awareness that we have of this evil; the remedy is provided by this awareness itself.

To start with, I want to tell you two things: firstly, you have nothing to fear; and secondly, the trial you are undergoing is providential; what happened to you had to happen, and it is for your good. For you had too much self-assurance and, as a result, you did not have enough prudence; you also had too much intellectual curiosity, without having enough faith; too much critical sense without enough of a sense of proportions.

Aurobindism is a heresy, like Teilhardism or Gurdjievism, and one must avoid it like the plague. There is no need for me to go into detail about this demented and frankly vile ideology; intellectually speaking, it is one of the most inane philosophies there is; Shrī Rāmana Maharshi made fun of it when people brought it up to him.

Obviously, you were under a bad psychic influence, but, in spite of your sufferings, this must not scare you, for such an influence belongs to the contingent whereas the *Mantra* pertains to the Absolute. [methodic recommendations follow. *Ed.*]

And one must realize holy monotony, holy poverty, holy childlikeness; knowing that you are acquainted with the essential principles of metaphysics, you must remain in the little garden of the *Japa*, without any curiosity and without the slightest ambition.

You ask me in your letter if your interpretation of Aurobindism is correct; it is perfectly exact; it is an evolutionism in which man makes himself a God, practically speaking. The encounter with those forces of darkness was, I repeat, a providential experience for you; do not regret it, and tell yourself that you were bound to have this experience so that you would be forever cured of certain temptations and certain dangers in your nature. I shall think of you in my prayers.

29 April 1984 · MĀYĀ

I am including here two texts which I have just written. What we have here, all told, are two classic problems: to forget the immediate and beatific application of the alternative *Ātmā-Māyā*, and to forget the fact that spirituality—the religion "of everywhere and of all time"—can be reduced essentially to this alternative; or that it can be reduced practically to this aspect of an "alternative", since one must choose between everything and nothing.

Another point to consider is the following: when one speaks of *Māyā*, without clarification and in the context of a spiritual path, it goes without saying that this is "illusion" as such.

But there is also *Māyā* in *Ātmā* and *Ātmā* in *Māyā*, and this is something completely different. The three *gunas* can be applied here: that is to say there is a *Māyā* according to *sattva*, another according to *rajas*, and a third according to *tamas*. There is also a divine *Māyā* and a cosmic or samsaric *Māyā*; and there is a heavenly *Māyā* and another that is earthly.

6 February 1992 · NUDITY

Regarding sacred nudity, I shall say it is based on the analogical correspondence between the "outermost" and the "innermost": the body is then seen as the "exteriorized heart", and the heart for its part "absorbs" so to speak the corporeal projection; "extremes meet". It is said, in India, that nudity favours the irradiation of spiritual fluids; and also, that feminine nudity, especially, manifests Lakshmī and thereby has a beneficial effect on the ambience. In an altogether general way, nudity expresses—and "realizes" virtually—a return to the essence, the origin, the archetype, hence to the celestial state: "And this is why, naked, I dance", as Lallā Yogishwarī said.

Unknown date n° 12 · DEVOTIONAL PATH AND GNOSTIC PATH

What confers a character of either *jnāna* or *bhakti* on the invocatory method is the invoker's intention, according to whether his spiritual nature is intellective or affective. That is, the *jnānī* is not *a priori* sensitive—as the *bhakta* is—to voluntarist, moral and sentimental arguments; on the contrary, it is the metaphysical

179

truths relating to the nature of *Ātmā* and *Māyā* which constitute the *primum mobile* for the jnanic spirit. While the *jnānī* discerns intellectually between the Real and the illusory, or between their reverberations in the midst of illusion or relativity, the *bhakta*, for his part, will choose volitively and sentimentally between a good and an evil; for him, concentration on the Real will become the ascetic momentum towards the Good; and he is less inclined to take the nature of things into consideration than to let himself be guided by moral or psychological opportunity. The *bhakta per se* is essentially dogmatist, dualist and moralist.

It is important not to lose sight of the fact that if on one hand there are men who are bhaktic in nature and others who are jnanic, on the other hand there are elements of *bhakti* and *jnāna* in every man, not to mention the fact that spiritual temperaments, so to speak, are sometimes mixed, in which case the Path is a question of destiny rather than choice. Moreover, the true *jnānī* is so detached that it can happen that he takes himself *a priori* for a *bhakta* under the pressure of his milieu, and only recognizes his true nature later and by force of evidence; inversely, many who take themselves for *jnānīs* from the outset are not *jnānīs* at all, and they only believe themselves to be so as a result of their reading, abetted by their *amour propre*.

Though our Path arises from *jnāna*, it does not exclude those of bhaktic spirit, for it is in the nature of *japa-yoga* to reconcile and enhance all aptitudes and all contemplative vocations; the supreme Name is both metaphysical Truth and saving Presence. Regarding the element of *bhakti* in *jnāna*, it refers to Beauty and Beatitude; the soul of the *jnānī* lives from these realities, and he perceives them on all planes, since essentially he has the sense of the metaphysical transparency of phenomena. There is no gnosis possible without beauty of soul.

Letters to Buddhist Correspondents

20 May 1948 · INVOCATORY PATH
to Marco Pallis

First of all, I want to thank you for the initiative you took concerning the precious robe of the holy Lama of Lachhen; this gift is highly symbolic, all the more since, as you may already know, I have received similar gifts from other saints, these being from American Indians: an eagle plume blessed by Black Elk, a bow that once belonged to Fast Thunder, and incense from the prairies sent by Medicine Robe; the first two are Oglala Sioux, the last is Assiniboine. I am sure you are aware of the affinities existing between the Tibetans and North American Indians. There are surely profound reasons for our works being known to both of them.

I believe you are right in persevering in the way you have undertaken; Shaykh Abd al-Wahid [René Guénon. *Ed.*] thinks likewise. This does not prevent the inward bond that unites you to me from corresponding to a reality; there are things that go beyond forms.

Do you know whether there is to be found in Tibet a way of *Buddhānusmriti* (the Chinese *nien-fo* and the Japanese *nembutsu*), namely a way that consists solely in the invocation of the saving Name of the Buddha? If you have received my book [*De l'Unité transcendante des Religions. Ed.*], you will find references to this method in the notes on pp. 147, 148, and 168. The "original Vow of Amida" is something that Tibetan Buddhists surely know of, and it must have been mentioned at least in some book or other; but what I would like to know above all is whether there exists a *gyüd* practising the incantational method; this is the method that would suit Westerners the best. I regret that no one from our community is in Japan where this method underwent a particularly important development.

As for the refusal of the government of Lhasa, this does not surprise me at all, I must say, given all that the Tibetans have experienced; the fact that you are a Buddhist does not constitute a sufficient guarantee. Be that as it may, this refusal is something that was to be expected; in any case, it does not affect you in a serious way since the essential is the contact with the Mahāyāna Buddhist civilization, the domain of which is not limited to the town of Lhasa; what I mean to say is that what matters above all, in your case, is not the contact with one of the greatest gurus, but the contact with a traditional authority understanding what you need and qualified to give it to you.

Your long letter is precious to me, and I hope to soon receive more news from you, that is to say, from Tibet, in reality.

May Peace be with you, with Thubden Shedub, and your family and friends.

September 1956 · REINCARNATION

If Hindus and Buddhists believe in reincarnation, it is because they interpret sacred texts literally, exactly as Monotheists do who believe, by following the literal meaning of certain texts, that Heaven is "above" and Hell "below", thus beneath the earth, and so on. For a Hindu, to believe that man is reincarnated is not more wrong than for a Monotheist to believe that God dwells behind the clouds, and that the souls of the elect "ascend" to Heaven; but what is wrong is to consider these two interpretations as dogmas.

At all events, it must not be forgotten that, according to Hindu and Buddhist texts, "human birth is difficult to obtain".

February 1958 · MODERN SCIENCE
to Sohaku Ogata, abbot of Chotokuin Monastery, Kyoto (original letter in English)

Easterners often underestimate the danger that lies in modern science. This science is in fact vitiated at its very core by two main misconceptions: "evolution" and "psychology". For a traditional mind, it is not difficult to see that the idea of evolution must be false, since the origin of a spiritual form is always better than its end. Without the preceding corruption of the "latter days", Lord Maitreya cannot come.

Europe was spiritually healthy in the so-called "dark" Middle Ages; it is our present age which is dark. As to the "psychologism" of modern universities, its error consists in reducing the spiritual to the psychological, and in believing that there is nothing beyond the realm of psychology—in other words, that this very limited science can attain to all inner realities, which is absurd. This view would imply that psychology, or even psychoanalysis, could comprehend *satori* or *nirvāna*. Modern science, like modern civilization as a whole, is thoroughly "profane", having lost all sense of the sacred, reducing everything to merely individual and trivial dimensions. Everything is "humanized", hence the concept of "humanism". An example of modern "scientific" confusion is the comparison made by the psychologist C.G. Jung between Buddhist mandalas and drawings by lunatics. The notion of the "spiritual" is entirely lacking; every phenomenon is reduced to mere "natural" causes. Sacred and traditional wisdom is put on the same level as profane and individualistic "philosophy". Modern science has discovered a large number of facts, but it has forgotten or discredited those truths, without which life has no value at all.

In Europe and America, and in the modern world in general, people frequently desire spirituality without tradition, which is an entirely false attitude, since the first condition of a serious spiritual development is the restoration of a traditional mind. Westerners want to "try" everything instead of commencing on the basis of metaphysical certainty. Truth is beauty, and beauty comes only through tradition. Okakura Kakuzo and Ananda K. Coomaraswamy understood this well.

In the West, all these criticisms have been developed by René Guénon and by myself, as also by Marco Pallis and others.

I write all this to let you know our position. It may be of interest to you, coming as it does from that very Europe which gave rise to the modern deviation.

28 April 1959 · THE CRITICAL AGE, INVOCATION, SADNESS

You allude to this "critical age"—between 45 and 60 years old—of which I have sometimes spoken. It is a time when a veil seems to descend between the world and ourselves, as if everything were called into question, and as if we would have to start from the beginning again. One must then find a new *modus vivendi* with relative things as well as with the Absolute; one must, through meditation, arrive at a definitive position with regard to life and its contents; this is obvious. Above all, we must not sacrifice concentration to our uncertainties, for certitude comes from concentration, precisely. If you want to know what you must change in your existence, how you ought to simplify it, which things are appropriate to renounce—because they become too invasive—you must start by resting in the *mantram*, as if you had no worries; this is what the Hindus call *prapatti*, and the Muslims *tawakkul*; then clarity will certainly come; problems resolve themselves to the extent that we detach ourselves inwardly.

There is also the question of the will with regard to the *mantram*: how does one strengthen it or determine it? The answer is simple: through the imagination; because the will obeys the imagination, or the "subconscious" one might say; it is our spiritualized imagination, our fundamental conviction, which renders concrete for us what we must will in an absolute manner. The themes of meditation play no other role, on the volitive plane, than to allow us to genuinely will what we have to do; they provide us with the arguments, as they do on all planes, moreover. When we base ourselves uniquely on the will as such, we are incapable of willing what surpasses us; but picture a man in the face of danger or of a seduction: in both cases, it is easy for him to act, that is to say, to obey the determination which comes from the object; it is easy to love beauty and to flee death. Thus, if we have the impression that our will is weak—our will-power for concentration or the *mantram*—it is that we do not sufficiently see, do not see "concretely" enough, the necessity for the *mantram*, nor its infinite beauty, nor our misery; and this proves also that we concern ourselves with things we should not concern ourselves with, that is to say, with things that lie outside our *dharma*. At the time of death, one may regret many things, but what one will never regret is to have omitted something in order to "think of the Buddha".

What we do in the morning is very important for the whole day; it is good not to leave the morning's invocation before having gained the certitude that it has determined our whole being and therefore our whole day. The brain is a sponge which pumps the river of appearances; it is not enough to empty it of the images from which it lives, one must also satisfy its need for absorption and its habitual movements; this is what psalmodies do, the reading of sacred texts, the meditations, the invocations. One must infuse into the mind, to the extent that it is able to bear it, the consciousness of the Real and of the unreal; this consciousness will be the framework for everything else. The world is a multiplicity which disperses and divides, at least *a priori*; the celestial Word—true "manifestation of the Void" (*shūnyamūrti*)— is on the contrary a multiplicity that gathers and leads to Unity, whence the importance of ritual recitations. The celestial Word absorbs the soul and transposes it imperceptibly, through a kind of "divine ruse"—in the sense of the term *upāya*—into the serene and immutable climate of the Absolute; the fishes of the soul enter without distrust into the divine net. In this sense, psalmodies of sacred Texts are very efficacious; in a way they show us what we should think and what we should be.

To combat sadness, we do not have any other means than to fix the gaze of the intelligence and the soul on the Infinite, which contains everything that is perfect and lovable. This point of view is easily realizable, it seems to me, in a perspective such as that of the Amidists, but in principle it is present everywhere; it is up to us to discover it. It is in this sense that S.N. told me recently: "Fundamentally, we should exult". To overcome the temptation of sadness, one should use the appropriate meditations and practise the invocation with the desired intention, for one or two hours, in a sanctuary or in virgin nature, depending on the circumstances. One must sever sadness at its root and not allow it to accrue; if it arises one day, it should disappear the same day; one must endeavour, by all available means, to overcome it; I mean to overcome it by ritual recitations, the *mantram*, meditation.

8 November 1959 · A CASE OF PSEUDO-REALIZATION

As for R. R., I can only be glad that he made a good impression on you. Perhaps these long travels will have opened new horizons for him. The question to be asked, in his case, is the following: are we dealing with a general human weakness—hence something easily forgivable—or with a spiritual anomaly, hence with something that does not fall immediately under the jurisdiction of charity? The answer is that we are dealing—or were dealing—with an anomaly due to a serious spiritual illusion; one can then be charitable only *a posteriori* and on condition of really recognizing the problem. I became all the more aware of this as R. R. confided in me about his state of realization; it is this "doctrine" that explains everything, but excuses nothing. The example of the Apostles sleeping in the Garden of Gethsemane does not apply here, because the case of the Apostles was that of a normal weakness—that of humankind—and not of an anomaly due to an error. Had I been R. R.'s guru, I could have helped him right away; but not being his guru, I had to abstain. I had to abstain even for the simple reason that the person in question would contradict me the moment I spoke. This is an altogether exceptional case, which cannot be explained by normal and legitimate reasons.

R. R. should start by realizing that he has everything to learn, and that a spiritual degree manifests itself otherwise than by pretentious attitudes, to say the least. His problem is not orthodoxy, it is heterodoxy. For to believe at his age that one no longer has need of men is heterodoxy and suicide. I have pondered at length whether I should write to him or not; but having weighed the matter, I cannot; he expects nothing from me. I do not know whether you can tell him that in my opinion, or rather according to my certitude, he is gravely mistaken about his own state.

It seems to me highly unlikely that another such case could be found among Eastern visitors; if it were just a matter of human weakness, of a psychological accident that a change in ambience could account for, I would be gravely guilty of not having noticed it. But in fact, this is something different, otherwise I would not have assigned friends to write letters on this subject. One can and must have pity for a man, but not for his pernicious errors; let him free himself from them, and we will love him without reservation. Had I been a Hindu, I might have been able to do something for him. If you cannot do anything—although your more neutral position grants you some advantages—I count somewhat on K.I., to whom I wrote along these lines some time ago already. But everything depends on Heaven. I once knew cases similar to this one, among Europeans; the causes are always the same, even if the style is different.

8 November 1959 · TRANSMIGRATION

Concerning the problem of transmigration, it seems to me that one does not take sufficiently into account the fact that between incarnations there are intermediary states—either celestial or infernal—whose duration is described in sacred Texts as being very long. The Bible and the Koran speak of the resurrection of the flesh, which is indeed a "re-incarnation"; but at that moment the present earth will have ceased to exist. In any case, the facile reincarnationism of most Easterners does not conform to their own Scriptures. Obviously there are widely diverse theories and symbolisms to be considered here, which indicates just how complex the problem is; perhaps it cannot be expressed in human language, since this language is terrestrial, at least in a certain way. In this sense, it is easier to speak of metaphysics than of cosmology; from a certain point of view, the Absolute is closer to us than are the other worlds.

26 February 1963 · JŌDO-SHINSHŪ, THE REDEMPTION

The incommensurable merit of Amida—or in a more real or less unreal sense, the merciful quality of the Absolute—can have the effect of instantaneously burning off the karmic layer of ignorance separating man from Nirvana; Nirvana is not "given", it is ignorance that is "removed".

Short of this perspective, Shinshu declares the existence of a bhaktic Paradise situated in the West, something that the simple faithful interpret literally.

In *Les Sectes bouddhiques japonaises* by Steinilber-Oberlin, one can read on pp. 224 and 225: "At the end of our earthly life, we cast off the last traces of this corrupted existence and, reborn in the Land of Purity and Happiness, we obtain the Buddha's Enlightenment."

Christian gnosis is directly analogous—in a certain sense—to Shinshu, in the sense that Redemption, hence the inexhaustible merit of Christ, is a manifestation—or the manifestation—of the merciful Power of the Infinite; Redemption does not "bestow" gnosis, but it removes that which separates us from it, if we know how to place ourselves in the necessary conditions. As in Jodo-Shinshu, there is in Christianity a literal and bhaktic application and a metaphysical and jnanic application.

Shinshu, in the end, is an ontological way; what must be found—among a thousand possibilities—is the thread linking us to the Absolute; this thread appears to be infinitesimal, but it suffices, because it is what it is.

31 January 1965 · CONFRONTING MENTAL DIFFICULTIES

When experiencing mental difficulties, it is important not to forget that there are three principal ways of confronting them, according to the ternaries *Makhāfah, Mahabbah, Maʻrifah*, and *Karma, Bhakti, Jnāna*: that is to say, one always needs 1. a measure of constraint, discipline, know-how, and of action despite everything, then 2. a measure of joy—for joy lies within us, so that it suffices to extract it from our substance and project it into the *mantra*—and finally 3. a measure of consciousness of the nature of things, hence discernment, analysis, a searching for the causes; and depending on our state, preeminence must be granted to one or another of these three means. Thus: when the mind is agitated, we must ask ourselves why it is so, and be aware of the illusory character of that which agitates it, or the disproportion between the object agitating us and the infinite Essence of our nature, or between the relative and the Absolute; for agitation cannot but cease, unfailingly so, when its cause is perfectly understood, and once it is reduced to its correct proportions; in any case, whatever the causes may be, we have no choice, since we are made for Eternity. Next—or first, depending on what sequence is more effective, it matters not—we must throw ourselves with perfect carefreeness into the *mantra*; let *Samsāra* be what it will, we shall not change it, and what is essential is that the Infinite welcome us. This is the point of view of faith and of trust, of joy and also of beauty; this is connected to the beauty of the sacred Image, the language of which is direct and somehow musical; we are husks, Reality is music. In any case, one must act, and thus at all cost practise the *japa*; the whole question, I repeat, is that of knowing which of the two other supports—one intellectual and the other affective—we shall give preference to, depending on circumstances or depending on our character.

Sometimes it is useful to change ambiences, to isolate oneself somewhere in nature, to go somewhere where we do not have the temptation of either reading or writing. Too habitual an ambience—a house for example—can sometimes be crushing in some fashion; but this is an altogether versatile contingency, for there are also sanctuaries that, for their part, always take us out of space and time.

February 1971 · SPIRITUAL AWAKENING
to Jean d'Encausse

The "doctrine of Awakening" that you present briefly at the beginning of your book is correct in its principle, this is obvious, but it becomes totally false and therefore spiritually inoperative, to say the least, once it becomes "agnostic", "iconoclastic", and "anti-religious", for in that case any religious dogmatism is more real or less false than it.

For it is the religions that adequately and efficiently provide the "doctrine of Awakening" in their esoterisms. As messages of salvation, they are situated in the dream world, of course, but that does not mean they are just anything, because there are distinctions to be made here: these messages realize, inside the dream, symbolically and horizontally what "Awakening" is totally and vertically; and they thus represent an indispensable point of departure for the "Awakening". It is impossible to escape the dream without the Will of Him who dreams—*saguna Brahma*—and without the Grace of Him who, within the dream, reflects Him who dreams: this reflection is the *Avatāra*; it is only through the *Avatāra* and, therefore, through God, that we can escape the dream. Otherwise our "doctrine of the Awakening" is nothing but inoperative philosophy and spiritual suicide. "Without me ye can do nothing" and also: "He who gathereth not with me scattereth". The *Avatāra*—whether Christ or Muhammad or the Buddha—is *Shūnyamūrti*, "Manifestation of the Void", hence of "Awakening"; and to follow the Buddha, for example, is absolutely not a question of imitating the model as he appears in books; it is to enter the Buddhist *Sangha* in one of its traditional forms, it is thus the "Triple Refuge" and integration either in the Theravada, or on the Mahayanic side in the Shinshu or Zen, by accepting all the liturgical consequences that this implies. An "Awakening" without the *Avatāra*, hence without religion, will turn into Satanism; it is the dream itself that will play the "Awakening", and this leads nowhere.

Moreover I absolutely do not see what harm there would be in salvation, simply because it is still part of the dream—but it is at the summit of the dream!—for, all told, the dream is not an unintelligible chaos, otherwise there would be no qualitative differences and the very notion of "Awakening" would not exist. Before one can leave the dream, one must prostrate oneself before the Lord of the dream, God, and before His central reflection and His spokesperson in the dream, the Revealer, the *Avatāra*.

2 June 1974 · PLATONISM, THE ABSOLUTE

I see that P.S. persists in his anti-Platonism; were he right—and I wonder if he is aware of this—all of Sufism and all of the Vedānta would collapse along with Plato, given that the idea of relativity in principial Reality—*in divinis*, if one wishes—is essential to all metaphysics. Hence, if the Platonists are mistaken, all of the East is mistaken along with them, including Buddhism, which also has the sense of relativity to the highest degree. P.S. believes that, for the Platonists, the idea of relativity in the Absolute—or the idea of a graduated Absolute—is true because it is logical, whereas in reality the relationship is the reverse: it is logical because it is true; no Platonist has ever said anything else.

31 May 1975 · THE EASTERN MASTERS, CHRISTIAN ESOTERISM, THE BUDDHIST PATH, RĀMANA MAHARSHI

Eastern masters almost never understand the situation of the Westerners they initiate; they almost always lose sight of two factors, even though they are fundamental—because this question really never arises in the East—namely the psychological conditions and the conditions of the ambience, which are difficult to meet in an abnormal world such as ours; I could almost say: the moral and aesthetic conditions of the path. That is why the practices of Zen for instance, grafted onto the mental trivialities engendered by modern life, are in general more harmful than useful; for one must be deeply imbued with the sense of the sacred, and also with a kind of holy childlikeness, to be able to benefit from initiatic graces, or spiritual graces as such.

And this obviously concerns Christians also, who in general live on the margin and not within their religion; to be a true Christian, one must become medieval again, psychologically and aesthetically speaking, but, quite clearly, without sacrificing any real and spiritually useful knowledge. *The Golden Legend* does not prevent us from understanding the *Bhagavad-Gītā*.

Be that as it may, here is what I would say to a Christian seeking an esoteric path, that is to say a path going beyond basic belief and also conventional mediocrity. Every religion is first of all a doctrine; now the fundamental content of this doctrine is the discernment between the Absolute and the contingent, or between the Real and the illusory; then comes the method, namely, and essentially, the so to speak continuous—or at least frequent—concentration on the Absolute or the Real. To doctrinal discernment and methodical concentration one must add, as a condition *sine qua non*, intrinsic virtue, that is to say beauty of soul; for the truth requires beauty. The Christian seeker must know that the quintessence of his religion is to be found in these elements, because this is the quintessence of all possible religion and all spirituality; the rest is *upāya*, "mythology", formal cladding. 1. Discernment (doctrine); 2. Concentration (method); 3. Virtue (moral beauty).

The question for you is that of knowing if, for God, you are Christian or Buddhist; assuming that your sense of the sacred and your intuition of spiritual forms have enabled you to assimilate the specific atmosphere of *Mahāyāna* to a sufficient degree, I shall tell you that the situation, in that case, is strictly analogous to what it is in Christianity, the central spiritual means being the *mantra*, in other words jaculatory orison, all the more as you have received the initiation referring to Amitabha Buddha, who corresponds metaphysically to Christ. And I would not advise any other path for a Western Buddhist than that of the invocation of Amitabha—be it in its Japanese form or its Tibetan form—assuming, of course, that one have in the eyes of God a valid reason for being Buddhist and embarking on a path that is so foreign to our traditional climate in the West. I suppose that this question is not entirely resolved for you.

I write few letters, for I am ailing, and this one is exceptionally long. For Buddhist questions, you could turn to my friend Marco Pallis, who was initiated in Tibet; for Christian questions, to my friend Leo Schaya, who, though not a Christian, is completely familiar with all the aspects of the problem.

If I understand correctly, it can happen that you take "metaphysical" Communion at church; now if you are validly affiliated with Buddhism and if you practise a Buddhist method, all Christian rites are excluded. Moreover, one does not take Communion "metaphysically"; one concentrates on God, the Absolute, the Real, or on the radiation of His Mercy, and one lets God do as He will. What you are doing, according to your letter, is doubly dangerous, first because it is a heterogeneous mixture of sacred forms and then because we have no right to impose a doctrinal program on Grace; Grace acts as it wills. Tibetans, not knowing Western religions, confuse them with secondary cults and are not competent in these matters. And you most certainly have not "passed beyond infidelity and religion"!

Rāmana Maharshi, being Hindu, could not give any advice to non-Hindus, and being a kind of *Pratyeka-Buddha*, he could not have disciples in the strict sense of the term. It is not possible, under any circumstance, to "go beyond doctrines"; moreover the Maharshi knew Vedantic doctrine very well. Having been born with a lofty spiritual degree—which is exceptionally rare—the Maharshi was a kind of incarnation of the Vedānta; but he knew only how to speak "for himself", so that not all of his utterances can be taken literally; his different kinds of "advice" do not lend themselves, in most cases, to concrete applications.

I suppose that you have read my book *Logic and Transcendence* and that you will read *Form and Substance in the Religions*; this work will be published very shortly. You will find in these two books all that one needs to know in metaphysics. Regarding jaculatory orison, perhaps you have read the *Russian Pilgrim* [*The Way of a Pilgrim*, anonymous work. *Ed.*], which deals with the "Prayer of Jesus".

9 June 1982 · FRITHJOF SCHUON'S CHILDHOOD

I have loved museums ever since my childhood, and I was able to spend hours visually assimilating the messages of various traditional worlds. In my case, visual assimilation came before conceptual assimilation; and I do not have just sacred art in mind, but also crafts, including the humblest, because they can sometimes transmit as much spirituality as sacred art proper. Man is "made in the image of God": I have therefore always been interested in man, races, castes, astrological types and others, and in types of dress, and different kinds of art; and in religions and the different kinds of wisdom, obviously, but this derives from the divine order as well as from the human; knowledge of Heaven does not *a priori* depend on knowledge of the earth, it is rather the reverse that takes place. I became interested in man, but not at first; there is a universal phenomenology of which man is but the centre yet not necessarily the key.

One of the part-human, part-divine phenomena that has fascinated me the most ever since my childhood is the *mudrā*; the one in which the hand is vertical, the thumb holding the middle finger so that they form a circle, the ring finger being half inclined, the other two fingers remaining nearly vertical; a *mudrā*-synthesis which seems to present a pearl, a jewel, a *cintāmani*, an elixir; a *mudrā* that teaches and communicates, not through a word, obviously, but through a divine or nirvanic gesture, precisely. A gesture that seems to extract—or to have extracted—what is the most precious, the most directly salvific, from a complex Message; this brings to mind that other *mudrā*, the Buddha's "Sermon of the Flower".

22 December 1982 · "DOSSIER H" ON RENÉ GUÉNON

I finally consented, after some hesitation, to give a French publisher my critiques of some of the Guénonian theses, notably those regarding the question of the Christian sacraments; you no doubt recall those more or less secret articles. The publisher is going to publish them at the end of a volume on Guénon. I thought that the time had come to make known to the public some of my divergences with Guénon. Likewise, the review *L'Herne*, which is dedicating a special issue to Guénonism, will publish a long letter by me on this subject, which I had originally sent to Professor L., the author of a book on Guénon; at the time, he humbly accepted my rectifications.

We now live in the direction of the "Western Paradise", on the continent of the American Indians; this clearly has some meaning in the sense of a return to the atmosphere of primordiality.

1 April 1985 · SHANKARĀCHĀRYA AND BUDDHISM

If Shankara's mission had been to account for traditional universality and thereby for the validity of all the forms of revelation and of spirituality, one could say that he was mistaken in passing judgment on Buddhism; however Shankara's mission was altogether intrinsic—not extrinsic as a study of the various traditional forms would have been—and there was thus no need for him to know the value of foreign traditions, and he had the right, on the altogether extrinsic plane of religious phenomena, to reject Buddhism, making use of symbolic formulations to do so; and he did this with the sole objective of protecting Hinduism as the providential ground for the mission of which he, Shankara, was the unique and incomparable instrument.

Shankarian Vedantism marked the inauguration of a millenary of intellectual and spiritual flowering; to speak of Hindu wisdom is to speak of Shankarāchārya. It was therefore a prospective work, not a retrospective one; it was an opening, not a testament. In short, on the plane of intrinsic metaphysics—not that of the "science of religions"—Shankara was one of the greatest masters that ever lived; his scope was so to speak "prophetic" or "apostolic"; he was, on his plane, as infallible as the Upanishads.

22 July 1985 · HAPPINESS

Echoes of Japan by Shastri has just been published in French; this little book is a gem. This reminds me of a large book, *Honen the Buddhist Saint*; this is a favourite with several of my friends; among spiritual books, it is what I would call a key to happiness.

This is exactly what matters in life: to know how to combine metaphysical science with an aspect of the real that makes us happy; or rather, to discover in spiritual realities a vital aspect that coincides with happiness. Now, as is proven by the notion of *Ānanda*, and by the peace-giving and beatific dimension of *Nirvāna*, it is not—strictly speaking—one aspect among others, but on the contrary a fundamental reality, to which we have the right—if I may say—owing to our own nature; or to our own essence, which coincides with That which is.

8 July 1989 · DEATH

One certainly does not have the right to complain about living on this earth, but when one learns that a friend has left this station of *Samsāra*, one cannot help feeling happiness for him; this is what I feel when I think of Thubten Tendzin [Marco Pallis. *Ed.*]. *Gate gate pāragate pārasamgate bodhi svāhā!* [*Mantra* of the *Prajñāpāramitā*: "(O thou who hast) Gone, gone; gone beyond; wholly gone. Oh blessed Enlightenment.", *The Heart Sūtra. Ed.*]

Unknown date nº 13 · HAPPINESS, THE EGO

Expressed in quintessential terms, the purpose of spirituality is the discernment between the Real and the illusory, and union with the Real; this union encompasses the impassive happiness that S.A. seeks, but it is not this happiness which is the motive, it is union; for union guarantees happiness, while the latter does not guarantee the former. The devil could give the happiness in question—not ontologically and definitively, of course, but empirically and transitorily—whereas God alone can give union; God is not implicit in happiness, happiness is implicit in God.

Every metaphysician should know that overcoming the ego is not—and cannot be—its annihilation, contrary to a certain literalist interpretation arising from ignorance of the elliptical dialectic of the Orient; there is no common measure between Deliverance and individuality, so that the latter could not be opposed to the former. The difference between the non-liberated and the liberated man is not that the latter no longer has any individuality, which would be a contradiction in terms, since he is a man; the difference consists simply in this, that the non-liberated man is enclosed in his individuality, whereas the liberated man is detached from it; he "possesses" individuality, but "is" not it. The *Avatāras* are unquestionably people, not only on earth, but also in Heaven; this in no way excludes their Supreme Identity, since, once again, there is no common measure here; this is what the *Mahāyāna* teaches through the doctrine of the Buddhas' "simultaneous bodies": *nirmāna-kāya, sambhoga-kāya* and *Dharma-kāya*; the third of these is nirvanic or divine. If this were not so, the liberated ones could not appear in visions or dreams after their death; and Heaven deceives no one. Thus individuality subsists as a dimension—until the Apocatastasis—like a house which one can enter and exit; during earthly life, it is subject to vicissitudes, whatever the person's spiritual degree.

Unknown date n° 14 · THE SOUL IN BUDDHISM

No Buddhist can deny that "the body is only the projection or outer shell of the soul", for the simple reason that this cannot be denied on the level of empirical facts; when a man falls gravely ill or suffers from physical pain, he is usually depressed, sometimes even desperate, even if he is a Buddhist. That the Buddhist doctrine is founded upon the theory of *dharma* changes nothing in practice. The word "soul" does not matter, it is the thing that matters; and if the thing does not exist, why hope to be reborn in a "Buddha Land"? That something which fears falling into hell because of a sin, or being reborn in a bad state, or which on the contrary aspires to the function of *Bodhisattva* or to *Bodhi*, is definitely what is called the "soul" in Western languages.

Letters to Native American
Correspondents
and Letters about the Native Americans

28 September 1947 · THE HOPI INDIANS
to René Guénon

I assume S.R. [Countess of Saint-Point. *Ed.*] will have shown you my letter meant for an Indian chief and concerning my brother. Our friend Brown [Joseph E. Brown. *Ed.*] is, at this very moment, visiting the Sioux with my letter; he is also, and above all, seeking intellectual contacts, in keeping with my instructions. Moreover, our efforts in this direction have already yielded results with other Indians, the Hopis: our friend J. Murray, who is here now, wrote a long letter to the Hopi Chief Katchongva—who is particularly hostile to the civilization of the "palefaces"—in which he made a very good exposition of the traditional point of view, by citing the examples of the East, and recommending that the Indians read your books, translated into English. As it happens, an Indian answered Murray several days ago in the name of the chiefs Katchongva and Ponyawima: *"Since I have written several letters for Chief Katchongva in his dealings with the government, he now wishes me to answer your letter. I was up at Hotevilla to see him and the other Chiefs to interpret the letter for them last week. I might say now that we all enjoyed your letter and are much impressed with your straightforward thoughts. And I am sure all of us are appreciative of your great interest in the Hopis. We went over several important statements you made in your letter comparing them with our thoughts and known* [sic] *facts. I will not go into detail about what was said now but will only say that you have hit the nail right on the head. It was decided that you send the books you mentioned* [of R. Guénon. *Ed.*] *and we will upon receiving them study them carefully. Because the Hopi believes that from the rising sun his true brother will come and will settle matters here in the land of the Hopis. This is the main reason why the Hopi will not take part in the white man's war at the present time. He is waiting for his true brother. He does not want to face his true brother with bloody hands and be guilty of killing another human soul which the Great Creator has made. He also knows that sooner or later the white man will suddenly come to the end of his trail. All his material wealth, inventions, great towers and skyscrapers, his might and power will come to naught. This "forcing others" to change their long established way of life will only quicken the end of the white man's way of life here. The Hopi knows that it is not very far off now. The Chief and others will be very glad to see you in person should you ever get a chance to come to Hopiland."*

What this letter shows is that the Hopis, like all Indians who are faithful to their tradition, await the Kalki-Avatāra; and they know that the end is near. To gain their trust one simply needed to speak to them of the idea of tradition, because, being proud and aloof, they normally open up to no one and often treat Whites with barely suppressed disdain.

According to a commonly known opinion, the American Indian tradition is shamanist and nothing else; what is overlooked is that those who are indistinguishably called "medicine men" are divided into several categories, only one of which corresponds perhaps to the Siberian, Tibetan, and Mongol shamans; and also that there is a spiritual element among these Indians that is completely independent from shamanism and plays a fundamental role in the lives of these people. One should add to this that witchcraft is severely forbidden in all the tribes and is punished as a crime.

I have just had a conversation with J.M., who saw Coomaraswamy for the last time in the spring [† 9 Sept. 1947. *Ed.*]. Coomaraswamy was of the opinion that the tradition of the North American Indians is not shamanism at all, but that it is metaphysical in essence; he even added that, in the absence of a Hindu initiatic connection, it is among the American Indians that he would seek such a connection.

7 October 1947 · MODERNITY, THE RELIGIONS
to Benjamin Black Elk, son of Chief Black Elk, Oglala Sioux

Most honoured Chief,

In my first letter, which our friend Mr Brown gave to you, I spoke of the affection that my brother and I have for the Indians; I have since learned that you have read my letter and that you have explained it to your saintly father [...].

I think Mr Brown has spoken to you of me and my activity. I quickly realized the falseness of modern civilization—the white man's way—for two reasons: firstly, I saw with my eyes and my heart the beauty, grandeur and spirituality of other civilizations, and the ugliness and egoism, the enslaving materialism of the modern civilization in which I grew up; secondly, I could never believe that only one religion in the whole world was the true one and that all the others were false. As a boy, when I read the books my father gave me, telling of non-Western peoples, I could not believe that so many noble, wise men could have been abandoned by God, and that on the other hand so many bad Western white men could have received the truth; how is it possible that God, in His desire to save every human soul, could have given the saving truth to one people alone, and condemned so many other peoples who are not worse than this one to remain for centuries and forever in the darkness of death? I sensed very quickly that this must be false, and that the Sacred Truth must have several forms, exactly as light can have several colours; God—the Great Spirit—has given this indispensable truth to each race in the form adapted to its own way of thinking. Naturally, there must have been peoples who forgot this Truth, as for example the ancient Europeans to whom God sent Christianity; but He did not send Christianity to all the peoples of the world, because many of them had not lost the profound meaning of their religion. A pagan is a man who worships idols and ignores or rejects God, the Great Spirit; with regard to the Indians, they have never worshipped idols or ignored or rejected God, the Great Spirit. Therefore the Indians are not pagans, and their religion, though not understood completely by every Indian, is a true religion, and God manifests Himself in it and gives His Grace. You know this better, of course. [...]

The Great Spirit gave the indispensable Truth to each race: He gave the Indians their way of praying, as He gave the Christians and the Muslims, the Hindus and the yellow races theirs. Each ancient, true religion is a necessary form of the eternal Truth, and a gift from God, the supreme Wakan Tanka. That is why nothing in Indian belief is simply a human invention or a thing empty of meaning; each symbol or rite known and practised by the Indians finds its analogous form and explanation in the traditions of other peoples—perhaps in the most direct manner in the Hindu tradition, because it is as ancient as that of the Indians, whereas the younger traditions are in a certain sense more simplified expressions of the same eternal Truth. All the "spirits" or "gods" invoked and known by the Indians— the "Sun", the "Sky", the "Earth", the "Rock", the "Moon", the "Winged-One", the "Wind", the "Mediator", the "Four Winds" and the other cosmic Powers—are universal Principles known in each Tradition, whatever forms the symbols may take; the "Angels" of the Christian, Muslim and Jewish religions are the same celestial beings as the "Powers" or "Spirits" of the Indians; the Indian "Thunderbird" is none other than the Muslim *Jibrail* and *Israfil*, or the Hindu *Shiva*. All the Indian rites, such as the very sacred Pipe, or the Sweat Lodge, or the fast and the call to the Great Spirit in the quest for a vision or a power or an illumination, the Sun Dance or other rites—without any doubt all this has its profound, metaphysical meaning, and thereby its spiritual efficacity. Not everything has the same central importance, of course, and the fact that the Sun Dance is no longer performed according to its earlier form implies that "the sacred tree is shrivelled". Besides the ritual transmission of a spiritual influence conserved and given by the priests, there is, as the essential element of each religion, the invocation of God when it is given in the right ritual conditions by a traditional priest (a "medicine man" invested with the relevant authority) and performed in a correct fashion, pronounced in a sacred language with a perfect concentration of the mind; this invocation of God, the Great Spirit, is the very essence of every religion.

31 OCTOBER 1947 · RETURN TO TRADITION
to Chief Medicine Robe, Assiniboine (original letter in English)

Most honoured Chief,

The ways of the Great Spirit are marvellous. It was a great pleasure to me to hear that our friend Mr Brown found the way to Chief Medicine Robe and the other wise men of the noble Assiniboine people. We, who belong to a sacred community of the

East, are happy to learn that the sacred tree of the Indian religion is still alive, and that it will not wither. In our time, which is approaching the end of times, all spiritual forces of mankind must strengthen each other. Therefore it is a joy for us to see that the Indians know this, and we do not doubt that the best among the young men of your people will understand the falsity of the White Men's way, which ultimately abases men to the level of animals; the young men must understand this, just as they must understand the grandeur and beauty of the ancient Indian civilization. This Indian civilization gave human life its full meaning, whereas modern civilization kills man's soul; man is no more a free child of the Great Spirit, but a mere slave of human society, and a slave of a deadly materialism; in such a life, man no longer has time to think of God. We should realize in ourselves that which gave ancient times their grandeur, beauty and happiness.

Every good thing begins in the secret of the heart; outer works mean nothing in themselves; they must be expressions of our inner light. No human soul may encounter the Great Spirit with empty hands. The Great Spirit gave His Red Children their religion at the beginning of the world, and when He appears at the end, He will ask His Red Children what they have done with the religion He bestowed on them; and He will ask the same question of every people He has created. Of course, not all Indians will return to the sacred tree of wisdom and virtue they inherited from their fathers; but when there is a community of men in every Indian nation who pray in the manner of their fathers, and whose hearts are steadily turned towards the Great Spirit, maintaining the holy tradition in its inner and outer forms—for the outer forms are very important too—, these men will represent before their Creator the whole nation.

In our time the ignorant and the wicked govern nearly everywhere, and their loud voices smother the quiet voice of truth; but God's is the last word, just as after every night the sun returns.

October 1959 · PRESERVING THE NATIVE AMERICAN TRADITION
to Chief Last Bull, Cheyenne (original letter in English)

Most honoured Chief,

Now that we are back from our travels to America, we think of the unforgettable visit we had with you and your family at Sheridan during the All-American Indian Days. While we know that all things of this world are imperfect and fleeting, and that perfection and eternity belong only to the heavenly world of the Great Spirit, our trip among the Indians was a great pleasure for us, and also a precious spiritual experience. For it allowed us once again to see that Truth is one, and that the religion of the Indians has the same truths and the same graces which the Great Spirit has put in the other ancient religions of humanity. All these truths and graces are but so many different expressions of the one Truth.

Everywhere in the world we see a materialistic "civilization" stamping out all that is spiritual and traditional. We came to the Indians to tell them that they are not alone in the world in their struggle for tradition and true spirituality, and that their venerable religion has many features in common with the ancient traditions of Asia, in particular with those of India and Japan; that there have always been diverse civilizations in the world, and that the civilization of the North American Indians is one of them. The young Indians must not forget that they have a sacred patrimony to safeguard, and that nothing is more misguided than to admire the modern world and scorn the ancient civilization of their race. If the former Indians had faults and made mistakes, it should be said that the same thing is true for all men, and that the imperfections of the Indians in former times were, in my opinion, far fewer than those of the men of today. The former Indians had a spirituality and virtues which placed them in the top rank among peoples.

If the Great Spirit wills, we shall come to your country again, some years from now. In the meantime, we pray for you, for your family, for your people, and for your people's religion.

May the Great Spirit bless you!

9 July 1961 · THE NATIVE AMERICAN RELIGION
to Chief Thomas Yellowtail, Crow (original letter in English)

Dear Friend,

Some people may have supposed that my interest in Indians and their holy traditions is a "scientific" one, but this is absolutely not the case; in fact, I did not come to America with the intention of writing a superficial book about the Indian religion. I am interested in spiritual truth and spiritual life, not in external classifications.

Religion is basically: first, to distinguish between what belongs to the Great Spirit and what belongs to this world of shadows, that is to say: to tell the vanishing from the Everlasting, or the illusory from the Real, or the finite from the Infinite; secondly, to remember the Everlasting always and to live with it and in it, that is to say: to have the mind always fixed on the divine Sun, which no eye can see, except the eye of the heart.

Old man Little Warrior once said to my friend Joseph Brown that some of the old Sioux were pronouncing very often or almost without interruption within the heart a name of the Great Spirit, such as *Tunkashila* or *Wakantanka* or some other name in Lakota; and old man Black Elk told my friend that the deep meaning of the Sun Dance is union with the Godhead. Man must always look at the divine Sun in his heart.

I was very happy to see the holy ceremony of the Tobacco Society, and I hope that many young people among the Crow understand not only the depth and beauty of tradition, but also its absolute necessity. I think the whole Plains Indian tradition is found in the Pipe and the Sweat Lodge and the Sun Dance, and also in the spiritual retreat in the mountains. There may have been many other practices, but it seems to me that these four are the most important, and that they must be kept under all circumstances. But all this you know better than I do.

5 October 1977 · THE NATIVE AMERICAN MENTALITY
to Joseph E. Brown

The difficulties in contacts between Whites and Indians are easy to understand. First of all, the white man does not have a sense of the sacred, insofar as he is a modern man, and almost all Whites are; if he asks an Indian questions, he does so usually out of curiosity, without realizing that an Indian has no motive for answering interrogations that he considers indiscreet and pointless.

To say that a white man does not have the sense of the sacred amounts to recognizing that he is full of false ideas; he does not know, intellectually and morally, the axioms of the traditional spirit or, in other words, of spirituality itself; he does not know metaphysics, cosmology, mysticism. Metaphysically, the modernist does not know that everything is a manifestation of the Self that is at once transcendent and immanent; he knows nothing of the doctrine of *Ātmā* and *Māyā*, even if he has read some Hindu books, because in that case he believes that these are concepts holding only historical, psychological, phenomenological interest—in short, things that can be left in a drawer. Cosmologically, he does not know that the world is made of a hierarchical series of regions—beginning with the Self and going all the way to matter—and that the evolutionist error is but a "horizontal" substitute for "vertical" emanationism that, for its part, unfolds starting from archetypes and through the animic or subtle world. That being the case, modern man also knows nothing of the sacred and its laws, and nothing of the psychology deriving from it and bearing witness to it.

Question: how can one study the metaphysics, cosmology, and spirituality of a people without having any idea of what it is all about? That is the whole problem. And that is why people go round and round in circles, indefinitely, while developing, by compensation, subtle or generous considerations that miss the point. I repeat: the white man does not offer the Indian sufficient, satisfying and acceptable motivations for the questions he asks, nor does he offer the mentality that, in the eyes of the Indian, constitutes the qualification required to deserve the answers he seeks. From the point of view of any traditional discipline, one does not have the right to speak of sacred things without a sufficient reason, or outside the master-disciple relationship; or again, there are things that lose their "power" if discussed without a plausible motive.

Yet there is more: an American Indian, apart from the fact that he has no motive for answering questions whose justification he does not perceive, cannot evaluate what the white man's need for logical explanations entails; and if, in spite of this, the Indian answers, he cannot do so by means of the abstract categories of classic European dialectics. He will do so therefore in a symbolist language that the white man, in turn, cannot understand, given that the modern mind does not understand symbolism, its principles and its methods.

If an American Indian has gone to a university, there is a very good chance that he will accept the errors and mental habits of Whites without discernment and, because of this, the abstract and differentiated language available to him will be of no avail to him for explaining the Indian mysteries. In an analogous manner, there are Easterners who think with two separate brains, a traditional one and a modern one, so that their thinking is either impeccable or absurd, depending on the brain with which they are operating. [...]

PS. How does one explain to an academic that Black Elk, in his subtle form, was reabsorbed into the world of the archetypes, passing through the subtle state and stopping at the threshold of the archangelic world; that certitude about the cosmic degrees and all the more so about the Principle resides in the very substance of the Intellect, which inserts itself into the individuality while being universal and principial in essence; that human ignorance derives from the scission, at once accidental and providential, between the Intellect and the ego; that the purpose of Revelation is the actualization of immanent knowledge, hence a knowledge that is connatural with the Intellect; that the goal of spiritual methods is the abolition of the scission between the individual consciousness and the universal Consciousness; how does one explain this to academics, and how can one understand the wisdom of the Indians without knowing all of that?

3 September 1983 · NATIVE AMERICAN AND MAGHREBI ATTIRE
to William Stoddart

The existence of princely and sacerdotal attire proves that garments confer on man a personality; that they express or manifest a function which transcends or ennobles the individual. By manifesting a function, dress represents thereby the virtues corresponding to it.

American Indian dress, embroidered with archaic symbols and ornamented with fringes, expresses at once victory and serenity: victory over the soul's weaknesses—the inner "holy war"—and sacerdotal dignity, which is serene and generous; the first element is represented by the variety of embroiderings, which "proclaim" heroism or the sacred, and the second by the fringes, which "bless" the earth.

In speaking of American Indian dress, I have in mind the archetypal intention—the "idea" that it projects through its formal language into the human world—and not the level this intention adopts or is subjected to *de facto* in the consciousness of a given majority. The forms bespeaking an ethnic genius, hence those that are more or less "revealed", are always greater than the median level of those who convey it; I have in mind here the profound and spiritual intention of these forms. Be that as it may, and from an altogether elementary point of view, I would say that the Indian genius, and therefore the general costume that exteriorizes it, is at the opposite end of weakness towards oneself and moral pettiness; when one wears an Indian dress, one is ashamed to entertain petty psychological problems.

It is said "the cloak does not a monk make," but it is also said "*Kleider machen Leute*" ("clothes make the man"); the costume does not change the man *ex opere operato*, certainly, but it actualizes in a normally predisposed man—thus one who is sensitive to duties and virtues—a given awareness of the norm and a given conformity to the archetype. And it goes without saying that a man can only don a vestment to which he is entitled in one degree or another; usurpation is as debasing as vanity; and "*noblesse oblige*".

The [Indian] women's dress expresses the archetypal "idea" in feminine mode; the essence of the symbolism and the style being always the integration into Virgin Nature combined with inward strength—victory over oneself—and the liberating serenity from Heaven.

To put on a traditional and sacral garment to which one is sufficiently entitled is to array oneself in an archetype and in a virtuality of perfection.

Maghrebi attire—like other non-worldly Muslim attire—suggests resignation to the Will of God, and more profoundly the mystery of Peace, *dār as-Salām*. And this calls for another comment: if it is true that Maghrebi attire, or any other analogous Muslim attire, manifests *de facto* a religious perspective, which is exclusivist by definition, along with the specific *barakah* it comprises, it is no less true—and necessarily so—that this attire manifests at the same time attitudes and mysteries appertaining to esoterism, and that in this sense it suggests no confessional limitation. Each civilization produces, by heavenly inspiration, several paragon phenomena; the representative dress of Islam is an example of this, as are the arabesques, the *miḥrāb* and the call to prayer.

The Plains Indians' dress represents a *jalwah*—a "sallying forth" or a "radiation"—the content of which derives from the concept of the "Holy War"; that of the Muslims indicates a *khalwah*, an "interiorization" consisting of holy poverty and divine Peace. I shall note in this context that partial nudity combined with a profusion of precious stones, found among the ancient maharajas, is not gaudy luxury, it is a quasi-celestial splendour befitting their status as demigods. Altogether different is the sumptuousness, part-bigoted, part-worldly, of many a Turkish sultan, which can scarcely be admired, except for the ceremonial robes when taken separately, the inspiration for which are fundamentally Mongol. [...]

PS. A fundamental quality of the American Indians is liberality combined with contempt for wealth; the Indian is not only very hospitable, he also likes to give, and sometimes gives away almost everything that he possesses; it is even a point of honour for the chiefs. Whence the "give-away" feasts where everyone shares presents with the greatest of generosity.

Strength, which vanquishes, and detachment, which gives. In the soul: victory over oneself and gift of oneself.

25 November 1983 · ADOPTION BY THE NATIVE AMERICANS

You ask me about the significance of being "adopted" by the American Indians. These adoptions have always existed among the Indians; there have always been Whites—or possibly men of other races—who have been adopted into an Indian tribe, or into a family, which amounts to the same thing practically speaking. From the Indian's point of view, this means that they consider you henceforth as one of theirs; and this implies, for the person who is adopted, a sufficient understanding of the mentality and spirituality of the Indians. In my personal case, this has even more meaning, given my spiritual function; this indicates a certain bond with a form—late but nonetheless real—of the primordial Tradition; and it is also like a marriage with virgin nature. [...]

PS. St Francis of Assisi had the sense of virgin nature, as well as that of poverty, which brings him close to the American Indian spirit.

8 August 1984 · THE INDIANS FACED WITH THE WHITES

The reason why so many Indians—including the famous medicine-man Fools Crow, whom I met at Wounded Knee—practise both religions at the same time—or rather, add the Christian religion to their own—is that the person of Christ strikes them as an irresistible spiritual reality, and they see no reason not to integrate him into their religious life; they see no contradiction in this. I am speaking here of the Indians who practise both religions, not of those who are entirely converted to Christianity, nor of those who totally reject it.

Of course, missionaries taught the Indians that everything in the Indian religion is the work of Satan, but many Indians did not believe that; Black Elk never did. Finally, out of weariness, the missionaries finally ceased insisting too much, and nowadays they have become completely indifferent on this subject.

There are even some who participate in the Indian rites, but this is a totally different story.

What caused the ruin, during the 19th century and at the beginning of the 20th, of the Red Race and its tradition, was the abrupt alternative between the two notions of the "civilized" and the "savage", each of the terms being taken as an absolute; this made it possible to attribute all possible values to the white man while leaving nothing to the red man; so that, according to this perspective, the latter no longer had any right to exist; and this is exactly the conclusion people were seeking. The "noble red man" has been greatly mocked—and this goes on even today; yet this idea is the only one to offer a counterweight to the stupid and criminal alternative which I have just pointed out, and this proves in a certain way the rightness of the idea in question. Indeed, nobleness is a value that lies completely outside the alternative mentioned, reminding us that man is man before being "civilized" or "savage"; and consequently that any normative human category possesses the dignity of being man, complete with the possibilities of value and greatness such dignity entails.

When the difference between the "civilized" and the "savage" is reduced to normal proportions, one arrives at the complementarity—and the equilibrium—between the "urban dweller" and the "nomad", of which Ibn Khaldūn spoke with much pertinence, recognizing a positive function for each society within the economy of human possibilities. And this applies also to a situation such as that in America where, clearly, each of the ethnic groups would have had something to learn from the other; but this is something, precisely, that the Whites were absolutely unwilling to admit. On the side of the Indians, the difficulty was not due to a prejudice of principle; it was due on the one hand to their mistreatment by "civilization", and on the other to the fact that the values of this civilization were—and are—mostly compromised by the modern deviation; the Whites, overly preoccupied with "things", have forgotten what man is, though being "humanists"; but that is exactly why they have forgotten it.

Unknown date n° 15 · THE NATIVE AMERICAN CIVILIZATION
(original letter in English)

For me, the ancient Indian civilization represents a most remark-able expression of man's attitude in the presence of the Absolute, and I can see in it certain analogies with the spiritual traditions of Asia. The American Indian genius has based its spirituality and its art on virgin Nature, on Nature's metaphysical symbol-ism and its beauty; given this perspective, it is evident that there is no need for temples or a written literature. This is a legitimate point of view—or one possible aspect of eternal Truth—among others.

By contrast, I see nothing legitimate in the civilization called "modern", whose beginning coincides on the whole with the "dis-covery" of America; this was the beginning of spiritual decline in Europe, and of the rationalist and "scientific"—and therefore materialistic—period of European history. In the modern world, the only criterion of value is that of physical—or superficially psychological—welfare, whereas in traditional civilizations, the criterion of value is that of the spiritual benefit involved, even if certain things must make us suffer for the time being. It results from this that ancient peoples—the American Indians like the others—were happier, in the main, than modernized peoples, in spite of all the calamities in ancient times; this is not a criteri-on in itself, of course, but it is a fact. At least they knew that calamities are all part of this life, that man as a collectivity de-generates without them; they did not have the false and fatal idea of indefinite "progress" and total "well-being". Actually, it is this illusion which brings on the greatest possible calami-ties, such as destruction of nature, mechanization, communism, Nazism, loss of tradition and true culture, overpopulation and degeneration as fruits of "science", then atomic bombs and so on. Modern-minded people will say that modern civilization im-plies many improvements and that the old Indian ways, or all traditional ways of life, imply too many evils; but such a way of reasoning makes no sense, for what counts are the tendencies of a civilization; a culture must be considered as a whole and not judged by its parts. In other words: if we consider the old Indian world as a whole, we see that its principles and its fundamental tendencies were good, and that the good things prevailed over the bad; but if we consider the modern world as a whole, we see that its principles and fundamental tendencies are false—in spite of certain partial and superficial improvements—and that the evil consequences prevail, after all, over the good ones.

Sometimes it is said that the Indians do not want to remain Indians and that they are partly responsible for their situation; this is hypocritical and murderous nonsense, for every people in the universe, treated as the Indians have been and living in the same conditions, would act in the same contradictory manner; it is not the Indians' fault that their traditional authorities have been abolished. We cannot put a ball on a slope as if it could remain in place, and then, seeing it roll down, pretend that it does so of its own will, without having been compelled.

One thing that struck me was the astonishing number of churches and missions on the Reservations; if you come to a desert with churches, you know you are in an Indian district. Of course, every Indian is free to adopt the religion that suits him, be it European Christianity or Japanese Buddhism or something else, but this freedom should manifest itself in a more effective way: the ancient religion of the Indians should have less pressure exerted against it, and the ancient Indian culture should play the role it merits in the education of the children. Actually, the schools are there to steal the children's souls, and make it possible to say afterwards that there are no more real Indians— or that there are only colourless and standardized "Americans".

In Europe, there are tiny independent states within large ones: for example, there is the minuscule principality of Monaco in France; and the tiny republic of San Marino within Italy. Why not turn the Indian "Reservations"—enlarging them at the same time— into small states which are relatively independent? Not to do so is to be charged, practically, with the responsibility of genocide.

What was wrong with the Indians of the olden times? Not their civilization as such, but perhaps a partial misunderstanding of the deep meaning of their religion, and also the fact that they were overly concerned with seeking their own glory, and often too forgetful of the Great Mystery; this may in part be the key to their calamities. Most white men do the same in a much worse way, and their end will come in its time.

It is difficult to bear the sight of all the injustices of this world. But this earthly world will disappear anyway, and the most important thing is always spiritual life; if we cannot change the world around us, we can at least change ourselves. The essential teaching of every true religion is that this world of vanishing phenomena is unreal, like a dream, and the unseen world of the Great Spirit is real. There are many degrees in the Unseen, but I just want to point out that there is more reality in the Unseen above than on this visible earth, and that God alone is absolute Reality.

Letters to Novices

10 October 1964 · THE SPIRITUAL PATH

Your two letters have reached me, and I am happy to know that you are firmly engaged on the Path, with Heaven's help.

Be assured that I do not forget to think of you, now that you have given a sign of life. Be patient on the Path, for you have your whole life in front of you. If ever you find a wall before you, say to yourself that it is your self—and not the Self—and persevere without worrying. Strictly speaking, there are no problems in spirituality, since one certitude alone suffices: *lā ilāha illā Llāh*. If there are obstacles, remember that everything is relative, and think of this verse: "Say *Allāh*! and leave them to their vain discourse" [Koran 6:91. *Ed.*].

What is certain in life is 1. death 2. the meeting with God 3. Eternity and 4. the present moment, when, pronouncing His Name, I find myself with Him, provided I do it through Truth, with a pure intention and good concentration; the latter is a function of the intention.

30 March 1981 · AT THE BEGINNING OF THE PATH

These few lines in reply to the questions raised in your letter. First of all, man being what he is, it is normal that at the beginning of the path it is difficult to maintain oneself in perfect equilibrium; to remain in beauty and grace and not fall back from time to time into the dispersion, heaviness and pettiness of profane life. What can be done? Always begin again from the beginning; this is why there are retreats. Then: ask for Heaven's help; this is why there is prayer.

But there is some perfectionism in you leading to nothing, and it needs to be replaced by a simpler and more normal attitude. When you emerge from a spiritual practice, a prayer, an invocation, do not try to transfer its grace into professional or simply practical life; do what you have to do as logically as possible, and repeat the invocation—divine Names or Formulas—when you can. One must not rigidify in an intention of perfection that is in fact unrealistic; we must remain simple and logical in our activities, and prayer will bear its fruits in time.

Emerging from the dispersion of profane life, you must not start asking yourself who you are—this is indifferent—you must start by invoking Heaven, here and now, in the midst of the chaos if necessary. Certainly, there is a contrast between spiritual life and profane life; but this contrast must not make you suffer, for God does not ask you to resolve the enigma of it. He simply asks you to invoke; and to accomplish your duties in life in conformity with what their nature requires; that is all.

For if there is a path of invocation, it is precisely because God in His Mercy wishes there to be a saving path that is adapted to all circumstances in life.

Do not ask yourself: wherefore is life? Do not ask yourself questions, for they can be innumerable, and your salvation does not depend on the answers. On one hand, you have the metaphysical Doctrine; on the other hand, you have the spiritual Method; this is sufficient. Moreover, the friends you mentioned in your letter will be able to resolve many questions of theory or practice for you. And I believe I have answered all the fundamental questions in my books.

Unknown date n° 16 · THE RELATIONSHIP BETWEEN MASTER AND DISCIPLE

To dissimulate the pettinesses of your soul, you hide behind subtleties that have only a quantitative value and thus do not alter your true nature in any way; one can be ignorant of your subtleties without mistaking what you are. If there were only weaknesses in you, quite human and simple things, I would not hold them against you, without thereby accepting them, of course; but you mingle calculation and pretension with your sentiments, as your letters amply prove.

You say that Mr B.'s [Titus Burckhardt. *Ed.*] criticisms of you "do not hold water". Mr B. never says things that "do not hold water". Mr B. is one of the most eminent of men, by his learning as much as by his spirituality; his treatises are among the most profound that we know. He did you the honour of writing to you, though his time is precious. [...] Mr B. has never spoken of your "intentions", only of your acts, always supported by precise facts; your adroitness in misrepresenting things has everything to displease me. Mr B. also told you that psychism does not count in the face of Reality, and that suffering which is not offered consciously or voluntarily to God has no spiritual value; you set no store by this, although these truths concern you most particularly.

If you say you are weak and you want to explain yourself in order that a helping hand be extended to you, I shall first ask you why, having read amply on what esoterism is, you have pretensions to this path, instead of keeping to ordinary piety, which by the way is rigorously incumbent upon you, as upon every human being; next, I shall point out to you that your exigent attitude, which always proceeds from the axiom "I am thus; kindly take it into account", has nothing to do with spontaneous weakness, apt to inspire pity, nor with a sincere search for God; for as Mr B. wrote to you, you are only seeking yourself. [...] You can be certain that where you find what flatters your natural tendencies, you will not find God. You hate your life, instead of hating your soul; you must pass through bitterness, voluntarily. Your letters prove to me that you did not listen to me when you visited, but I hope you will listen to me now, and surmount your subtle pride, which makes you say, for example—in your letter to Mr B.—that your words are only "foam", so as to remove you from their consequences by humiliating your interlocutor, who, in this instance, is supposed to be incapable of penetrating your mysteries.

If it is true that you seek God, as you affirmed when it was a matter of gaining my trust, prove it to me by your attitude. You must begin a new life, as we have all had to do; above all you must thank God daily for the troubles of your past and present life; you must bless your destiny, which has led you towards the Truth, where you see your misery face to face; all the rest is indifferent. Then you must respect the community, and make an effort to see the value of others; the community is an important element in the spiritual life; one must adapt to others and learn from them, since it is not for the Master to say everything. In inner difficulties, one must ask others' advice, for the community as such is an inspirational support; one must be able to see the Master in the most modest disciple, and know how to humiliate, to efface, oneself before him. Finally, one must submit to the Master, in an unconditional manner. Such is the rule. Once again, do not make me regret my trust; do not make Heaven close before you.

Unknown date n° 17 · TRIALS, INJUSTICE, DESTINY

Injustice is a trial, but a trial is not an injustice. Injustices come from men, whereas trials come from God; what is injustice and therefore evil on the part of men is trial and destiny on the part of God. One has the right, and possibly the duty, to fight a given evil, but one must resign oneself to trials and accept destiny; this is to say that one must combine the two attitudes, given that every injustice that we undergo on the part of men is at the same time a trial that happens to us on the part of God.

In the horizontal or earthly dimension, one can escape evil by fighting it and conquering it; in the vertical or spiritual dimension, on the other hand, one can escape, perhaps not the trial as such, but at least its heaviness, by accepting the evil as the divine Will, while transcending it inwardly as a cosmic play, as one can spiritually transcend any other manifestation of *Māyā*. For the din of the world does not enter the divine Silence, which we bear in the depths of ourselves and in which both the world and the "I" are extinguished or reabsorbed, as accidents into the substance.

Man has the duty to resign himself to God's will, but by the same token he has the right to overcome the soul's suffering spiritually, to the degree possible for him; and this is not possible, precisely, without a prior attitude of acceptance and resignation, which alone fully releases the serenity of the intelligence and opens the soul to Heaven's aid.

Letters to His Brother

Erich Schuon, Trappist Monk at Scourmont
Abbey, near Chimay in Belgium

8 May 1942 · MORTAL SIN, HELL

The several allusions made, during our last conversation, regarding the question of Hell, have prompted me to return to the subject in writing so as to show you the reasons that incline me to accept that there is nothing paradoxical in the fact that an individual who dies in a state of mortal sin goes to Hell. The most decisive argument is the following, which I had as a matter of fact set forth in my article on predestination: an individual is damned not because of a mortal sin, nor because this mortal sin was committed in the last moment of life, but uniquely because of the fundamental tendency of his nature, a tendency of which mortal sin, and the destiny preventing this sin from being atoned for before death, are but the culminating manifestations; given that these manifestations have the character of a criterion, the religious point of view, placing itself as it does always and by definition at the standpoint of the individual, considers them as causes. In other words, an individual is not damned because he has committed a mortal sin, but because he has demonstrated through this mortal sin that he is damned; to think otherwise is to think that God is limited by time.

Some object that a temporal fact cannot lead to a perpetual outcome; but precisely, if sin is indeed a temporal fact, namely the fundamental tendency of a being, a tendency which is either in conformity or contrary to the pure Essence of Divine Reality, then this tendency is no more limited than perpetuity; if the soul is perpetual, then so too is its fundamental tendency, and sin will simply be its signature. Only that in the human state, unlike what takes place with spirits (that is to say angels and demons) and also with animals, it is difficult to determine an individual's fundamental tendency, so long as it has not been manifested by means of a touchstone of a spiritual order. Such a touchstone is always the contact the individual has with Divine Reality, by means of a spiritual reality; it is then the individual's reaction that betrays his fundamental tendency; yet even then, it is usually difficult or even impossible to determine what this tendency is as long as the person is still alive; all that can be said is that a given individual, if he dies without a repentance accepted by God, is damned [the end of this sentence is illegible. *Ed.*]. That he may die without this repentance and without grace is not certain; but that he will be damned if he dies without this repentance and without grace, this is absolutely certain.

Another objection formulated against Hell adduces Divine Goodness and human misery (namely, human irresponsibility). This is a very feeble objection hardly meriting consideration, since Divine Goodness, though unconditional in itself, is conditional in manifestation, and on the other hand, human responsibility exists, given that, metaphysically, man is necessarily free by his ontological participation in Divine Freedom; this is the fundamental character of the human species; the existence of Heaven and Hell proves this, precisely. One likes to blame Hell for its atrocious aspect and its definitive aspect; but what is forgotten is that the atrocious and the definitive are cosmic possibilities. A secondary cycle always reflects a total cycle; now earthly life is a secondary cycle, and the existence of the soul is a total cycle. There are atrocities that are definitive for an earthly life; this indicates that they can be so for a total cycle also. Imagine a child who, while playing, has an accident that results in the loss of a hand; no supplication can make an amputated hand grow back; this is therefore definitive, in spite of Divine Goodness, which goes to show that there are things whose definitive character results from their specific nature; the same applies to Hell and Paradise.

16 December 1958 · NATURAL PHENOMENA FOR THE NATIVE AMERICANS

In the context of the Indian tradition there is nothing surprising about the story of the buffalo pronouncing the name of Sitting Bull. The beings we call "guardian angels" have often been manifested through animals or other natural phenomena. "He was a buffalo" refers to a "cosmic genius", an "angel", if you will; the ultimate prototype of this is a divine aspect, what the Muslims call a "Name" of God; the animal—or the wind, or the morning star, etc.—is thus the earthly, perceptible trace of a divine reality, with a supreme angel, then a guardian angel, as intermediaries.

Indian metaphysics is based upon the geometric symbolism of three superimposed planes and four directions; there is thus a vertical ternary and a horizontal quadernary, the latter being reflected on each of the planes. Man—or the Pipe—is the mediator between earth and Heaven, and even between earth and the Great Spirit, which forms the upper plane. All the differentiated qualities of the cosmos come from the four quarters or their combinations, hence the idea of the "four winds". Like certain Asiatics, the Native Americans possess the sense of the "metaphysical transparency" of things in the highest degree.

7 July 1969 · THE VIRTUES, PRAYER

Thank you for your wishes for my birthday. I take this occasion to formulate mine for yours without remembering exactly when it takes place; this may seem surprising, but I have never been able to remember the birthdays of people in my family. Thank you also for your interesting letter. What always surprises me, with people discussing spirituality, is that they are not aware of the essential, or lose sight of it and, in the absence of the one centre, get lost in the multiple periphery. One would like to cut them short every time with this question: "What is at stake?" Then remind them that what matters first is discernment between the world and God, the transitory and the permanent, the relative and the absolute, the illusory and the real; and then union, through quasi-permanent prayer, to what has been recognized as being absolute, hence real. All the rest is but a question of means or of cladding. Essential in this context are the extrinsic as well as the intrinsic virtues, such as patience, trust, gratitude, generosity, in short, humility and charity; I mean real humility and charity, not their childish simulacrum. For without the beauties of the soul, truth remains sterile in us and it becomes impossible for us to pray, not occasionally, but all the time, and fruitfully. What counts in prayer is the fact of praying, and praying with sincerity; apart from that, there are the sensible graces and there are the illusions; however, in the end, what makes life worth being lived, or what allows one to live with trust and without despair, is the quasi permanence of sincere prayer. There are also, as a so to speak sacramental quintessence of prayer, the divine Names, in themselves bearers of a certain salvific Presence.

In a certain sense, all of Christ's message is in these words: "The Kingdom of Heaven is within you." To pray is to remain "inside", in "holy inwardness", something that presupposes "holy silence". Quintessentially speaking, to live from prayer is to remain blessedly enclosed in the Name of God.

Thank you for all of your reflections about the liturgical chaos and more, and also for those on Judaism.

Here summer started two days ago; today it is raining again, but at least it is not so cold any more.

13 April 1974 · THE MODERN MENTALITY

What primarily killed basic intelligence in the West is existentialism and psychoanalysis, without forgetting Marxism. When someone affirms that two plus two equals four, his pulse is taken or he is asked what social milieu he comes from. Logic is replaced by relativistic psychology which moreover is false in its root, and then by a so-called sociology. One claims there is no truth, and one asserts that this is true; one says that man cannot know anything, but one considers that one is cognisant of this, hence knows it; one claims that "life" takes precedence over thought, and yet this claim is itself a thought! People are so stupid that they fail to notice these contradictions.

3 August 1977 · MGR LEFEBVRE

I have read the decisive decrees of the Council—in which Mgr Lefebvre had an important function—then all the speeches and books of this archbishop, just as I have read all the documents of Rome about him, and in a general way a pile of texts and speeches emanating from the pope, the cardinals, post-Conciliar theologians, etc., and I consider that Mgr Lefebvre is entirely right; he is simply content to be and do what he has always been and has always done (and he refuses to enter into the game of modernism, Freemasonry, Teilhardism, Marxism, Freudianism, etc., which are fashionable in the Modernist Church of "our times").[1]

What is the Church that the pope is meant to represent? It is Tradition that is 1. immutable; 2. universal 3. timeless; and the pope is identified with the Church insofar as he is identified with the immutable, universal and timeless Tradition. That a pope might not identify himself with this Tradition is an apocalyptic possibility that has always been recognized by theologians and that has no connection with *ex cathedra* infallibility. Like the majority of monks—I know this from experience—you do not seem to be informed about what is happening in the Church outside the monasteries, the Church that the simple faithful must endure. In practice, there is no Paul VI Mass, for the simple reason that the majority of the priests—but this can vary depending on the countries—make up liturgies as they please, something that is graced with the name of "liturgical creativity". Everything is called into question, theology is crumbling, and what is being taught in seminaries is above all social action, the cult of man; there is almost no doctrine any more, confession is neglected, everything is in flux, except the hatred directed against Tradition and Mgr Lefebvre.

I had no wish to bring up this subject, but in spite of myself I must provide some basic answer. In order to have an opinion on these issues, one must be a witness to what is happening in the world; one must be exactly informed about the theses of the former archbishop of Dakar; one must be in contact not only with modernists and countless semi-modernists, but also with authentic traditionalists; *audiatur et altera pars*.

21 July 1984 · THE CATHOLIC CHURCH

I am answering your letter from last month; thank you for your good wishes. It is true, we are becoming older; this was to be

---

[1] In the years that followed, some of Mgr Lefebvre's statements led the author to modify his opinion, without however ceasing to recognize that the bishop's two great merits were the maintenance of Tradition and the forming of true priests. *Ed.*

expected. Fortunately, we are in good health, and life for us has a meaning that transcends it.

You should not brood too much over the extravagances of the new liturgy, etc.; and there are several reasons for this. Firstly for the most general, as well as fundamental, reason that evil cannot not exist and that one must accept its existence as a metaphysical necessity; and God will not call us to account about things for which we are not responsible. Secondly: if we must accept "evil as such" because it is ontologically necessary, we must also accept "a given evil" because it enters into our destiny; this is what is known as "accepting the will of God". We must not make ourselves ill because we cannot change others; and in any case life does not last forever. We would like to be in Paradise, but we must resign ourselves to the fact that we are not there yet, and leave no stone unturned to arrive there; moreover, we are there already in and through prayer, to which we have access at each moment.

Certainly, the disorders in today's Church have causes, that we may know or not know; our opinions will not alter this; but we cannot avoid noticing the phenomenon. Monks readily believe that this evil is to be found only in their monastery; they are often unaware that the evil is everywhere. Be that as it may, one must not have too simplistic a notion of the "Church", a notion that Christ did not have. That the Catholic Church cannot disappear—nor the Orthodox Church, moreover—this is obvious, but there is a wide margin between "everything" and "nothing"; when confronted with the question of knowing "where the Church is", one should not answer it in too schematic a fashion, and one must not lose sight of certain elements of the Apocalypse. Final victory belongs to God, this is what is essential. Consolation can be found in reading the Psalms.

It is getting hotter and hotter here. Bloomington is on the same circle of latitude as Washington, Lisbon, Cagliari, and Smyrna; thus compared to Lausanne it is a southern city, and one notices this.

22 November 1989 · MARXISM AND RELIGION

The quasi collapse of Communism can be explained by its fundamental lack of realism, namely by the sheer excess of bureaucratic centralization and by the abolition of religion. Without religion, individuals no longer have any moral conscience. Religion is natural to man. The religious phenomenon is, by definition, supernatural; artificial religions are ineffective. In other words: the "supernatural" is "natural" for man. There are certainly religions that have degenerated by the fault of men—the paganisms in the Bible bear witness to this—but there are no religions as such without a divine origin. It is useless to "construct" a human society without religion; the construction will not succeed. And when religion is rationalized, it is destroyed. Marxism forgets that society is made for men and not conversely, and that religion enters into the very definition of the human being.

Letters to Miscellaneous
Correspondents

11 September 1945 · IRONY

I recently had to write to someone: "I will not be a party to any confidential tone"; you can see what this means: one must stay clear of any sentimentality or "sectarian" partiality and never allow oneself an attitude of facile irony because one believes one has the right to speak *pro domo*. For instance, when one is obliged to notice an error or a weakness on the part of a representative of the Church, one must do it with regret, and not with malicious delight; the ills afflicting the Church could make an atheist or a heretic cackle, but never a sage. I could say, paraphrasing what a French prince of our times has said, that "All that is traditional is ours."

21 January 1947 · CHRISTIANITY AND FREEMASONRY, EXOTERISM AND ESOTERISM, AL-HALLĀJ

I do not think there is any imminent danger of the Orthodox Churches condemning Masonry, and as for the union of the Churches, this does not seem to be realizable; efforts made in this domain have no chance of succeeding.

I am not as sure as you are that the Roman Church has exceeded its powers in excommunicating Masons for, precisely, the question of knowing whether or not Masonry is an esoterism does not apply here at all. According to the greatest Sufis, including Ibn 'Arabī, the condemnation of Al-Hallāj was legitimate, and had nothing to do with the intrinsic quality of the saint; likewise, when a movement is harmful to the Church's interests—and these interests are legitimate like those of exoterism itself—the Church will always have the right to deal ruthlessly; now there is no question that the Church could not consider legitimate an organization that, by placing all religions and with them irreligion on an equal footing, presented itself in practical terms either as a super-religion, or as a non-religion—or as a secular pseudo-religion based on a humanitarian and liberal moralism—risking thereby the engendering of a religious egalitarianism and, as a result, religious indifference, something that from the exoteric point of view is inadmissible. Guénon said somewhere that, for the exoterists, esoterism is as something that does not exist; in that case, how can we reproach them for condemning esoterism as such? Islam, in this respect, provides an instructive example: for the religious authorities, the initiatic brotherhoods are simply organizations of pious or scholarly men, who sometimes exaggerate in the expressions of their zeal; however, each time initiates have openly displayed their independence, the aforementioned authorities have cracked down; yet they did so only in the case of individuals and not against the brotherhoods which for their part, precisely, had their quasi-organic place in the exoteric system. I would say the same thing about Masons: the Church had no need to exert control over them so long as they built cathedrals and did not draw attention to themselves for anything else, save their Christian piety; moreover they were indispensable for Christianity and their numbers were proportionate to their utility; they did not constitute a movement and did not accept anyone except Christians in their ranks—this being of course the universe of the Latin Church. As for modern Masons, they do not play any intelligible role in the Christian world, and their existence does not correspond to anything; that said, they are quite numerous and constitute a real movement, based on a philosophical morality separate from Christian doctrine. Given such conditions, can one truly say that it is an "esoterism" that Rome has condemned?

The rapid spread of Freemasonry has not brought any new light in the world where it took place, and the fact that it coincides with one of the phases of Western degeneration even allows one to think that it had causes that were not at all spiritual; who would therefore affirm that this rapid diffusion is due to an upsurge of initiatic aptitudes in the epoch of people such as a Voltaire and a Rousseau? Have not some of the most harmful authors of the modern darkening of the world been Masons? Be that as it may, this unexpected diffusion of an initiatic organization in an essentially profane world, at a time in which this organization, namely Masonry, had ceased to be "operative" and had, strictly speaking, lost its reason for being—such a diffusion does not strike me as corresponding to anything very legitimate. Moreover, Guénon said somewhere that Masonry became a victim of modern tendencies and, in part, of the counter-initiation that has infiltrated some of the Lodges and succeeded in turning Masonry away from its spiritual goals; if such is the case—I am repeating my earlier question—can the Church be accused of having condemned an "esoterism"?

Turns of phrase such as these: "…Masons… cannot receive sacraments simply because they are initiates"—such formulations, I say, strike me as being inappropriate, for neither would you say: "Al-Hallāj was executed simply because he was an initiate"; neither Al-Junayd nor Ibn ʿArabī ever dreamt of speaking of "an abuse of authority", even though the matter was far graver than the condemnation of a Masonry become purely "speculative". Thus this "quality as initiates" of which you speak is not at all at stake. It seems to me that, had Masonry remained within its normal limits, and had it not become the victim of the anti-traditional spirit, the Church would never have condemned it, any more than it did in preceding centuries; but faced with such an abnormal phenomenon, from the exoteric or simply traditional point of view, as the expansion of Masonry, could exoterism have reacted any differently than it did? The following is something you ought to carefully take into account: in a civilization having a religious form, esoterism must necessarily base itself, be it only in appearance, on that form; when it does not do so, it violates the laws of such a civilization, and must bear the repercussions. The rapid expansion of Freemasonry was favoured by the religious wars, then by the philosophical century; if this expansion had had a spiritual cause, it should have had a positive meaning for the ambience in which it took place; however, in the modern world it has not been noticed anywhere that there was the slightest influence harbouring a spiritual power of an initiatic nature. I am speaking, of course, of the two centuries between the establishment of the Great Lodge of London and the works of Guénon, and not of these last years, leaving aside the fact that the Eastern influences following in the wake of these works could not constitute a "force" such as Masonry.

That being the case, it seems to me that, starting from the idea that Rome did not condemn Masonry for being an esoterism, but uniquely for being a movement dangerous for the credence of the faithful, then one can, when one wants to belong to Masonry insofar as it corresponds to an esoterism precisely, place oneself at an intemporal point of view and rightly consider that Rome's condemnation is not aimed at us; but this point of view only applies so long as one belongs to a non-federated Lodge.

In keeping with the wish formulated in your letter, I am writing to you what I think, without wishing to get involved in things that do not concern me directly.

13 January 1948 · THE ART OF TRANSLATING FRITHJOF SCHUON'S FRENCH WRITINGS

You will have the text in a few days. If you will, please translate it as literally as possible; I am sure that you will not seek to make me speak like an average Englishman, as did S. and D., by attributing short and naïve sentences to me. I am not an Englishman, and there is no reason for me to appear as such, even in a translation; what matters in a translation is to avoid mistakes in grammar and syntax while remaining as faithful as possible to the original text. I am not asking the English translators to use Gallicisms, but an English that is correct and that violates no shade of meaning of the French text. It is not enough that the ideas be true, the style too must be intelligent.

February 1970 · CHOOSING AN ESOTERIC PATH

[For a Westerner,] the only traditional forms available, practically speaking, for an esoteric affiliation are Islam, Greek Christianity, and the Shinshu branch of Japanese Buddhism (not Zen). In principle, an analogous path can also be followed in Catholicism, but the current disorders in the Church—which are unprecedented—present extremely grave problems.

At all events, whether it is Catholicism or any other traditional form, an affiliation in view of esoterism is not possible if one does not have certain precise directives at one's disposal which the representatives of the various traditions are generally unable to provide. Without these directives, there is a risk, on the one hand, of sinking into a conversion pure and simple—which has nothing to do with esoterism and the *Religio Perennis*—and, on the other, to be incapable of taking advantage of the esoteric elements.

It is impossible to join Hinduism; one must be born in it. It is all the more useless to seek a Hindu affiliation given that Hinduism offers nothing essential that cannot be found elsewhere—on the esoteric plane, that is. Moreover, there is a glut of false gurus in contemporary Hinduism and most Europeans who yield to the Hinduist temptation become incapable of intellectual discernment, imagining that "direct experience" is all that matters, whereas in such conditions it is nothing.

The choice of a tradition does not depend completely on individual initiative, and the sentiments of "affinity" are often disproportionate, pretentious and illusory. Our choice must be approved by Heaven, in other words there must be a sufficient reason for it that is valid in the eyes of God, if one may express things thus.

1 March 1971 · STRUCTURE OF THE SPIRITUAL PATH

Finally I have a moment to answer you. There is no need for you to apologize beforehand for an appearance of "banality", or a lack of education; there is no such thing for me, what alone matters is the distinction between the true and the false, the good and the bad, the noble and the vile. The only fault in your letter is that you do not always express yourself with the simplicity allowed—or required—by the subject under discussion.

Thus, already in your youth, you have asked yourself certain questions; this is a good sign for you, and now it is a matter of drawing the appropriate conclusions. But what I do not like in your style is a tone that is both familiar and ironic, and often misses the mark; say that the believers you knew seemed superficial to you, but do not say that they were "morons", and so on; for this term not only does not reflect well on the writer or show respect for the reader, but is rather ill-chosen in this case; it is verbal hyperbole. Likewise when you speak of the "imbecility of great men who massacre women and children", etc.; this is not "imbecility", it is something else; and nationalism is not just a "label". Who do you think you are? In short: if you think that you have to criticize men or attitudes, do it coldly, calmly, soberly, with dignity, without adding either irony or familiarity. This is a spiritual question, a question of principle.

You mention your readings: Rāmakrishna, the Maharshi, Swāmi Rāmdās; this is very good. But you also mention Gurdjieff, Krishnamurti; this is horrible. This has nothing to do with spirituality, either from the point of view of truth or from that of the path.

There is first of all the crucial question of traditional orthodoxy; there is nothing valid outside this orthodoxy. That is to say, metaphysical truth and the spiritual method can only be found within intrinsically orthodox traditions: Latin and Greek Christianity, Islam, Hinduism, Northern and Southern Buddhism. Hinduism is excluded for Westerners, because in order to be able to practise a Hindu method, one has to be born a Hindu, hence belong to a caste; and certain methods are accessible only to Brahmans.

It is true that metaphysical truth transcends all forms, and thus all religions by definition; but man is a form, and he cannot attain to the non-formal except from within form; otherwise religions would not exist. The religious form must be transcended within religion itself, in its esoterism. "Without me ye can do nothing", Christ said, and he knew whereof he spoke. And Muhammad said that "none shall meet Allah who hath not first met His Prophet"; now the Prophet is the sacred Form. Nothing can be done outside form, except vain philosophy and pseudo-spirituality.

The spiritual search must start with the following truths/principles. First of all, metaphysical truth is essentially the discernment between the Real and illusory: *Ātmā* and *Māyā*, *Nirvāna* and *Samsāra*, God and the world; all relative truths derive from this fundamental discernment, which is to be found in the esoterism of every intrinsically orthodox religion. Secondly, this truth requires quasi-perpetual concentration on the Real—but do not attempt this under any circumstance! In Hesychasm, this is the role of the "prayer of Jesus" or "prayer of the Heart"; it is the "remembrance of *Allāh*", the *japa-yoga*, the *nembutsu*. Thirdly, there is the practice of virtues, which is essential, for "vertical" realization requires "horizontal" perfection; and it also requires, apart from the moral virtues, the qualities of dignity and nobility. Fourthly, all of this is situated in the framework of a traditional orthodoxy, with all of its liturgical conditions; and sacred art, in the broadest sense, is part of those conditions.

This is what matters. You have read far too much and without discernment, as reflected by the philosophical and psychological reflections in your letter; you think too much, and haphazardly. You say for instance, like Kant, that we can never see things the way they are because of the limitations of our senses, and so on; you are wasting your time. I have moreover responded to this error in my book *Logic and Transcendence*; this book dismantles the whole notion of relativism.

You say that you are looking for an active path to follow, but that you are not looking for "a spiritual master who works for me", and you add: "for I alone know my tasks, my symbols, my attachments, my mechanism." This is absurd and profane; you know nothing at all. You have everything to learn, and it is up to the master to decide what you need. The great evil of Western searchers is that they always search outside orthodoxy and with false masters, so that the value of their experiences is nil.

I shall not tell you anything more specific this time; you must first answer me and ask me some questions, if such is your wish.

One more remark: we do not need to know how to imagine God; we are men and we have the right to be so; God knows this and He does not expect us to manifest ourselves in any other way towards Him than in the manner of human creatures. When we speak to God, He becomes man for us, and we do not have to ask ourselves how, although metaphysics explains this to us. But before God, it is first of all necessary to be a man, I would even say a child; otherwise we shall never find wisdom. We cannot do anything without God's help, and we must ask Him for it. It is absurd to say that by personifying God we limit Him; first of all, we have no choice and God knows this, and secondly, God Himself personifies or limits Himself. He is at once personal and impersonal.

17 January 1976 · THE RACES

As for the question of races, I start from the idea that in the cross, the two poles on the vertical axis mark a fundamental difference, an opposition if one will, whereas the poles on the horizontal axis mark a relative difference, or a complementarity; depending on the perspective, one can accept that there are four poles here, or that there are only three if one considers the horizontal axis as just one intermediary pole—or one plane—comprising two secondary modes. Applied to the races, this diagram means that either there are four races, the white, the black, the yellow and the red, or that there are three, the white, the black and the Mongol race; by analogy, I shall say that the difference between the North (white race) and the South (black race) is quasi-absolute, whereas the difference between the East (yellow race) and the West (red race) is relative, that is to say it indicates a complementarity rather than an opposition.

To all that, I have to add that the racial differentiation of humanity into three absolute races or, according to a more relative viewpoint, into four races—and not forgetting the intermediary types stemming from ancient admixtures—is the only one possible for man and that there are no others, unless one wants to consider for each race, depending on the cycle, typological modalities that are particular to each but do not break the framework of the three fundamental types.

In writing all this, I do not want either to knock down open doors or speak of things that do not directly concern the problem that you brought up in your letter. In any case, for obvious historical reasons there cannot be any traditional theory about the races; as for speculations on cosmological analogies, these are a very delicate matter, it seems to me, and it is better not to become overly fixated on one thesis or another; unless one clearly specifies the viewpoint at which one is placing oneself.

18 January 1976 · THE FOUR AGES OF MAN, LIMBO

Your classification is certainly plausible according to a certain perspective; but it is no less plausible that differences in perspective can bring about differences in the allocation of the symbols, if one may say. For example, Guénon paradoxically attributes childhood to the North and to winter, youth to the East and to spring, maturity to the South and to summer, and old age to the West and to autumn; one could just as easily attribute childhood to the East and to spring, youth to the South and to summer, maturity to the West and to autumn, and old age to the North and to winter; for childhood, like spring, is incontestably the time of blossoming forth and of joy; summer is the time of heat, love, passion, which corresponds well to youth; maturity, like autumn, is the time of the harvest, plenitude, achievement; and old age, which has always been compared to winter, is the time of detachment, contemplation, purity.

Guénon wrote to you that he doubts "that one can establish a strict correspondence with the faculties"; I suppose he has mental faculties in mind. But one can hold a different opinion and attribute reason to the North, sentiment to the South, imagination to the East, and memory to the West. For reason is cold, static, and objective, sentiment is hot, dynamic, and subjective; imagination is active and creative; memory is passive and conservative.

To return to the quaternary of ages distributed according to that of the cardinal points, I shall add that, astrologically speaking, the cycle of the signs of the zodiac begins in the spring with childhood, and ends in winter with old age. Be that as it may, the fact that each thing contains several aspects is enough to account for the divergences of perspective; there seem to be some also regarding the allocation of the elements (earth, air, fire, water) and the qualities (cold, dryness, heat, humidity).

You allude in your letter to the silence of Hinduism and Buddhism on the resurrection. I shall say that the silence of the transmigrationists on the resurrection is answered by the silence of the resurrectionists on transmigration. But there must be, in Hinduism, at least traces of the monotheistic dogma, just as conversely the monotheistic doctrines must contain traces of the Hindu and Buddhist dogma, in the notion of "limbo" for instance; "limbo", not being either Heaven or Hell, evokes transmigration implicitly. The concrete difference between eschatologies is moreover one of the greatest of mysteries—I mean the differences one finds between posthumous states depending on the traditional systems. [...]

Having returned home after a stay in an alpine hamlet, I find on my desk your kind message for the New Year, which I forgot to mention at the beginning of this letter. In turn, I send you my best wishes of health and prosperity for this new year.

The epoch we are living in is certainly not luminous, but there are compensations, and Mercy is more available than ever for those who attach themselves to the "one thing needful".

April 1976 · INTELLECTUALISM, ATTRACTION TO ESOTERISM

Intellectuality is one thing, intellectualism another; intellectuality, if it is integral and not fragmentary, requires and produces moral nobility, whereas intellectualism is no guarantee against self-complacency nor against puffing oneself up, to say the least. [...]

Esoterism attracts not only men of the elite but also mediocre people suffering from an inferiority complex for which they seek to compensate through some kind of sublimation or other; there are also psychopaths in search either of a dream space or of a shelter affording a sense of security.

3 February 1978 · INFALLIBILITY

Infallibility concerns firstly principles and secondly known facts; it cannot be extended to include facts that are insufficiently known nor *a fortiori* facts that are virtually unknown. Doctrinal infallibility entails not only intellectual discernment, but also, on the one hand, a sufficient knowledge of the facts about which this infallibility claims to be knowledgeable, and on the other hand an awareness of the limits either of experience, or of competence, or also of information; in certain instances, competence can make do with fragmentary information—"one can know the whole world without leaving one's house", said Lao Tzu—whereas in other instances the information must complete or else compensate for a limitation in competence. Be that as it may, there is no such thing as an infallibility that encompasses *a priori* all the contingent orders possible; omniscience is not a human possibility. No one can be infallible with respect to phenomena that are unknown, or insufficiently known to a particular type of perspicacity; therefore it is important to know the limits of the information as well as those of our intuitive capacity; in short, it is possible to have intuition for pure principles without having any for this or that phenomenal order, that is to say without being able to apply principles spontaneously to this or to that mental phenomenon, physical or other. For example, it is legitimate to have a type of intelligence that is above all mathematical—a particularity which obviously does not hinder fundamental metaphysical intuitions—but it is not legitimate to be unaware of the unidimensional character of this predisposition and to believe that one is qualified for grasping everything at first glance, merely because one understands principles, or more precisely because one understands them conceptually or "mathematically". Certainly, "he who can do more can do less": the authentic metaphysician can grasp all the aspects and all the applications, but only in principle; for some applications he will need either special gifts—and it is obviously possible and desirable that he have them—or at least sufficient information, and the willingness, of course, to take advantage of it.

6 May 1978 · TRANSLATING POEMS

Given that I have very rigorous ideas about poetic art, I allow poems to be translated in only two ways: either the translation is rendered word for word, thus in prose but respecting the lines of the original, or else the poem is translated by strictly applying to it the rules of metrics or of prosody, in which case the translation is inevitably freer, but then it must be a work of art. A third possibility is rhythmic prose, but then it must be truly rhythmic and not merely fitful. As for my poems—if one absolutely holds to publishing a few to fill out *Sophia Perennis*—the best would be to include the German text and, facing it, the literal English version.

Our garden is now a true paradise, with its flowering trees and bushes, the grass dotted with daisies and patches of tulips and myosotis. The neighbours' garden is another paradise, without forgetting S.A.'s, which is tiny, but it is still a garden; and

245

as it is bounded by a slope, the landscape beyond, along with the lake and mountains, seem to prolong it. I can visualize your two gardens in W., which also prolong on earth aspects of the celestial Paradise.

21 April 1980 · THE MESSAGE OF RENÉ GUÉNON

But since all of this puts into question Guénon's work, then let me say this: the importance of this work lies in its informative function; in other words, Guénon has provided us with essential information on the following realities: tradition, the traditional spirit, traditional values, orthodoxy, pure intellectuality, metaphysics, esoterism; hence also, in reverse order: the anti-traditional mentality, the profane spirit, heterodoxy, rationalism, ideological sentimentalism, theology, exoterism. These realities, or notions—those which are positive—do not belong to Guénon at all, because they are, needless to say, universal—they have existed everywhere and always—though the modern world, in which we live, has mostly lost sight of them, by definition so to speak since it is because of this loss that it is the modern world and not a world like others. Now Guénon had the merit of recalling these realities or truths in the midst of a world which had forgotten them or rejects them—to recall them in a precise and quasi-exhaustive way; in short, he had the merit of formulating in a masterful way the principles upon which all spirituality and all civilization rest. The entire value of the Guénonian *opus* resides in this informative function; which amounts to saying that this value derives from the objective reality, and the crucial importance, of the information. Thus, it is a question of truths that we must accept, with or without Guénon, just as they were accepted everywhere and always outside the modern world, the originality of which is precisely that it does not accept them, and that it is alone in not accepting them.

Unknown date n° 18 · PRINCIPLES OF TRADITIONAL PSYCHOLOGY
  to Mark Perry

First question: is the person intelligent? Is he very intelligent? Moderately? Somewhat? Is his intelligence speculative (ideas)

246

or practical (realizations) or psychological and social (human contacts)?

Second question: does the person have a strong will? Abundantly, moderately or minimally so? Is his will primarily forceful or perseverant: is he primarily energetic or tenacious?

Third question: is the person virtuous? Are his virtues lofty, average or mediocre? Is he unscathed by pride or egoism?

Fourth question: is the person normal? Or is he abnormal, either by asymmetry or by disequilibrium? Asymmetry is the combination of a hypertrophy and an atrophy: it can happen that people who are very gifted in a certain respect are strangely underdeveloped in another. Disequilibrium is a psychic passivity that results in a man being subject to phases, highs and lows, and being duped by them, which does not go without a form of individualism, indeed narcissism. There is also degeneration, manifested by a character that is either infantile or senile, or both at once; it is often very secondary, but it is helpful in understanding certain anomalies, however slight. Sometimes degeneration gives rise to a certain moral idiocy, even when the person is very intelligent and gifted.

Fifth question: is the person distinguished? For he has no right to be vulgar or trivial, or blasé. The distinguished, or noble, person is one who masters himself and loves to master himself; who detests laxity; who loves integrity of form; whose sentiments, *ipso facto*, are noble, which by the way brings us back to the question of the virtues. But anyway, when one speaks of distinction, or an aristocratic bearing, one means above all a culture of formal expression.

Sixth question, but it should be the first in a certain respect: is the person spiritual? That is: is he pious rather than worldly? Does he tend toward attaching himself to God and the hereafter? Is he naturally spiritual, or—if not—does he make laudable efforts to re-educate his imagination and will? [...]

A man can also be either a natural idealist or a materialist; if he is an idealist, he is called to be spiritual, otherwise the quality of idealism is valueless; but anyway, it is a condition.

When one analyses a person, one must be careful not to elaborate on a psychological phenomenon that is common to all men, and risk attributing it to the person being analysed; every man bears within him certain tensions, certain reflexes, certain paradoxes. One must only speak of these to the extent that these phenomena bring about particular moral outcomes. In a basic analysis, it is essentially a matter of discovering whether a phenomenon, for example a character trait, is substantial or accidental; in the first case, it is an aspect of the person, whereas in the second, it is an element that is superimposed. To discern this connection is an obligation of a sense of proportions.

Unknown date n° 19 · THE SOUL
to Vintila Horia

Regarding the subject you intend to treat in your book, my perspective is of course very different from that of psychologists and other empiricists. Proceeding from the idea that the absolutely Real is essentially Being, Consciousness and Beatitude, and accepting that the Real, due to its very infinity, produces relativity and consequently a multitude of reverberations, I see in the human soul a reflection of absolute Consciousness, determined by a fabric of cosmic contingencies. Now since by definition the human soul is commensurate with the Absolute—which is its *raison d'être* and the sole explanation for its characteristic faculties—man is made for transcendence, which explains the religious phenomenon and all spiritualities.

January 1991 · SPIRITUAL LIFE

In sum, life is simple: we stand before God from birth until death; to be aware of this and draw the consequences from it is everything. The consciousness of the Sovereign Good is the greatest of consolations, it should always keep us in equilibrium. From this comes first of all the quality of resignation, the constant acceptance of God's will; this virtue is difficult to the extent that we want to force the world to be other than what it is, to be logical, for example. The complement to resignation is trust; God is good, and everything is in His hands. There is also gratitude, since every man has reasons to be grateful; we must remember the good things we enjoy, and not forget them because we lack something. Finally, one must do something in life, since man is a being who acts; and the best of actions is that which has God as its object, namely prayer.

Glossary

afrād (Arab.): see *fard*.

aham brahmāsmi (Skt): "I am Brahma (the Absolute, the Principle)".

ākhirah (Arab.): end, last; the hereafter.

'alayhi l-ṣalātu wa l-salām (Arab.): "on him be blessings and peace".

Allāhu karīm (Arab.): "God is good (beneficent, generous)".

anā l-ḥaqq (Arab.): "I am the Truth".

ānanda (Skt): beatitude.

ātmā (Skt): the Self (which is both transcendent and immanent); by extension, the Absolute, the Principle, Beyond-Being (*brahma*). ◊ *ātmā vs māyā*: the Real, the Absolute, the Principle, *vs* respectively the illusory, the relative, manifestation.

audiatur et altera pars (Lat.): "let the other side be heard as well".

avatāra (Skt): descent; divine incarnation on earth.

avidyā (Skt): unawareness, ignorance.

barakah (Arab.): blessing, spiritual influence.

barzakh (Arab.): isthmus (connecting two states, two levels).

basṭ (Arab.): dilation, spiritual state of expansion.

bhakti (Skt): devotion. ◊ *bhakti-mārga, bhakti-yoga*: way of love, of devotion. ◊ *bhakta*: devotee; one who follows the way of love, of devotion.

bodhi (Skt): awakening, enlightenment; supreme knowledge.

bodhisattva (Skt): enlightened being on the path to becoming a buddha, having vowed to save all sentient beings in advance (*mahāyāna* Buddhism).

brahma (brahman) (Skt): the Absolute, the Principle. ◊ *nirguna brahma*: unqualified *brahma* (supra-personal, intrinsic; Beyond Being). ◊ *saguna brahma*: qualified *brahma* (personal, extrinsic; Being).

brāhmana (Skt): member of the first caste (India): Brahmin, priest; the human type that is intellective, speculative, contemplative and sacerdotal, tending towards wisdom or sanctity *buddhānusmriti* (Skt): ceaseless remembrance (invocation) of Buddha.

buddhi (Skt): spirit; the Spirit or the Intellect as such, microcosmic as well as macrocosmic or universal, but always microcosmic when opposed to *mahat*—or *ātmā mahān*—as in Shankara's teachings.

chintāmani (Skt): Jewel of thought.

dār al-salām (Arab.): abode (haven) of peace.

darshana (Skt): live vision, contemplation, esp. of a saint (pronounced *darshan* in Hindi).

Deo juvante (Lat.): "with God's help".

dharma (Skt): law (universal and individual), order, norm, duty, religion, morality.

dharmakāya (Skt): the first of the three Bodies (*trikāya*) or hypostases of the Buddha: the universal or divine Body; corresp. to the Essence, to Beyond Being.

dhikr (Arab.): remembrance, mention, invocation. ◊ *dhikr al-ṣadr*: remembrance of the breast; danced invocation.

et verbum caro factum est (Lat.): "and the Word became flesh"

faqīr, pl. *fuqarā'* (Arab.): poor [in God]; one who follows a contemplative path.

faqr (Arab.): spiritual poverty.

fard, pl. *afrād* (Arab.): isolated, unique; used esp. of certain saints.

fiat lux, et lux fuit (Lat.): "Let there be light: and there was light".

filioque (Lat.): "and of the Son": an element added to the original Nicene Creed by the Latin Church—and contested by the Greeks—affirming that the Holy Spirit proceeds from the Father "and the Son" within the Trinity.

guna (Skt): quality; cosmic tendency (of which there are three: *sattva, rajas, tamas*).

guru (Skt): person who has authority; spiritual master.

gyüd (Tib.): tantra.

hadīth (Arab.): a saying or act of Muhammad, transmitted by one of his Companions. ◊ *hadīth qudsī*: hadith in which God speaks in the first person by the intermediary of the Prophet.

al-hamdu li-Llāhi wa l-shukru li-Llāh (Arab.): "praise [be] to God and gratitude to God".

haqīqah (Arab.): truth, reality.

hatha-yoga (Skt): yoga of force; a path to Union introduced by postures and techniques of breathing and concentration.

ḥuḍūr (Arab.): [divine] Presence.

īshvara (Skt): the creative Being, the personal God, the Lord.

isrāfīl (Arab.): Raphael (archangel).

jalwah (Arab.): radiation.

jamrah, pl. *jamarāt* (Arab.): pillar stoned by pilgrims in Mina, where Satan appeared to Abraham and his family three times during preparations intended for the sacrifice of Ismael.

japa (Skt): invocation. ◊ *japa-yoga*, *mantra-yoga*: invocatory path.

jibrā'īl or *jibrīl* (Arab.): Gabriel (archangel).

jinn (Arab.): subtle being, genie, spirit of the animic world.

jīvan-mukta (Skt): one who is delivered in this life.

jñāna (Skt): gnosis, knowledge. ◊ *jñāna-mārga*, *jñāna-yoga*: way of Union through knowledge. ◊ *jñānī*: one who follows a path of knowledge; one who has realized Union via the path of knowledge.

al-ka'bah (Arab.): the cube; the Kaaba, principal sanctuary of Islam, situated in the centre of the great mosque of Mecca, towards which Muslims orient their prayers.

kali-yuga (Skt): the fourth world age, age of conflicts, the dark age, corresp. to the Iron Age of the Greeks. Cf. *yuga*.

Kalki-*avatāra* (Skt): name of the last *avatāra* of Vishnu, who will appear at the end of the current human cycle, and whose advent will bring the *kali-yuga* to an end.

karma (Skt): action; sacrifice; causality; destiny; law of cause and effect (chain of actions and concordant reactions); in an individual destiny, consequences of past thoughts, words, attitudes and actions. ◊ *karma-mārga*, *karma-yoga*: path of action and good works.

khalwah (Arab.): solitude, spiritual retreat.

kshatriya (Skt): member of the second caste (India): warrior; the human type that is active, combative, noble, heroic, ready to overcome himself by action, including spiritual action.

lā ilāha illā Llāh (Arab.): see *shahādah*.

lā jamīla illā Llāh (Arab.): "[there is] no beauty save [that of] God".

līlā (Skt): divine play.

maḥabbah (Arab.): love, spiritual love.

mahāyāna (Skt): "great vehicle"; one of the two main branches of Buddhism.

Maitreya (Skt): the Gracious, the Beneficent; name of the Buddha awaited at the end of time.

makhāfah (Arab.): fear, spiritual fear.

malāmatī, pl. *malāmatiyyah* (Arab.): man of blame, a saint dissimulating his state by reprehensible acts.

mandala (Skt): circle; by extension: sphere, environment, community; book, chapter; a geometric and symbolical representation of the cosmos, or of the sacred entourage of a deity, a buddha or a bodhisattva, which can serve as a support for meditation.

mantra (Skt): sacred word; verse; hymn; a sacred formula for invocation.

maqām ilāhī (Arab.): a divine station.

ma'rifah (Arab.): gnosis.

mā shā'a Llāh (Arab.): "what God wanted [has happened]".

mauna-dīkshā (Skt): silent initiation.

māyā (Skt): universal unfolding, divine art, power of illusion; veil concealing the Divine, cause of the dualist illusion. ◊ *ātmā vs māyā*: the Real, the Absolute, the Principle *vs* respectively the illusory, the relative, manifestation.

miḥrāb (Arab.): prayer niche.

moksha (Skt): deliverance (from ignorance, from the dualist illusion); realization of identity with the Self.

mudrā (Skt): seal; symbolic posture or gesture, especially of the hands and fingers.

mukta (Skt): delivered. ◊ *jīvan-mukta*: one who is delivered in this life.

munāfiq, pl. *munāfiqūn* (Arab.): hypocrite, impostor, deceiver.

murshid (Arab.): guide, [spiritual] master.

al-nafs al-ammārah (Arab.): "the soul which commands", i.e. the passional and egoistic soul, the soul which incites to evil (correl. with *al-nafs al-lawwāmah*, "the soul which blames", i.e. the soul conscious of its imperfections; and to *al-nafs al-muṭma'innah*, "the appeased soul", i.e. the soul reintegrated into the Spirit, reposing in certitude).

nembutsu (Jap.): remembrance (invocation) of Buddha.

nirmānakāya (Skt): the third of the three Bodies (*trikāya*) or hypostases of the Buddha: the earthly or transformative Body; corresp. to the human manifestation of the Buddha.

nirvāna (Skt): extinction in uncreated Beatitude, implying an exit from *samsāra*; state of beatific emptiness.

oratio et jejunium (Lat.): prayer and fasting.

paria (Port.): from the Tamil *parayan*, tambourine player; one who is without caste, untouchable (India).

philosophia perennis (Lat.): the perennial—i.e. intemporal, essential, primordial, universal—philosophy; the science of metaphysical principles.

pontifex (Lat.): one who makes a bridge, pontiff.

prājña (Skt): wisdom, knowledge; in *mahāyāna* Buddhism, the last of the six *pāramitā* (virtues, perfections) of the *bodhisattva*.

prapatti (Skt): trusting surrender in God.

pratyeka-buddha (Skt): solitary buddha who has neither master nor disciples.

purusha (Skt): the masculine ontological pole of manifestation: determining Spirit or Essence, correl. with the feminine pole, the primordial Substance *(prakriti)*.

qabd (Arab.): contraction, spiritual state of tightening.

al-rahīm (Arab.): "He who manifests his mercy", the Merciful (divine name).

rahmah (Arab.): mercy, clemency, infinite goodness, radiating beatitude.

al-rahmān (Arab.): "He whose nature is mercy", the Clement (divine name).

rajas (Skt): one of the three *guna*: the cosmic quality of expansiveness; corresponding in man to the passional tendency, to outward activity.

religio perennis (Lat.): the perennial—i.e. intemporal, essential, primordial, universal—religion, underlying every religion; doctrinal and methodical esoterism, implying the intrinsic virtues.

sādhanā (Skt): method; set of practices on a spiritual path.

sādhu (Skt): good, virtuous, saintly; person who has renounced the world in order to devote himelf to the spiritual life, wandering through India, generally on foot.

sakīnah (Arab.): divine Presence, inner peace.

salām (Arab.): peace.

ṣalāt (Arab.): blessing; prayer, canonical prayer.

ṣalla llāhu ʿalayhi wa sallam (Arab.): "may God bless him and give him peace!"

samādhi (Skt): state of ecstatic Union.

sambhogakāya (Skt): the second of the three Bodies (*trikāya*) or hypostases of the Buddha: the Body of beatitude or celestial Body; corresp. to the divine Personification.

samsāra (Skt): the fact of flowing or passing, esp. from one state to another; world, cycle of rebirths, universal manifestation, impermanence.

samyak-sambuddha (Skt): he who has attained perfect awakening; name of the Buddha.

sanātana-dharma (Skt): perennial or primordial law; perennial religion.

sangha (Skt): assembly, community; in Buddhism: the community of the awakened ones, the saints, and by extension the community of all the monks and the faithful.

sannyāsī (Skt): ascetic, monk, generally itinerant, having formally and definitively renounced the world.

satori (Jap.): awakening, illumination.

satsanga (Skt): frequenting saints or men with a spiritual tendency.

sattva (Skt): one of the three *guna*: the ascending, luminous, pure cosmic quality; corresp. in man to the tendency towards the good, spirituality, knowledge.

shahādah (Arab.): testimony of faith ("*lā ilāha illā Llāh muḥammadun rasūlu Llāh*: there is no god but God; Muhammad is the envoy of God").

shakti (Skt): power, force; feminine personification of the energy or power of a divinity.

sharī ʿah (Arab.): sacred, revealed law.

shaykh (Arab.): old man; sage; spiritual master.

shūdra (Skt): member of the fourth caste (India): servant; the human type that is concupiscent, materialist, with no ideal other than pleasure, refusing to master and surpass himself; whose virtue will be obedience and fidelity.

shūnyamūrti (Skt): manifestation of the Void (a name of the Buddha).

sirr (Arab.): secret [of the heart], intimate mystery [where man and God are one].

sophia perennis (Lat.): perennial—i.e. intemporal, essential, primordial, universal—wisdom; knowledge of Reality, Truth.

sunnah (Arab.): custom, prophetic tradition based on the hadiths.

tamas (Skt): one of the three *guna*: the descending, tenebrous cosmic quality; corresp. in man to ignorance, inertia, downward tendency.

tanzīh (Arab.): abstraction, distance, affirmation of divine transcendence.

ṭarīqah (Arab.): path, initiatic path; Sufi brotherhood.

taṣawwuf (Arab.): Sufism.

tashbīh (Arab.): comparison, resemblance, affirmation of divine immanence in creation.

ṭawāf (Arab.): circumambulation.

tawakkul (Arab.): trust [in God], resignation, abandonment of self.

tawbah (Arab.): repentance; penitence.

tawḥīd (Arab.): affirmation of divine Unity; unification.

theravāda (Skt): "old teaching" or "doctrine of the Ancients"; the principal branch of the Buddhist school that Mahayanists call *hīnayāna*.

upāya (Skt): procedure, means, stratagem by which God seeks to capture souls.

vacare Deo (Lat.): to be empty for God.

Veda (Skt): generic name of the four oldest major collections of sacred hymns of the Brahmanic religion.

Vedānta (Skt): literally, the end of the *Veda*, the *Upanishads*; name of one of the six *darshana*—or viewpoints—of the Hindu doctrine, containing the metaphysical doctrine of non-duality (*advaita*).

vincit omnia veritas (Lat.): "the truth triumphs over everything".

wa Llāhu a'lam (Arab.): "and God knows better".

al-wujūd al-muṭlaq (Arab.): absolute Being.

yoga (Skt): yoke; union; technique or alchemy aimed at opening the human microcosm to the divine influx in view of realizing Union; the art of perfect concentration.

yogī (Skt): a person who follows a path of *yoga*; a person who has attained its goal, namely supreme Union.

yuga (Skt): name of a cosmic cycle. Every *mahā-yuga* (great cycle) is comprised of 4 *yuga* (ages): *krita-yuga* or *satya-yuga*, corresp. to the Golden Age of the Greeks; *tretā-yuga*, corresp. to the Silver Age; *dvāpara-yuga*, corresp. to the Bronze Age; *kali-yuga* (the age of conflicts, the dark age), corresp. to the Iron Age.

zāwiyah (Arab.): angle, corner; gathering place of a Sufi brotherhood.

Index of Letters

LETTERS TO CHRISTIAN CORRESPONDENTS 1

13 May 1949 · Spiritualizing suffering. 3
12 July 1950 · Spirituality 3
31 May 1955 · Christian initiation 4
31 May 1955 · The Eucharist, invocation 5
1 June 1955 · *Bhakti* and *jnāna* in Christianity 7
1956 · Certitude, invocation, faith. 8
7 February 1956 · Spiritual life, concentration, death. 9
1959 · The right attitude towards a spiritual experience 11
1960 · Evil, solitude, our life .12
1960 · Bitterness, confession, spiritual sincerity 13
2 May 1960 · In Germany. 14
7 October 1960 · The Incarnation. 14
23 April 1962 · Overcoming bad habits 16
10 January 1968 · Modern science, transubstantiation 16
9 February 1968 · Truth is not everything. 17
29 April 1968 · The spiritual path. 18
16 November 1969 · Formal religions and Perennial religion. 18
6 September 1970 · The Christian invocatory path 19
5 December 1970 · Marial graces, the spiritual master 21
4 May 1971 · The essential in the spiritual life. 21
24 August 1971 · Taoism, Chinese medicine, Christian esoterism. . . . 22
12 January 1972 · A thorny problem. 23
9 December 1972 · The sacraments, the Blessed Virgin, conversion . . 25
20 December 1972 · A disagreement 28
1973 · Invocation and sobriety 29
19 April 1973 · The resurrection of the flesh, the posthumous destiny
    of animals, hell 30
4 August 1973 · Sexuality, the fall of Adam 31
15 February 1974 · The fall of Adam, concupiscence, sexuality,
    marriage 33
21 November 1975 · The perennial philosophy, the ternary intelligence-
    will-soul, Christian esoterism. 34

23 November 1975 · Catholicism and discernment 37

January 1976 · Metaphysics, attachment to God 39

22 February 1976 · Salvation, the Crucifixion and the Blessed Virgin
according to Islam, ecumenism 39

30 April 1976 · Integralism and modernism, confessional exclusivism,
the Koran. 42

30 April 1976 · Dogma. 43

1 September 1976 · Modern Catholicism and Holy Spirit 43

8 November 1976 · Christianity and Islam 44

27 February 1978 · Entering the path 44

17 July 1978 · Invoking like the birds 44

4 September 1978 · Maladjustment to one's milieu, resolving a
problem. 45

10 September 1978 · *Habemus papam?* 46

24 January 1979 · Becoming a monk today 46

24 January 1979 · God owes nothing to those who are lukewarm . . . 47

4 May 1979 · Esoterism, the sacraments and legislation in Christianity 48

4 May 1979 · The early Church 49

4 May 1979 · The ego 49

25 February 1980 · The esoteric path 49

1 March 1980 · Esoterism and religion 50

24 November 1980 · Christ and the Blessed Virgin. 51

9 January 1981 · Marital discord. 51

July 1981 · The resurrection of the flesh, Christian sacred art. 54

3 September 1981 · The choice of a spiritual path. 54

15 October 1981 · Serenity 55

22 March 1982 · Prayer, asceticism 55

22 April 1982 · The Orthodox Church 57

2 May 1982 · Dogmatic divergences, purgatory 57

30 June 1982 · Catholicism and Protestantism 58

30 June 1982 · Apostolic succession and heavenly mandate 59

30 June 1982 · Eucharist and Communion 60

2 July 1982 · Exoterism 61

2 July 1982 · Protestantism 62

2 July 1982 · Luther 63

2 July 1982 · Christian art, civilizationism 63

2 July 1982 · Protestant piety 65

2 July 1982 · The Orthodox and Protestant Churches 66

14 August 1982 · Transubstantiation, the French Revolution, Napoleon 67

26 January 1983 · Meditation and invocation, distraction and
concentration 68
27 March 1983 · The virtues 69
27 March 1983 · Esoterism, Christianity, Islam 71
29 March 1983 · Esoterism, exoterism, Christian esoterism 72
7 September 1983 · The spiritual master 74
7 September 1983 · Absolute and relative esoterism 74
6 January 1984 · Esoterism, Jesus Christ 76
25 July 1984 · The pneumatic, the gnostic, Oriental art 77
25 July 1984 · Divine inspiration, theophany, esoterism 79
15 September 1984 · The Christian esoteric path 80
15 March 1985 · Morality and aesthetics. 82
5 August 1985 · Baptism, the fall of Adam 82
28 September 1985 · Penitential path and gnostic path, the graces,
the Curé d'Ars. 83
12 November 1985 · Overcoming passivity 84
6 December 1985 · Traditional art, prayer. 84
9 December 1985 · The ternary truth-path-virtue 85
9 December 1985 · Religious orthodoxy 86
9 December 1985 · Spiritual realization. 87
29 January 1986 · Obstinacy 87
9 May 1986 · Jaculatory prayer 87
6 September 1986 · Exteriority and interiority 88
27 October 1987 · Christian esoterism, René Guénon 89
31 March 1988 · Character. 89
Summer 1988 · The origin of the soul. 90
1995 · Contemplative life 90
Unknown date n° 1 · The true esoterist 91
Unknown date n° 2 · Faith, intellection, certitude 92
Unknown date n° 3 · Hamlet 94
Unknown date n° 4 · Warning to a disciple. 94
Unknown date n° 5 · God determines man. 96
Unknown date n° 6 · The saint and the world 96

LETTERS TO MUSLIM CORRESPONDENTS. 99

29 April 1940 · Laughter and weeping 101
1 May 1940 · Laughter, primordial man. 101
21 December 1947 · The art of writing. 102

17 January 1950 · Happiness and sanctity, the fast 103
22 October 1950 · Spiritual functions. 103
19 March 1951 · An article about René Guénon 103
6 May 1951 · A trial 104
1951 · Trials 104
4 October 1951 · Florence and Siena 105
15 March 1955 · Adam 105
26 January 1955 · The fall of Adam 106
28 January 1956 · Faith, invocation 106
28 January 1956 · Esoterized exoterism. 107
31 January 1956 · Spiritual life. 108
7 March 1956 · Love and fear on the path. 108
14 November 1956 · Early Islam. 109
5 January 1957 · Why invoke? 109
1 August 1957 · Man, the supreme Name 110
June 1958 · Old age 110
17 December 1960 · The human condition, divine Mercy. 111
31 May 1963 · Henri Corbin and Frithjof Schuon. 112
1964 · Here and now. 113
22 June 1964 · Modern science 113
12 December 1964 · The spiritual heart 113
1 June 1965 · The world and the ego, happiness. 114
7 November 1965 · Spiritual company, the spiritual man. 114
11 January 1966 · Spiritual life. 115
15 June 1967 · Being oneself. 115
26 December 1967 · Frithjof Schuon speaks of his health 116
7 January 1968 · Old age, invocation 116
February 1968 · Invocation, fear of God, happiness 116
16 October 1968 · Trust in God 117
14 April 1970 · Invocation and sincerity. 118
26 June 1970 · René Guénon's *opus* 118
9 September 1970 · Jesus and Muhammad 119
27 November 1970 · Universalism and exclusivism. 119
12 January 1971 · Poetry 120
16 June 1971 · Work 122
3 August 1971 · When faced with injustice 122
10 January 1972 · Sanctity, visions, humility 123
8 February 1972 · Muhammad 124
29 March 1972 · The quaternary Name-Heart-Invocation-Poverty . . . 124

29 March 1972 · Frithjof Schuon discusses his paintings 125

31 October 1972 · Susceptibility 125

31 October 1972 · The jinns 126

21 November 1972 · Poetry 126

10 March 1973 · Canonical prayer, the Greater pilgrimage 127

19 July 1974 · Correct attitude 128

20 November 1974 · The soul's fluctuations 128

12 December 1974 · The divine Name, faith 129

29 January 1975 · Spiritual death 130

12 March 1975 · Frithjof Schuon's written message 130

19 August 1975 · Sincerity, cynicism, hypocrisy, pride, virtue,
perfection, the spiritual man 131

14 July 1976 · Accepting postulants, reading souls 133

2 October 1976 · Detachment, faith 134

6 July 1977 · On the subject of a vision 135

28 September 1977 · The disorders of the soul 136

17 June 1978 · Gnosticism, paths of love and knowledge, exoterism's
rights 137

7 August 1979 · Intellection and revelation 137

7 August 1979 · Shankarāchārya and the Buddha 138

18 September 1979 · Esoterism and exoterism, knowledge, Islam . . . 139

17 January 1980 · The Islamic mentality 142

7 February 1980 · Ambient absurdity 143

24 December 1980 · Faith 143

3 August 1981 · Frithjof Schuon's emigration to the United States . . . 144

4 December 1981 · Evil, the Koran 144

January 1982 · Inverness 145

17 March 1982 · Old age 146

26 May 1982 · Truth and Reality 146

13 October 1982 · Protestantism 146

6 February 1984 · Old age 148

25 February 1984 · The esoteric exegesis of the Scriptures 148

16 December 1984 · Faith and invocation 148

28 March 1985 · Intelligence and objectivity of thought 149

8 November 1985 · Overcoming a trial 150

26 May 1987 · The *shahādah* 150

22 October 1987 · The two dimensions of esoterism 151

13 November 1987 · Branches of the primordial Tradition 152

Unknown date nº 7 · The Greek philosophers 152

Unknown date n° 8 · The soul, psychology. 153
Unknown date n° 9 · The ternary intelligence-will-character. 154
Unknown date n° 10 · Bitterness, injustice, destiny 154
Unknown date n° 11 · Distraction and concentration. 155

LETTERS TO HINDU CORRESPONDENTS 157

1945 · Rāmana Maharshi, initiation, the castes 159
5 May 1945 · Rāmana Maharshi, concentration. 161
1949 · The path of knowledge. 163
7 October 1954 · Swāmi Rāmdās, Hari Prasad Shastri 166
1955 · Reincarnation. 168
September 1955 · We are all one. 168
28 February 1956 · Condolences 168
18 October 1957 · In favour of tradition. 168
14 February 1960 · Important books 169
15 March 1961 · Maharishi Mahesh Yogi 169
24 April 1961 · Invocation and its modes 170
1962 · Grace 171
25 April 1962 · The *Rāma-mantra* 172
29 May 1964 · The unity of the religions, ecumenism 173
22 June 1970 · Christian sanctuaries in India, the Blessed Virgin . . . 174
13 July 1974 · Good and evil. 175
17 February 1978 · Liberation in this life 175
3 March 1978 · Hatha-yoga 177
19 May 1978 · A maleficent psychic influence, Aurobindo 178
29 April 1984 · *Māyā*. 179
6 February 1992 · Nudity 179
Unknown date n° 12 · Devotional path and gnostic path 179

LETTERS TO BUDDHIST CORRESPONDENTS 181

20 May 1948 · Invocatory path 183
September 1956 · Reincarnation 184
February 1958 · Modern science. 184
28 April 1959 · The critical age, invocation, sadness 185
8 November 1959 · A case of pseudo-realization 187
8 November 1959 · Transmigration 189
26 February 1963 · Jōdo-shinshū, the Redemption 189
31 January 1965 · Confronting mental difficulties 190

February 1971 · Spiritual awakening 191

2 June 1974 · Platonism, the Absolute. 192

31 May 1975 · The Eastern masters, Christian esoterism, the Buddhist
path, Rāmana Maharshi 192

9 June 1982 · Frithjof Schuon's childhood 195

22 December 1982 · "Dossier H" on René Guénon. 195

1 April 1985 · Shankarāchārya and Buddhism 196

22 July 1985 · Happiness 197

8 July 1989 · Death 197

Unknown date n° 13 · Happiness, the ego 197

Unknown date n° 14 · The soul in Buddhism. 198

LETTERS TO NATIVE AMERICAN CORRESPONDENTS 199

28 September 1947 · The Hopi Indians 201

7 October 1947 · Modernity, the religions 202

31 October 1947 · Return to tradition 204

October 1959 · Preserving the Native American tradition 206

9 July 1961 · The Native American religion 207

5 October 1977 · The Native American mentality 208

3 September 1983 · Native American and Maghrebi attire 210

25 November 1983 · Adoption by the Native Americans 212

8 August 1984 · The Indians faced with the Whites. 212

Unknown date n° 15 · The Native American civilization 214

LETTERS TO NOVICES 217

10 October 1964 · The spiritual path 219

30 March 1981 · At the beginning of the path. 219

Unknown date n° 16 · The relationship between Master and disciple . 220

Unknown date n° 17 · Trials, injustice, destiny 222

LETTERS TO HIS BROTHER. 223

8 May 1942 · Mortal sin, hell 225

16 December 1958 · Natural phenomena for the Native Americans. . . 226

7 July 1969 · The virtues, prayer 227

13 April 1974 · The modern mentality 228

3 August 1977 · Mgr Lefebvre 228

21 July 1984 · The Catholic church 229

22 November 1989 · Marxism and religion 231

LETTERS TO MISCELLANEOUS CORRESPONDENTS 233

11 September 1945 · Irony 235
21 January 1947 · Christianity and Freemasonry, exoterism and
   esoterism, Al-Hallāj. 235
13 January 1948 · The art of translating Frithjof Schuon's French
   writings 238
February 1970 · Choosing an esoteric path 238
1 March 1971 · Structure of the spiritual path 239
17 January 1976 · The races 242
18 January 1976 · The four ages of man, limbo 242
April 1976 · Intellectualism, attraction to esoterism 244
3 February 1978 · Infallibility 244
6 May 1978 · Translating poems. 245
21 April 1980 · The message of René Guénon. 246
Unknown date n° 18 · Principles of traditional psychology 246
Unknown date n° 19 · The soul 248
January 1991 · Spiritual life 248

Index

Abd al-Qādir, Emir, 142
Abū Bakr, caliph, 109, 124
Adam, original sin, Fall, 31, 33, 54, 82, 105, 106
aham Brahmāsmi, 159
Alī, caliph, 124, 162
Amida, Amidism, *Jōdo*, *Jōdo-Shin-shū*, 57, 110, 147, 187, 189, 193, 238
angel, 3; guardian, 226
Angelus Silesius, 4
Anglican Church, 147
animal, 19, 30, 72
Anthony of Sourozh, Mgr, 28
Apostle, 124, 162
art, Baroque, 64; Byzantine, 64; Christian, 64, 105; Far Eastern, 79; Hindu, 79; sacred, 241; traditional, 84
asceticism, 56
Ātmā, 14, 81, 153
attire, clothing, 210
Aurobindo, 178
avatāra, 70, 151, 176, 191, 198

Bādarāyana, 124
baptism, 4, 48, 55, 82
Baroque art, 64
beauty, 151
Bellarmine, Robert, 46
Berthier, R. F., 33
Bhagavad-Gītā, 169, 174
bhakti, devotion, 7, 83, 137, 179
bitterness, 13, 154
Black Elk, 209
Black Elk, Benjamin, 202
Bloomington, Indiana, 55, 144, 230
bodhi, 15
bodhisattva, 124
Boehme, Jacob, 147
Borella, Jean, 76

Bossuet, Jacques B., 37
Brown, Joseph E., 201, 202, 204, 208
Buddha, 15, 138, 191
buddhi, 14
Buddhism, 86, 181, 238, 240; Japanese, 108, 110
Burckhardt, Titus, 110, 166, 220
Byzantine art, 64

Cajetan, 46
Calvin, John, 67
Cana, Marriage at, 32
cardinal points, 70, 242, 243
caste, 142, 160
Catholic Church, 21, 37, 58, 60, 73, 86, 229, 230, 238
Catholic fundamentalism, 42
Catholic Mass, 36, 73, 229
celibacy, sacerdotal, 48
certitude, 8, 87, 92, 115
character, 89; nobility of, 70, 241
charity, 22
childbirth, 34
China, 59
Chinese medicine, 22
Chodkiewicz, Michel, 139
Christian art, 64, 105
Christian esoterism, 48, 73, 89, 189, 193
Christian initiation, 48
Christianity, 50, 107, 240
civilizationism, 64
civilization, modern, 203, 206, 208, 213, 214; traditional, 107, 113
Clement of Alexandria, 4, 137
complex, 132
concentration, 10, 18, 19, 35, 68, 161, 170
concupiscence, 33
confession, 13, 74

confirmation, Christian, 4, 48
contemplation, 90, 145
conversion, 18, 27, 50
Coomaraswamy, Ananda, 84, 185, 202
Coomaraswamy, Rama, 21
Corbin, Henry, 112
Council of Nicaea, 7
Council of Trent, 63
Council Vatican II, 65, 228
crafts, 195
crucifix, 54
Crucifixion, 40
Curé d'Ars, 4, 83
cycle, cosmic, 159
cynicism, 131

Dante, 101, 121
death, 11, 36, 168, 197; spiritual, 130
degeneration, 247; of humanity, 86
deliverance, 128, 198
destiny, 154
devil, demon, 87, 106, 197
dhikr, see invocation
Diderot, Denis, 67
dignity, 241
discernment, 35, 38, 77, 113, 170, 227, 240
disequilibrium, 247
distractions, 68, 104, 155, 190
doctrine, 35, 80, 161, 193
dogma, 43, 57

Eckhart, Meister, 4, 48, 76, 80, 137
ecumenism, 41, 174
Edenic tree, 32
ego, 49, 110, 114, 115, 155, 197
Elias, 54
Eliot, Thomas S., 121
emperor, 59
Enoch, 31, 54
esoterism, 34, 35, 49, 50, 71, 72, 74, 76, 80, 91, 107, 139, 148, 151, 237, 238, 240, 244; Christian, 48, 73, 89, 189, 193
Eucharist, Holy Communion, 4, 5,

20, 56, 60, 67, 74, 75, 194
Eve, 72
evil, 12, 143, 144, 175
evolutionism, 184, 208
exclusivism, religious, 140
existentialism, 228
exoterism, 61, 71, 76, 140

faith, 9, 56, 92, 106, 108, 129, 135, 143, 155
fard, pl. *afrād*, 152, 159, 162
Far Eastern art, 79
fasting, 103
fear of God, 108, 117
Fedeli d'Amore, 34
fiat lux, 14
filioque, 67
Florence, 105
Fools Crow, 212
Francis of Assisi, 212
freedom, human, 226
Freemasonry, 235

gaiety, 102
generosity, 172
Germany, 14
al-Ghazālī, 107
Gnosticism, 137
God, 96, 117, 241
grace, 6, 11, 15, 20, 21, 29, 82, 83, 111, 123, 135, 174
gratitude, 150, 248
Gregory Palamas, 138
Guénon, René, 4, 49, 77, 82, 89, 103, 118, 185, 195, 201, 243, 246
guna, 179
Gurdjieff, George, 240

al-Hallāj, 79, 235
Hamlet, 94
happiness, 103, 114, 149, 169, 197
Hari Prasad Shastri, 167, 168, 197
hatha-yoga, 177
heart, 113, 124
heaven, 26
Heaven, Paradise, 111
Hell, 30
Henry VIII, 147

heredity, 89, 90
heresy, 103
Hesychasm, 240
Hindu art, 79
Hinduism, 86, 138, 142, 152, 239, 240
Hōnen, 197
Horia, Vintila, 248
human being, 19, 35, 72, 110, 111
humility, 22, 123, 150, 172
hypocrisy, 131

Ibn 'Arabī, 76, 137, 139, 145
Ibn Khaldūn, 213
icon, 54
identity, supreme, 176, 198
imagination, 186
impassiveness, 45
Incarnation, 14
Indians, North American, 152, 183, 199, 226
infallibility, 244
initiation, 4, 159; Christian, 48
injustice, 122, 154, 222
inspiration, 138
integralism, Catholic, 42
intellect, 4, 7, 137, 153
intellection, 71, 93
intellectualism, 95, 244
intelligence, 149, 245, 246
intelligence-will-soul, 35, 38, 71, 72, 153, 154
intention, 68, 81
interiority-exteriority, 88, 176, 228
invocation, jaculatory prayer, prayer of the heart, *japa*, *dhikr*, 5, 9, 16, 19, 29, 44, 68, 74, 81, 88, 96, 106, 108, 109, 115, 116, 118, 124, 128, 136, 148, 155, 170, 173, 179, 186, 204, 220, 227; *see also* prayer of Jesus
irony, 235
Īshvara, 14
Islam, 38, 39, 44, 55, 60, 61, 72, 76, 86, 99, 142, 236, 238, 240
Islamic mentality, 142

Jagadguru of Kanchipuram, 68th,
169, 175
Jannat al-Dhāt, 128
Japanese Buddhism, 108
Jesus Christ, 5, 7, 14, 19, 31, 42, 49, 51, 54, 56, 79, 81, 101, 119, 124, 228, 240
jinn, 126
jīvan-mukta, 175
job, profession, 122
John of the Cross, 87
John the Apostle, 162
Judaism, 76, 166
Judgment, Last, 54, 109
Jung, Carl G., 185

khalwah, 118
knowledge, gnosis, *jñāna*, 7, 77, 83, 139, 163, 179
Kolbe, Maximilian, 40
Koran, 15, 43, 145; sura *al-Tīn*, 105, 106
Koranic exegesis, 105
Krishna, 176
Krishnabai, 167
Krishna Menon, 163
Krishnamurti, Jiddu, 240

Lakshmī, 175
Lallā Yogishwarī, 179
Lao Tzu, 136, 244
Last Bull, 206
Last Judgment, 54, 109
laughter, 101
Lefebvre, Mgr Marcel, 228
Liguori, Alphonsus, 46
limbo, 243
Lings, Martin, 119, 130
liturgical language, 6
Logos, 40, 81
Lord's Prayer (*Pater Noster*), 6
love of God, 109, 150, 164
Luther, Martin, 63

Mā Ānanda Moyī, 108
maharaja, 211
Mahārāmāyana, 169
Maharishi Mahesh Yogi, 169
malāmatī, 123

marriage, 34
Marxism, Communism, 228, 231
Mary the Blessed Virgin, 19, 22, 26, 31, 39, 40, 49, 51, 54, 72, 80, 81, 84, 85, 89, 174
Mass, Catholic, 36, 73, 229
Massignon, Louis, 40, 43
māyā, 14, 81, 116, 179
Medicine Robe, 204
meditation, 69, 169
Mercy, divine, 111
metaphysics, 39, 53, 61, 80, 91, 128, 139
method, spiritual, 3, 35, 54, 80, 193
Michelangelo, 64, 122
Michon, Jean-Louis, 144
Middle Ages 112, 184
modern civilization, 203, 206, 208, 213, 214
modern science, 16, 113, 184
monasticism, 46
monastic vows, 81
mudrā, 195
Muhammad, 119, 124, 134, 138
Muslim prayer, 127

Name, divine, 69, 73, 108, 109, 110, 129, 130, 180, 228
Napoleon, 68
Nasr, Seyyed Hossein, 112
nudity, 179

objectivity, 149
Okakura Kakuzo, 185
old age, 110, 114, 116, 146, 148, 243
Omar, caliph, 142
oratio et jejunium, 19, 29, 76
Origen, 137
Orthodox Church, 21, 54, 57, 59, 66, 238
orthodoxy 86, 240
Osborne, Arthur 159

Pallis, Marco, 183, 185, 194, 197
papacy, 46, 48, 229
Paradise, 111
pariah, 134
Pārvatī, 175

passivity, 84
peace, 145
perfection, 108
Philokalia, 6
philosophia perennis, 34
pilgrimage to Mecca, 127
Planck, Max, 53
Plato, 77, 152, 192
Plotinus, 77, 152
pneumatic, 77
poetry, 120, 126
pontifex, 88
Pope Paul VI, 47
Pope Pius XII, 41
Possibility, All-, 144
poverty, spiritual, 136
pratyeka buddha, 124
prayer, 6, 35, 55, 85, 136, 143, 249; Islamic, 127; jaculatory, *see* invocation.
prayer of Jesus, 5, 22, 36, 76, 195, 40
primordial man, 101, 132, 176
prophecy, prophet, 152
Protestant Church, 58, 60, 62, 65, 66, 67, 146
psalmody, 187
psychoanalysis, 228
psychology, 154, 184, 246
Ptolemy, 113
Purgatory, 57
Pythagoras, 77, 152

al-Qaranī, Uways, 124

races, human, 242
Rāma, 172, 176
Rāmakrishna, 108, 240
Rāmana Maharshi, 113, 124, 159, 161, 164, 175, 176, 178, 194, 240
Rāmdās, Swāmi, 108, 166, 172-73, 240
reality, 146
realization, spiritual, 21, 27, 87
Redemption, 82
reincarnation, 168, 184, 189
relativism, 241
religion, 19, 34, 39, 42, 49, 50, 72,

76, 120, 140, 173, 193, 207, 231, 240
religio perennis, 18
resignation, 18, 248
Resurrection of the Flesh, 30, 54, 189, 243
revelation, divine, 138
rite, 162, 204, 207
Rousseau, Jean-Jacques, 67

sacraments, 4, 26, 36, 48, 74, 89
sacred art, 241
sadness, 101, 187
Saint Peter's Basilica, 64
Saladin, 142
salvation, 40, 57, 87, 128, 191
samyaksam buddha, 124
sanctity, 37, 103, 123
Saraswatī, 175
Sat-Chit-Ānanda, 153
satsanga, 114
Satya-Yuga, 159
Schaya, Leo, 194
Schuon, Erich, 223
Schuon, Frithjof, 82, 112, 114, 116, 125, 130, 134, 144, 195
science, modern, 16, 113, 184
scriptures, monotheistic, 79
scriptures, sacred, 173
Self, 110, 153
sentiment, 139
serenity, 55, 145
sexuality, 31, 33
shahādah, 79, 108, 117, 150
Shakespeare, 121
shakti, 175
Shamanism, 202
Shāmil, Imām, 142
Shankarāchārya, 77, 110, 138, 164, 196
sharī 'ah, 139
Shiism, 138
Shiva, 14, 172
Shivānanda, 108
Siena, 105
Sieyès, Abbé, 67
sincerity, 118, 131, 134

sin, mortal, 225
sobriety, 29
Socrates, 152
Sohaku Ogata, 184
solitude, 12
sophia perennis, 21
soul, 90, 153, 198, 248
spirituality, spiritual life, spiritual path, 3, 5, 9, 18, 19, 21, 29, 35, 44, 49, 54, 69, 71, 84, 85, 90, 96, 103, 104, 108, 112, 115, 124, 125, 128, 130, 134, 154, 163, 170, 185, 197, 219, 238, 239, 248
spiritual master, guru, *murshid*, 21, 50, 74, 103, 160, 163, 170, 192
Srīmad Bhāgavatam, 169
Stoddart, William, 210
stubbornness, 87
subconscious, 186
suffering, 3
surpassing of oneself, 53
susceptibility, 125
symbolism, 75, 91

Tagore, Rabindranāth, 121
tanzīh, 151
tanzīl, 15
Taoism, 22
tarīqah, 133
tashbīh, 151
tawḥīd, 124
Teilhard de Chardin, 24
Tersteegen, Gerhard, 147
theology, 4, 92
Therese of the Child Jesus, 3
Thomas Aquinas, 138
Tibet, 183
today's world, end time, 43, 54, 104, 159, 170, 184, 202, 205, 244
traditional art, 84
traditional civilization, 107, 113
transcendence-immanence, 151
translation, 238, 245
transmigration, 31, 90, 189
Transubstantiation, 16, 67
travel, 191
tree, Edenic, 32

trial, 3, 104, 117, 150, 178, 190, 222
Trinity, 61
troubadour, 34
trust in God, 55, 111, 118, 248
truth, 124, 146, 172

union, spiritual, 197
Upanishad, 169

vacare Deo, 124
Vâlsan, Michel, 122
Vedānta, 146
vice, defect, 131
virtue, 9, 18, 20, 22, 35, 70, 164, 227,
    241
Vishnu, 14
Vivekānanda, 174
Voltaire, 67

The Way of a Pilgrim, 6, 80, 195
Whitman, Walt, 121
will, 247
Will, divine, 96

Yellowtail, Thomas, 207
yoga, 177
Yoga-Vāsishtha, 169
Yogaswāmi, 175
yogī, 177

Zen, 54, 193, 238
Zwingli, Ulrich, 67, 147

By the same author

The Transcendent Unity of Religions, Faber & Faber, 1953; revised edition, Harper & Row, 1975; introduction by Huston Smith, Quest Books, 1984, 1993

Spiritual Perspectives and Human Facts, Faber & Faber, 1954; Perennial Books, 1969; new translation, Perennial Books, 1987; new translation with selected letters, World Wisdom, 2007

Gnosis: Divine Wisdom, Perennial Books, 1959, 1978; revised, Perennial Books 1990; new translation with selected letters, World Wisdom, 2006

Language of the Self: Essays on the Perennial Philosophy, introduction by Venkataraman Raghavan, Ganesh Madras, 1959; Select Books Bangalore, 1998; revised and augmented, World Wisdom, 1999

Stations of Wisdom, John Murray, 1961; Perennial Books, 1980; new translation, World Wisdom, 1995, 2003

Understanding Islam, Allen & Unwin, Penguin, Unwin Hyman, Routledge, 1963, 1964, 1965, 1972, 1976, 1979, 1981, 1986, 1989, 1993; World Wisdom, 1994, 1998, 2003; new translation with selected letters, foreword by Annemarie Schimmel, World Wisdom, 2011

Light on the Ancient Worlds, Perennial Books, 1965; World Wisdom, 1984; new translation with selected letters, World Wisdom, 2006

Treasures of Buddhism (formerly *In the Tracks of Buddhism*, Allen & Unwin, 1968; Unwin Hyman, 1989); World Wisdom, 1993; new translation with selected letters, World Wisdom, 2018

Logic and Transcendence, Harper & Row, 1975; Perennial Books, 1984; new translation with selected letters, World Wisdom, 2009

Esoterism as Principle and as Way, Perennial Books, 1981, 1990; new translation with selected letters, World Wisdom, 2019

Sufism, Veil and Quintessence, World Wisdom, 1981; new translation with selected letters, foreword by Seyyed Hossein Nasr, World Wisdom, 2006

From the Divine to the Human, World Wisdom, 1982; new translation with selected letters, World Wisdom, 2013

Castes and Races (this book's 3 chapters are also included in *Language of the Self*), Perennial Books, 1982; World Wisdom, 1999

Christianity/Islam: Perspectives on Esoteric Ecumenism, World Wisdom, 1985; new translation with selected letters, World Wisdom, 2008

Survey of Metaphysics and Esoterism, World Wisdom, 1986, 2000

In the Face of the Absolute, World Wisdom, 1989, 1994; new translation with selected letters, World Wisdom, 2014

The Feathered Sun: Plains Indians in Art & Philosophy, introduction by Thomas Yellowtail, World Wisdom, 1990

To Have a Center, World Wisdom, 1990; new translation with selected letters, World Wisdom, 2015

Roots of the Human Condition, introduction by Patrick Laude, World Wisdom, 1991, 2002

The Play of Masks, World Wisdom, 1992

The Transfiguration of Man, World Wisdom, 1995

The Eye of the Heart, foreword by Huston Smith, World Wisdom, 1997; new translation with selected letters, World Wisdom, 2021

Form and Substance in the Religions, World Wisdom, 2002

Primordial Meditation: Contemplating the Real, The Matheson Trust, 2015 (translated from the German)

POETRY
Written in English

The Garland, Abodes, 1994

Road to the Heart, World Wisdom, 1995

Translated from German

Adastra & Stella Maris, foreword by William Stoddart, bilingual, World Wisdom, 2003

Songs Without Names, Vol. I-VI, introduction by William Stoddart, foreword by Annemarie Schimmel, World Wisdom, 2006

Songs Without Names, Vol. VII-XII, introduction by William Stoddart, foreword by Annemarie Schimmel, World Wisdom, 2006

World Wheel, Vol. I-III, introduction by William Stoddart, foreword by Annemarie Schimmel, World Wisdom, 2006

World Wheel, Vol. IV-VII, introduction by William Stoddart, foreword by Annemarie Schimmel, World Wisdom, 2006

Autumn Leaves & The Ring, introduction by Patrick Laude, bilingual, World Wisdom, 2010

Written in German (no translation)

Sulamith, Urs Graf, 1947

Tage- und Nächtebuch, Urs Graf, 1947

Liebe / Leben / Glück / Sinn, 4 vols, Herder, 1997

PAINTINGS

The Feathered Sun: Plains Indians in Art & Philosophy, introduction by Thomas Yellowtail, World Wisdom, 1990

Images of Primordial & Mystic Beauty: Paintings by Frithjof Schuon, Abodes/World Wisdom, 1992

ANTHOLOGIES OF SCHUON'S WRITINGS

The Essential Frithjof Schuon, edited by Seyyed Hossein Nasr (formerly *The Essential Writings of Frithjof Schuon*, Amity House, 1986; Element Books, 1991), World Wisdom, 2005

Echoes of Perennial Wisdom, World Wisdom, 1992; new translation with selected letters, World Wisdom, 2012

Songs for a Spiritual Traveler: Selected Poems, bilingual, World Wisdom, 2002

The Fullness of God: Frithjof Schuon on Christianity, edited by James Cutsinger, foreword by Antoine Faivre, World Wisdom, 2004

Prayer Fashions Man: Frithjof Schuon on the Spiritual Life, edited by James Cutsinger, World Wisdom, 2004

Art from the Sacred to the Profane: East and West, edited by Catherine Schuon, foreword by Keith Critchlow, World Wisdom, 2007

Splendor of the True: a Frithjof Schuon Reader, edited by James S. Cutsinger, foreword by Huston Smith, State University of New York Press, 2013

www.ingramcontent.com/pod-product-compliance
Lightning Source LLC
Chambersburg PA
CBHW030528030726
47495CB00004B/896